101
CAKE
DESIGNS
by
Mary Ford

Published by Mary Ford Cake Artistry Centre Ltd
who wish to offer sincere thanks to Tate & Lyle Refineries
for their encouragement with this edition.

Printed and bound in Great Britain by Purnell Book Productions Ltd.

ISBN 0 946429 00 6

Mary was born in Wick Village, near Bristol. Her interest in cake icing started when her father, a flour miller, encouraged her to take up the craft.

On leaving school, therefore, Mary went straight into a bakery on a four-year apprenticeship, with a day release each week to attend a course at Bristol Technical College, where she gained her Final City and Guilds in Bread Making and Flour Confectionery.

Having moved to London to gain greater experience, Mary finally settled in Bournemouth where she started teaching cake icing in Bournemouth and Southampton Colleges. That eventually led to private tuition.

She met and married Michael and as their business increased, so ever larger premises were found to accommodate larger classes. Mary, throughout this period, continued icing cakes to order and instructing students who were arriving from all parts of the World.

Mary makes no secret of the fact that cake decoration is the consuming passion of her life. She has won innumerable awards in the craft.

The ambition to write a book in cake icing followed the success of Mary's correspondence courses. She has created, stage by stage, each of the one-hundred-and-one cakes in this book and so has fulfilled that ambition.

Michael was born in Croydon, Surrey. His ambition to succeed in the culinary arts began at school, where he was the only boy to study cookery. This led to a three-year course in bread making and flour confectionery at Plymouth Technical College. There Michael achieved the Final City and Guilds in the subject.

He then travelled the country to further his practical experience in various hotels, restaurants and bakeries. He visited Bournemouth to work in a bakery and there met and married Mary in 1970.

His ambition to manage his own business came to fruition 12 months later when, with Mary, he created the forerunner to the Mary Ford Cake Artistry Centre.

Michael introduced a number of ideas in order to expand the company, including mail order, correspondence courses throughout the World and the development and manufacture of cake artistry tools.

A natural follow-up to the correspondence courses was the production of this book, in which Michael has been responsible for all the photography.

Preface

For many years now our friends and customers have asked us to produce a cake icing book — so much so that during 1981 we circulated a questionnaire on the subject. The result is here for you to see. We sincerely hope the end-product meets with your approval and gives not only easy instruction for amateur and professional alike, but also encourages the development of your own ideas in cake artistry.

We dedicate this book to all who have supported us over the years in our endeavours and thank our staff for making this publication possible. Our special appreciation goes to Stan and Betty Oddy for their help in the preparation of the book.

Michael and Mary

Foreword

Brilliant in conception and comprehensive in its presentation this book must prove of absorbing interest and of immense value to all who enjoy and practice the art of cake decoration.

It is unique among the range of books on this subject currently on sale and epitomises the teaching of the Mary Ford Centre in that simplicity, allied to imagination and some natural ability, form the basis of creative art.

Each of the one hundred and one cake designs in this book is not only presented in full colour but every stage of each design is described in illustrated detail.

All the ingredients, tools and decorations necessary to complete the cakes pictured can be obtained from the Mary Ford Centre. For those who wish to receive personal instruction from experts, courses in the art of cake decoration are a regular feature there.

It is with confidence, pleasure and admiration for the way this book has been produced that I recommend it to those who are interested in or appreciate the artistry of cake decoration.

William Jennings.
Feature writer to the Bakery Trade Press.

Introduction

The Mary Ford story is a fairy tale come true. No waving of a magic wand however has brought about the success and quality of product which is synonymous with the Mary Ford Cake Artistry Centre. Hard work, dedication, perseverence and consistently high standards of product have achieved this.

Michael and Mary Ford manage their enterprise from premises in Southbourne, Bournemouth. From this base they bake and sell their own bread and confectionery; ice celebratory cakes to order and give, amongst other things, instruction in cake icing as well as bread, pastry, cake and chocolate making. Demonstration classes are also held and, last but not least, they sell, by mail order and over the counter, all manner of cake icing articles and tools.

All this is a long way from the one small room in an hotel annexe where, in 1971 Mary commenced instructing just six pupils each session. Michael and Mary progressed to their first retail outlet and then to their present address. To raise part of the capital they then needed, their home had to be sold — such was the faith in their own ability and urge to succeed.

The quality of the Mary Ford Centre work is a byword to professionals and amateurs alike and culminated in 1981 in the making, icing and presentation of a magnificent four-tier wedding cake gift to Prince Charles and Lady Diana.

This book is the latest in a comprehensive list of outstanding goods to come from Mary Ford and, as is only to be expected, is produced in a highly professional manner. Consequently its contents are easily read, digested and understood by all who desire to make and ice cakes for those special occasions or wish to model in sugar paste.

Without fear of contradiction, it can be said that this beautifully presented book is unique in the field of cake icing and fills a much needed gap in the range of icing books currently on sale. Each of the one-hundred-and-one cake designs in the book enjoys a full-page colour photograph and every stage of each cake design is amply described in easy-to-follow writing and picture.

What is also unique is the ability to obtain from the Mary Ford Centre all the ingredients and decorations necessary to complete the cakes illustrated in this book and, if necessary, receive instruction in the art of icing and modelling at the centre.

This book is thoroughly recommended to all who are interested in or appreciate cake icing artistry.

S & B

We stress the importance of all aspects of cake artistry, but always give special emphasis to the basic ingredient and unreservedly recommend the use of "Tate & Lyle" Icing Sugar.

Index/Contents

Glossary.
Glossary of terms, abbreviations and basic instructions.

Abbreviations –
- cm – centimeter
- ° – degree
- diam. – diameter
- f – farenheit
- ' – foot/feet
- g – gram
- hrs – hours
- " – inches
- (L.D. 10m) – leave to dry ten minutes – see (L.D.)
- lbs – pounds
- m. – minutes
- ml – millilitre
- (No. 1) – indicates piping tube to be used – see *p 11*
- pt. – pint
- Rd – round
- Sq – square
- (T) – indicates cake should be tilted during piping
- tbsp. – tablespoon

American terms –

English	American
Baking powder	– Double-acting baking powder
Baking tin	– Baking pan
Baking tray	– Baking/cookie sheet
Bicarbonate of Soda	– Baking soda
Cake board	– Cake plate/tray/circle
Cake mixture	– Batter
Cake tins	– Cake pans
Cocktail stick	– Wooden toothpick
Colouring	– Food colors
Flour	– All purpose flour
Greaseproof paper	– Parchment paper
Icing	– Frosting
Icing bag	– Frosting cone/decorating cone
Icing sugar	– Confectioners' sugar
Icing tube	– Nozzle/tip
Marzipan	– Almond paste
Palette knife	– Spatula
Turntable	– Turntable/lazy Susan
Vanilla essence	– Vanilla extract

Cake base. This indicates where the bottom edges of the cake meet the cake board.

Cards. Thin cake boards.

Colouring. (Coloring) *Granulated sugar* – carefully add edible colouring to the sugar, mix thoroughly. Allow to dry for 24 hours.
Marzipan – fold and mix colour into marzipan.
Partial mix – where colouring is not fully mixed into medium used.
Royal Icing – mix colour in Royal Icing after it has been made.

When coloured coated cake is required, the following sequence is recommended.
1. Keep the first coat white.
2. Second coat to be a pale shade of the the colour required.
3. Final coat/s to be actual colour required.
Sugar paste – fold and mix colour into sugar paste.
2 colours of Royal Icing – see page 12.

Cow Gum. Artist's glue.

Curved Pieces. Usually made from a piece of soft metal or a plastic mould and used for shaping some runouts.

Diam. Diameter.

Disc. A circle of Royal Icing, sugar paste (Cold Fondant) or marzipan. – A thin cake board.

Drying. *(L.D. 10m)* – means leave to dry for 10 minutes in a temperature of 65°F (18°C) or for the minutes stated.
(L.D. 24 hrs.) – means leave to dry for 24 hours in a temperature of 65°F (18°C) or for the hours stated.
Note: In high humidity a longer drying time may be needed.

Figure piping. Use of Royal Icing without glycerine of various consistencies piped on waxed paper. A piping tube not always required.

Filigree. Piping an irregular line over an area.

Fix. *To join* – use water when fixing sugar paste to sugar paste, (Cold Fondant to Cold Fondant).
– use apricot jam when fixing cake to cake or marzipan to cake.
– use Royal Icing when fixing to Royal Icing.
– use media in use for all decorations.

Flood-in. The use of Royal Icing being held in place with a previously piped line. The Royal Icing should be softened with cold water to a dropping consistency and contain NO glycerine.

Flowers. Moulded – see pages 15 & 16.
– piped – see page 17.

Glycerine. Table for use – see page 8.

Graph. For templates and instructions – see page 9.

(L.D. 20m). See Drying.

(No. 1). This indicates the use of a no. 1 piping tube. Other bracketed numbers indicate the appropriate piping tubes to be used.

Outline. A piped line which holds soft runout royal icing (referred to as flood-in). Unless stated otherwise a no.1 tube should be used for general outline work.

Pipe-in. Piping medium in use without an icing tube.

Plaques. An outlined shape filled with soft Royal Icing on waxed paper, dried and then decorated.

(Pt.). Pint. (8 flu oz + 4 tablespoons).

Runouts. A runout is soft Royal Icing held in position with a piped line on waxed paper, or on the cake, and being allowed to dry in the specified time.
– drying – see Drying.
– remove – when completely dry, carefully peel off the waxed paper from under the runout.

Scallops. Curved lines piped in series.

Size. As a general guide measure size of cake. Reduce measurement by 1", this will be the inner size of the runout. The width of the runout must not extend the overall size of the cake board.

Stiffened Icing. Royal Icing with additional icing sugar added.

Stipple. To spread Royal Icing over area with a palette knife (metal spatula) and touch lightly with a fine domestic sponge.

Sugar Paste. (Cold Fondant) To colour – see Colouring.
– to make – see page 8.
– rosebuds – see page 15.
– roses – see pages 15 & 16.

Suspended Lines. A piped line held in position at each end.

" symbol. Inch.

(T). Indicates that the cake should be tilted during piping.

Template. Is an aid for designs.
– how to make – see page 9.

Tilting. Supporting the cake at an angle when piping on the side is necessary. Use a substantial block for the cake to lean on.

Waxed Paper. Specially prepared paper for figure piping and flood out work.

Wedge. Can be cut from any shaped cake – see page 14.

Reference table to cake designs.

CAKE No.	NAME	OCCASION	STYLE	PAGE No.	FRUIT CAKE SIZES (inches)	SPONGE SIZES (inches)	BOARD SIZES (inches)	MARZI-PAN (lbs)	ROYAL ICING (lbs)	SUGAR PASTE (lbs)	BUTTER-CREAM (lbs)
1	TANIA	Wedding	1 tier square	18	9	–	15, 12	2½	3	–	–
2	PETAL	Wedding	2 tier round	21	10, 7	–	13, 10	3½	4	¼	–
3	BETTINA	Wedding	3 tier square	24	11, 8, 5	–	15, 11, 8	6½	7	–	–
4	PAULA	Wedding	2 tier hexagonal	27	10, 7	–	13, 10	3½	3½	–	–
5	ANDREW	Christening	square	30	9	–	12	2½	3½	–	–
6	PENELOPE	Birthday	doll	33	–	9" round	13	–	1	1½	½
7	JOHNNY	Birthday	bulldozer	36	–	10" sq	14	–	½	2	1
8	SYLVIA	25 Anniversary	square	39	8	–	11	2	3	½	–
9	CUPID	Valentine	double heart	42	–	4@8" heart	16	1½	3	½	–
10	EDWARD	Birthday	square	45	8	–	11	2	2½	–	–
11	PETULA	Birthday	round	48	8	–	11	1½	2	–	–
12	CLAIRE	Engagement	heart	51	8	–	11	2	3	–	–
13	LISA	Wedding	3 tier round	54	11, 8, 5	–	14, 11, 8	5	5	–	–
14	ELAINE	Wedding	2 tier heart	57	9, 6	–	13, 10	3½	4½	–	–
15	LOUISE	Wedding	1 tier round	60	9	–	12	2	2½	–	–
16	WEDGWOOD	Wedding	3 tier round	63	12, 9, 6	–	15, 12, 9	6½	7	–	–
17	MOTHER	Mother's Day	round	66	8	–	11	1½	2½	–	–
18	CLAUDE	Birthday	calculator	69	–	10"×6"	12	–	½	1	½
19	ALBERT	Birthday	Daddy	72	6	–	9, 9	¾	2	–	–
20	FELICITY	Confirmation	Bible	75	8	–	14	2	3	½	–
21	POLLY	Celebration	floral	78	7, 7	–	9	2	4	1	–
22	EASTER	Easter	square	81	8	–	12	3½	3	–	–
23	PEARL	30 Anniversary	cushion	84	–	2@8" sq	11	–	1½	1½	1
24	ROSEMARIE	Wedding	4 tier round	87	11, 9, 7, 5	–	15, 12, 10, 8	6½	7	2	–
25	DAISY	Wedding	2 tier square	90	9, 6	–	12, 9	3½	4	–	–
26	PATRICIA	Wedding	3 tier square	93	12, 9, 6	–	15, 12, 9	7½	8	–	–
27	REBECCA	Wedding	3 tier hexagonal	96	12, 9, 6	–	15, 12, 9	7½	7½	–	–
28	CATHRYN	Christening	twins 2 tier	99	10, 6	–	13, 6*	4	5	–	–
29	MONTY	Birthday	vintage car	102	–	2@8" sq	14	–	½	2½	1
30	PETER	Father's Day	fishing	105	8	–	11	2	3	½	–
31	COURTNEY	Retirement	crossword	108	9	–	12	2½	2	2	–
32	SUSAN	25 Anniversary	2 tier round	111	9, 6	–	12, 9	3	3½	–	–
33	PEDRO	Holiday	sombrero	114	2pt basin	–	16	1	3½	–	–
34	VINCENT	Bon Voyage	square	117	9	–	12	2½	3	–	–
35	ANNE	Wedding	3 tier round	120	12, 9, 6	–	15, 12, 9	6½	7	1	–
36	WENDY	Wedding	3 tier heart	123	12, 9, 6	–	16, 12, 9	7½	8	½	–
37	KATE	Wedding	2 tier round	126	9, 6	–	12, 9	3	3½	–	–
38	SARAH	Wedding	2 tier square	129	9, 6	–	12, 9	3½	5	½	–
39	MORGAN	Birthday	treasure chest	132	–	3@7"×5"	10	–	½	2	1
40	NAOMI	Birthday	figure 5	135	figure 5	–	13	1½	2	2	–
41	LAURA	40 Anniversary	1 tier round	138	9	–	12	2	3	1½	–
42	WILLIAM	Birthday	open book	141	8	–	14	2	3	–	–
43	KATRINA	18th Birthday	key	144	4, 4	–	15	1½	3½	–	--
44	GEORGIANA	Welcome Home	round	147	8	–	11	1½	2	–	--
45	APRIL COTTAGE	Birthday	cottage	150	–	2@11" sq	12	–	1	2½	1½
46	PRINCESS	Wedding	4 tier hexagonal	153	12, 10, 8, 6	–	16, 13, 11, 9	8½	10	½	–
47	ADELINE	Wedding	1 tier square	156	9	–	12	2½	3	–	–
48	ROSETTA	Wedding	3 tier round	159	10, 8, 6	–	16, 13, 8*, 6*	5	5	3	–
49	HEATHER	Wedding	3 tier square	162	10, 8, 6	–	13, 11, 9	6	6	–	–
50	MARGUERITE	50 Anniversary	1 tier round	165	10	–	13	2½	3½	–	–

* Thin boards.

This reference table is a guide to the materials used to produce the actual cakes featured in this book. You can, of course, choose whatever material quantities and sizes you wish. Refer to the main photograph in each instance for the appropriate shape of board and cake.

N.B. As you will see in our step-by-step photographs, there are some instances in which we have used coloured Royal Icing instead of white, since this shows the build-up of decorative work more clearly. Naturally, any colour choice is up to you.

Reference table to cake designs.

CAKE No.	NAME	OCCASION	STYLE	PAGE No.	FRUIT CAKE SIZES (inches)	SPONGE SIZES (inches)	BOARD SIZES (inches)	MARZI-PAN (lbs)	ROYAL ICING (lbs)	SUGAR PASTE (lbs)	BUTTER-CREAM (lbs)
51	ERNIE	Retirement	chair	168	–	2@10"sq	14	–	½	1½	1
52	TRACY	5th Birthday	round	171	6	–	9	¾	2	2	–
53	BRIAN	Birthday	round	174	8	–	11	1½	2	–	–
54	VICTORIA	Celebration	crinoline	177	2pt basin	–	10	1½	1½	2	–
55	SCOTT	Birthday	train	180	–	9" sq	13"×6"	–	1	2	1
56	VERONICA	Birthday	mother	183	8	–	11	2	3½	–	–
57	CARMEN	Wedding	2 tier round	186	10, 7	–	13, 10	3½	4½	–	–
58	JOY	Wedding	4 tier square	189	12, 10, 8, 6	–	16, 13, 11, 9	10	10	–	–
59	SANDRA	Wedding	1 tier round	192	8	–	13, 11	1½	3	–	–
60	SONIA	Wedding	3 tier square	195	11, 8, 5	–	15, 11, 8	6½	7	–	–
61	JANE	Christening	round	198	8	–	11	1½	2½	–	–
62	GRAHAM	Birthday	spanner	201	–	10" sq	14	–	1	2½	1
63	VIOLET	Birthday	round	204	8	–	11	1½	2½	–	–
64	ARTHUR	Birthday	Grandad	207	8	–	11	2	2	–	–
65	TIFFANY	Anniversary	table	210	9, 7	–	12, 9*	3	3½	2	–
66	MARTINA	Birthday	twins	213	8	–	11	2	2	2	–
67	JEANETTE	Celebration	round	216	8	–	11	1½	2	–	–
68	KEVIN	Birthday	football pitch	219	8	–	11	2	2	1	–
69	LUCILLE	Wedding	3 tier horseshoe	222	10, 8, 6	–	14, 11, 9	4½	7	–	–
70	SHARON	Wedding	2 tier square	225	9, 6	–	13, 9	3½	4½	–	–
71	AMELIA	Wedding	3 tier round	228	12, 9, 6	–	15, 12, 9	6½	7½	–	–
72	VANESSA	Wedding	3 tier hexagonal	231	12, 9, 6 †	–	15, 12, 9	6½	7½	–	–
73	KIM	Celebration	good luck	234	10	–	14	2½	3	–	–
74	TONY	Birthday	mug & bottle	237	–	2@8" sq	–	–	–	2½	1½
75	DELIA	Presentation	closed book	240	7	–	11	1½	2½	½	–
76	TINA	Birthday	typewriter	243	–	2@10" sq	12	–	½	2½	1
77	OLIVER	Birthday	circus	246	8	–	12	3	1½	1	–
78	FAYE	Birthday	round	249	9	–	12	2	3	–	–
79	RICHARD	18th Birthday	figure 18	252	4, 4, 4	–	16	2	3	½	–
80	CHERYL	Celebration	congratulations	255	12	–	15	4	6	–	–
81	DIANA	Anniversary	square	258	8	–	11	2	3	–	–
82	AMY	40 Anniversary	1 tier square	261	9	–	13	2½	3½	–	–
83	ELIZABETH	50 Anniversary	2 tier square	264	9, 6	–	12, 9	3½	3½	2	–
84	ESTELLE	55 Anniversary	octagonal	267	9	–	12	2½	3½	–	–
85	NANCY	60 Anniversary	1 tier diamond	270	8	–	13	2	3½	–	–
86	SIMON	Birthday	square	273	8	–	11	2	3½	–	–
87	RUTH	Birthday	letter R	276	–	–	12	2	3½	½	–
88	SALLY	Engagement	square	279	9	–	13	2½	3½	–	–
89	GRISELDA	Halloween	round	282	9	–	12	2	3	–	–
90	KAREN	Birthday	square	285	8	–	11	2	3½	–	–
91	ELIZA	Celebration	flower basket	288	2pt basin	–	10, 7	1½	3	3	–
92	CAROL	Christmas	round	291	8	–	11	1½	2	–	–
93	ANGELA	Christmas	square	294	8	–	11	2	2	1	–
94	CHRISTINE	Christmas	round	297	8	–	11	1½	2	½	–
95	CRISPIN	Christmas	hexagonal	300	8	–	12	1½	3½	–	–
96	CANDICE	Christmas	round	303	8, 4	–	12	3	3½	–	–
97	SANTA	Christmas	sleigh	306	–	10" sq	14	1	1	2	1
98	NOEL	Christmas	round	309	8	–	11	2	3	–	–
99	ROBIN	Christmas	round	312	8	–	11	1½	3	–	–
100	CHARLOTTE	Christmas	square	315	8	–	11	2	3½	–	–
101	ISABEL	New Year	double bell	318	2pt basin	–	16, 15	2½	3	1½	–

* Thin boards.   † Vanessa requires double quantity of cake in each tin.

This reference table is a guide to the materials used to produce the actual cakes featured in this book. You can, of course, choose whatever material quantities and sizes you wish. Refer to the main photograph in each instance for the appropriate shape of board and cake.

N.B. As you will see in our step-by-step photographs, there are some instances in which we have used coloured Royal Icing instead of white, since this shows the build-up of decorative work more clearly. Naturally, any colour choice is up to you.

Basic Cake Recipe

Imperial/Metric	American
2 oz/57 g plain flour	½ cup all purpose flour
2 oz/57 g brown sugar	⅓ cup brown sugar
2 oz/57 g butter	¼ cup butter
2½ oz/71 g currants	½ cup currants
2½ oz/71 g sultanas	½ cup seedless white raisins
1 oz/28 g seedless raisins	3 tablespoons seedless raisins
1 oz/28 g glacé cherries	3 tablespoons candied cherries
1½ oz/42 g mixed peel	4½ tablespoons candied peel
¾ oz/21 g ground almonds	2½ tablespoons ground almonds
½ fluid oz/2 teaspoons brandy or rum	2 teaspoons brandy or rum
1 large egg	1 large egg
pinch nutmeg	pinch nutmeg
pinch mixed spice	pinch apple pie spice
pinch salt	pinch salt
¼ lemon zest and juice	¼ lemon zest and juice

Preparation. First line your tin with a double layer of buttered greaseproof paper. Then clean and prepare the fruit, halve the cherries. Mix all fruit together with lemon zest. Sift flour, spices and salt.
Method. Beat the butter until light. Add sugar to butter and beat again until light. Gradually add egg, beating in thoroughly after each addition. Stir in ground almonds. Fold in flour and spices. Finally add fruit together with brandy or rum and lemon juice. Mix well together and transfer to tin.

It is most important to follow the exact measurements and mixture of the foregoing ingredients.

In baking the cake initially, if one pint of water is placed in a meat tray in the bottom of the oven, this will create sufficient humidity to keep the top of the cake moist and ensure level results in baking. Remove water after half baking time.

When the cake is baked, leave it in the tin (pan) for one day, remove from tin (pan) then sprinkle the appropriate quantity of soaking mixture. Wrap cake in waxed paper and leave in a cupboard for three weeks. When the waxed paper becomes sticky, this means that moisture is seeping out, a sure sign that the cake is mature. If more liquid is required, add just before marzipanning. A cake needs no more than three weeks to mature.

CAKE PORTIONS: TO CALCULATE SIZE OF FRUIT CAKE REQUIRED 8 PORTIONS ARE GENERALLY CUT FROM EACH 1 LB OF FINISHED ICED CAKE.
Soaking mixture. Equal quantities of Rum, Sherry and Glycerine or spirits of choice. 1 tbls. per 1 lb of cake when required.

Glycerine – Table for use

For soft-cutting icing (per 1 lb or 454 g or 3½ cups of ready-made Royal Icing) use 1 teaspoon of glycerine for the bottom tier of a 3-tier wedding cake.
2 teaspoons of glycerine for the middle tier.
3 teaspoons of glycerine for the top tier, or for single tier cakes.
(N.B. Glycerine only to be added after Royal Icing has been made.)
NO GLYCERINE IN ROYAL ICING FOR RUNOUTS OR No. 1 WORK.

Royal Icing Recipe

Imperial/Metric
1½ ozs/42 g powdered egg white
½ pint/284 ml cold water
3½ lb/1½ kg best icing sugar sieved
OR
½ oz/14 g powdered egg white
3 fluid ozs/3 tablespoons cold water
1 lb/454 g best icing sugar, sieved
OR
3 egg whites (separated the day before)
1 lb/454 g best icing sugar (approximately) sieved

American
¼ cup powdered egg white + 2 tablespoons
1¼ cups cold water
10 cups confectioner's sugar sifted
OR
1½ tablespoons powdered egg white
3 tablespoons cold water
3½ cups confectioner's sugar, sifted
OR
3 egg whites (separated the day before)
3½ cups confectioner's sugar (approximately) sifted

Preparation. All equipment used must be perfectly cleaned and sterilised. Pour water into a jug and stir in powdered egg white. This will go lumpy and necessitates standing the mixture for one hour, stirring occasionally. Then strain through a muslin.

Method. Pour solution or egg whites into a mixing bowl and place the icing sugar on top. A drop of blue colour (color) may be added for white icing. Beat on slow speed for approximately 15-20 minutes or until the right consistency is obtained. (If powdered egg white is used the Royal Icing will keep in good condition for 2 weeks. Fresh egg whites will deteriorate quicker). Store Royal Icing in sealed contained in a cool place.

Buttercream
(Referred to as CREAM in the Book)

Imperial/Metric
4 ozs/113 g butter
6-8 ozs/170-227 g icing sugar
1-2 tablespoons warm water
essence or flavouring of choice

American
½ cup butter
1⅓-2 cups confectioner's sugar
1-2 tablespoons warm water
extract or flavouring of choice

Method. Sift icing sugar. Soften butter and beat until light. Gradually add the icing sugar beating well after each addition. Add essence (extract) or flavouring (flavoring) of choice and water (carefully).

Heavy Genoese Sponge Recipe

Imperial/Metric
3 oz/85 g butter
3 oz/85 g margarine
6 oz/170 g caster sugar
3 eggs, lightly beaten
6 oz/170 g self-raising flour sieved

American
6 tablespoons butter
6 tablespoons margarine
¾ cup sugar
3 eggs, lightly beaten
1½ cups self-raising flour sifted

Preparation. First line your tin (pans) with greased greaseproof paper.

Method. Cream butter and margarine. Add sugar and beat until light in colour and fluffy in texture. Add the egg a little at a time beating after each addition. Carefully fold in the flour.
Bake: 190°C, 375°F, Gas 5. 20-25 minutes.

½ recipe makes	1 @ 8″ Rd sponge
	or 1 @ 7″ Sq
1 recipe makes	1 @ 10″ Rd sponge
	or 1 @ 9″ Sq
1½ recipe makes	1 @ 12″ Rd sponge
	or 1 @ 11″ Sq

Sugar Paste Recipe (Cold Fondant Recipe)

Imperial/Metric
1 lb/454 g icing sugar, sieved
1 egg white
2 ozs/57 g liquid glucose
(Slightly warmed)

American
3½ cups Confectioner's sugar, sifted
1 egg white
4 tablespoons liquid glucose
(Slightly warmed)

Method. Add egg white and glucose to icing sugar. Blend all ingredients together. Knead well until a smooth paste is obtained.
Keep in a polythene bag or sealed container and in a cool place. Colour and flavour (flavor) as required.

CONVERSION TABLES			
WEIGHT		SIZE	
IMPERIAL	METRIC	IMPERIAL	METRIC
½ oz	14 g	5 ins	12.5 cm
1 oz	28 g	6 ins	15 cm
2 oz	57 g	7 ins	18 cm
3 oz	85 g	8 ins	20.5 cm
4 oz	113 g	9 ins	23 cm
5 oz	142 g	10 ins	25.5 cm
6 oz	170 g	11 ins	28 cm
7 oz	198 g	12 ins	30.5 cm
8 oz	227 g	13 ins	33 cm
9 oz	255 g	14 ins	35.5 cm
10 oz	284 g	15 ins	38 cm
11 oz	312 g	16 ins	40.5 cm
12 oz	340 g		
13 oz	369 g		
14 oz	397 g		
15 oz	425 g		
16 oz	454 g		

LIQUID		
IMPERIAL	METRIC	AMERICAN
1 tsp.	5 ml	1 tsp
1 tbsp	15 ml	1 tbsp
1 fl.oz	28 ml	⅛ cup
2 fl. oz	57 ml	¼ cup
3 fl. oz	85 ml	⅜ cup
4 fl. oz	113 ml	½ cup
¼ pint	142 ml	⅝ cup
½ pint	284 ml	1¼ cup
1 pint	568 ml	2½ cup

Note: AUSTRALIAN TABLESPOON
4 tsp. 20ml 1 tbsp (AUS)

		CAKE SIZES AND QUANTITIES WITH APPROXIMATE BAKING TIMES							
		(QUANTITIES ARE STATED IN MULTIPLES OF EACH OF THE BASIC RECIPES)							
	Basic Fruit Cake Recipe (Bake at 275°F, 140°C, Gas Mark 1)						Heavy Genoese Sponge Recipe (Bake at 375°F, 190°C, Gas Mark 5)		
SIZE ins	ROUND	SQUARE	HORSE SHOE	HEART	HEXAGONAL	APPROX TIMING	ROUND	SQUARE	APPROX TIMING
5	1	1½	-	1½	1	1½-1¾ hrs	-	-	-
6	1½	2	1¼	2	1½	1¾-2 hrs	-	-	-
7	2	3	-	3	2	2½-3 hrs	-	½	20-25 mins
8	3	4	2½	4	3	3½-4 hrs	½	-	20-25 mins
9	4	5	-	5	4	4-4½ hrs	-	1	20-25 mins
10	5	6	4½	6	5	4¼-4¾ hrs	1	-	25-30 mins
11	6	7	-	7	6	4½-5 hrs	-	1½	25-30 mins
12	7	8	6½	8	7	5-5½ hrs	1½	-	25-30 mins

Template graph and instructions.

(Do not remove or draw directly onto this graph.)

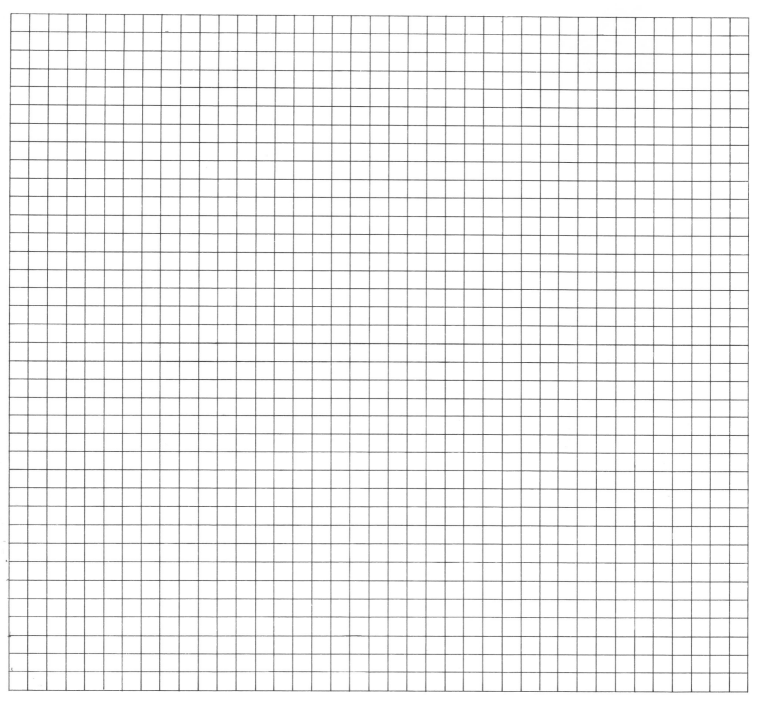

Explanatory note:
Most cakes in this book include artwork necessitating the use of graphs (for an example please refer to the drawing of the lovebirds template in picture No.13 of the cake 'Tania' on page 19). All graphs, such as that in picture No.13, *need to be adjusted to obtain the correct scale*. This can be achieved by using the following instructions.

Instructions:
1. Count and record the number of squares in the picture.
2. Cover the MASTER-GRAPH with a sheet of greaseproof paper and count out, mark and trace the equivalent number of squares on the greaseproof paper.
3. Remove the greaseproof-paper graph and reopen book to the relevant page (i.e. page 19 for picture No.13).
4. Wherever the drawing in that picture crosses a line, mark the identical crossing point on the greaseproof-paper graph.
5. Still using the picture as a guide, join the marks on the greaseproof-paper graph to create the template required.

Equipment.

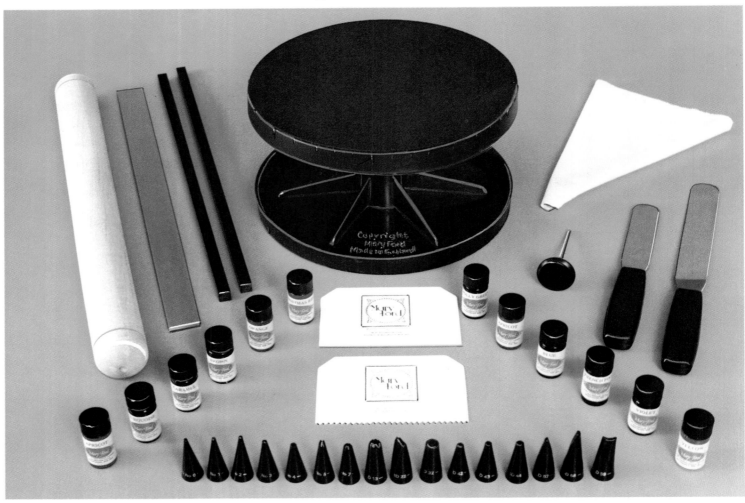

Turntable	Straight edge	Plain scraper	Flower nail
6" Palette knife	Rolling pin	Serrated scraper	Edible colourings
4" Palette knife	Pair of marzipan spacers	Nylon piping bag	Icing tubes

The above are the items of equipment used in making the cakes that appear in our book. Most of them were designed by us, and they are all obtainable through the Company's Mail Order Department.

You will find each item, and many more, featured in our catalogue, which can be obtained from:

Mary Ford Cake Artistry Centre Ltd.
28–30 Southbourne Grove, Southbourne,
Bournemouth BH6 3RA.

**Cake decorating courses are held at the Mary Ford Centre.
For further details please apply to the above address**

Mary Ford Tube No.'s showing their shapes.

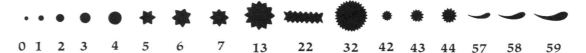

| 0 | 1 | 2 | 3 | 4 | 5 | 6 | 7 | 13 | 22 | 32 | 42 | 43 | 44 | 57 | 58 | 59 |

**The above are all the icing tubes used in this book.
Please note that these are Mary Ford tubes, but comparable tubes may be used.**

Piped Designs.

1. 1st stage of 6-dot sequence, pipe 3 dots.
2. 2nd stage, pipe 2 further dots.
3. 3rd stage, pipe last dot to complete sequence.
4. Graduated bulbs.
5. Shell.
6. Cone-shaped shell.
7. Rosette.
8. 'C' line.
9. Bold 'C'.
10. 'S' line.
11. Rope.
12. Curved rope.
13. Spiral shell.
14. 'C' scroll.
15. 'S' scroll.
16. Left-to-right scroll.
17. Right-to-left scroll.

Various Writing Styles.

ABCDEFGHIJKLMNOPQRSTUVWXYZ ÆØ 1234567890

ABCDEFGHIJKLMNOPQRSTUVWXYZ ÆØ 1234567890

A A ABCDEFGHIJKLMNOPQRRSSTTUVWXYZ

ABCDEEFGHIJKLLMNOPQRSTUVWXYZ 12345678890

ABCDEFGHIJKLMNOPQRSTUVWXYZ 1234567890

ABCDEFGHIJKLMNOPQRSTUVWXYZ 1234567890

ABCDEFGHIJKLMNOPQRSTUVWXYZ ÆØ 1234567890

ABCDEFGHIJKLMNOPQRSTUVWXYZ

ABCDEFGHIJKLMNOPQRSTUVWXYZ 1234567890

ABCDEFGHIJKLMNOPQRSTUVWXYZ 1234567890

ABCDEFGHIJKLMNOPQRSTUVWXYZ 1234567890

ABCDEFGHIJKLMNOPQRSTUVWXYZ

Making and filling a greaseproof piping bag

1. A sheet of greaseproof paper – 12"×8" – required.

2. Cut sheet diagonally as shown.

3. Turn one triangle to position shown.

4. Fold paper from right to centre.

5. Lift corner from left to right.

6. Fold under and pull into shape.

7. Fold in loose ends and cut section. Fold back to secure.

8. Cut off tip of bag and drop in tube.

9. Using a palette knife, half fill bag with Royal Icing.

10. Carefully fold and roll the open end to seal bag, which is then ready for use.

11. To make a LEAF BAG repeat 1–7 and then flatten tip.

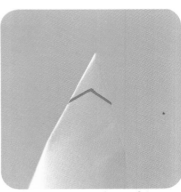

12. Picture showing shape of tip to be cut.

13. Now cut tip.

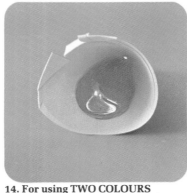

14. For using TWO COLOURS partially fill one side of bag with one colour.

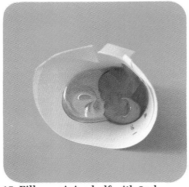

15. Fill remaining half with 2nd colour. Repeat 10.

16. Picture showing effect of using two colours of Royal Icing.

How to marzipan

17. Picture showing a matured fruit cake with lining paper removed.

18. Upturn cake, place on board (3″ larger) and if required brush on spirits and glycerine.

19. Using icing sugar for dusting, roll marzipan between spacers (approx: ⅜″ thick), as shown.

20. Cut marzipan to size using the cake tin (in which the cake was baked) as guide.

21. After removing surplus marzipan brush off any loose icing sugar.

22. Jam the marzipan with boiling apricot puree by applying it with a palette knife.

23. Lay cake onto the jammed marzipan.

24. Upturn cake and replace on board.

25. Picture showing a square cake (which is prepared in the same way as a round cake).

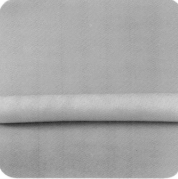

26. Form remaining marzipan into a sausage shape.

27. Now roll the marzipan into a thin strip (wide enough to cover the cake side).

28. Cut marzipan for side (length=approx: 3 times diameter) and then jam as in 22.

29. Fix marzipan to cake side and trim off surplus (L.D. approx: 3 days).

30. For a square cake roll out a sheet of marzipan to cover the 4 sides.

31. Cut the sheet into 4 separate strips to fit sides.

32. Jam and fix each strip then trim (L.D. approx: 3 days).

HOW TO CUT A WEDGE
33. After marzipanning, cut wedge from cake, as shown.

34. Replace wedge.

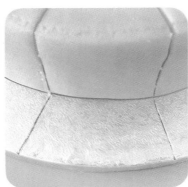

35. Mark board to show position of wedge. Place cake on turntable.

HOW TO COAT A CAKE
36. Spread Royal Icing around side of cake with a palette knife.

37. Place hands in position shown (holding the scraper against the cake side).

38. Holding scraper steady with one hand, revolve the turntable one complete turn with the other hand.

39. Repeat 36–38 until side is smooth.

40. Using the palette knife, remove surplus icing fom cake.

41. Immediately remove wedge.

42. Clean sides of wedge and replace (L.D. 12 hrs).

43. Using the palette knife, place Royal Icing on top of the cake.

44. Using the palette knife in a paddling movement, spread the icing evenly over the cake top.

45. Using a stainless steel rule, start to level the icing.

46. Continue to use the rule in a backwards and forwards motion to level icing.

47. Picture showing coated cake.

48. Remove surplus icing from edges of cake top and wedge (L.D. 12 hrs). Repeat 36–48 twice more.

49. 1½ yards of satin ribbon on a piece of greaseproof paper – approx: 8"×6" required.

50. Fold the paper over the centre of the ribbon.

51. Fold the paper and ribbon in half and place to wedge.

52. Replace wedge.

53. Roll up equal lengths of ribbon ends and fix to side of cake.

HOW TO COAT A BOARD.
54. Picture showing hands and scraper in readiness to coat board.

55. Holding scraper steady in one hand, revolve the turntable one complete turn with the other (see picture 38).

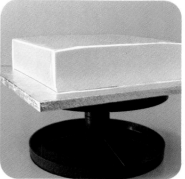

56. For coating a square (or hexagonal, etc.) cake, coat the opposite sides (L.D. 12 hrs).

57. Now coat remaining sides (L.D. 12 hrs).

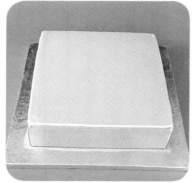

58. Coat the top as for round cake (L.D. 12 hrs). Repeat 56–58 twice more.

HOW TO MAKE A SUGAR PASTE ROSE BUD.
59. Roll a piece of sugar paste into the shape shown.

60. Flatten back to form sharp edge.

61. Roll up the sugar paste as shown.

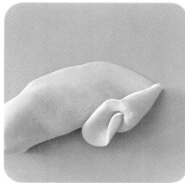

62. Continue rolling, as shown.

63. Fold over remaining sugar paste.

64. Remove surplus sugar paste, then bend back edge to form bud.

HOW TO MAKE A SUGAR PASTE ROSE.
65. Repeat 59–64 but finishing with bud in upright position.

66. Roll out sugar paste and flatten one end.

67. Cut away surplus leaving the petal.

68. Wrap petal around the bud and slightly dampen with water to fix.

69. Repeat 66–68 for the second petal.

70. Repeat 66–68 making and fixing larger petals until size of rose required is obtained.

MAKING ROYAL ICING BIRDS.
71. Pipe wings on waxed paper, working from left to right (No.1) (L.D. 12 hrs).

72. Pipe tail on waxed paper (two types shown) (No.1).

73. Pipe body against tail (No.1).

74. Lifting icing bag pipe neck, head and beak (No.1).

75. Immediately fix wings to body (L.D. 12 hrs).

MAKING SUGAR BELLS
76. Pipe a bulb on waxed paper (No.3).

77. Pipe a second bulb on top (No.3).

78. Sprinkle granulated sugar over the bulbs (then leave until outside of bulbs are dry).

79. Scoop out unset Royal Icing from centre of bell.

80. Pipe-in hammer (No.1).

PIPING SUGAR FLOWERS & ROSES

PIPING SUGAR FLOWERS
81. Picture showing items required=flower nail, waxed paper and piping bag with petal tube (No.58).

82. Fix a square of waxed paper to top of flower nail and hold in position shown.

83. Keeping thick end of tube to the centre of flower, pipe 1st petal.

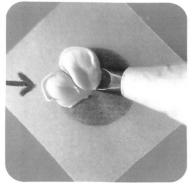

84. Turn nail and pipe next petal.

85. Turn nail and pipe 3rd petal.

86. Turn nail and pipe 4th petal.

87. Turn nail and pipe 5th petal.

88. Turn nail and pipe the last petal.

89. Picture showing the piped petals.

90. Pipe a centre bulb (No.2) (L.D. 24 hrs).

PIPING SUGAR ROSES
91. Form a cone of marzipan.

92. Using stiff Royal Icing, pipe the centre of the rose (No.57).

93. Pipe a petal behind the centre (No.57).

94. Pipe the next petal starting inside the 1st petal (No.57).

95. Pipe the 3rd petal, starting inside the 2nd petal and ending over part of the 1st petal (No.57) (L.D. 15 m).

96. Repeat 93–95 for 5 petals around outside of rose (L.D. 24 hrs). Remove from cone.

17

Tania

NOTE: Before attempting to decorate this cake, please study the whole sequence of photographs and notes and ensure you have the proper equipment and materials, as well as sufficient time. Additional information can be found on pages 5–17.

1. Prepare a 9″ square cake on 12″ and 15″ boards in normal way.

2. Turn cake and board upside-down and place on support.

3. Pipe 18 loops along each cake edge (No.1).

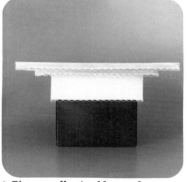

4. Pipe equally sized loops along each board edge (No.1).

5. Pipe larger loops on each edge, as shown (No.1).

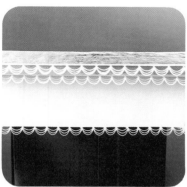

6. Pipe larger loops on each edge, as shown (No.1).

7. Repeat 3–4 between each loop.

8. Repeat 5.

9. Repeat 6 (L.D. 2 hrs).

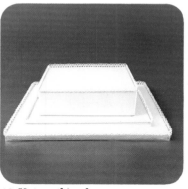

10. Upturn the cake.

11. Pipe 5 outer petals on waxed paper to form flower (No.1) (L.D. 2 hrs) (52 flowers required).

12. Pipe a central dot on each flower (No.1) (L.D. 24 hrs).

13. Drawing showing template of lovebirds (5 pairs required).

14. Pipe-in bird breasts, beaks and tails on waxed paper (No.1) (L.D. 1 hr).

15. Pipe-in heads and bodies (No.1) (L.D. 1 hr).

16. Pipe-in the wings (No.1) and paint the eyes in edible colouring (L.D. 24 hrs).

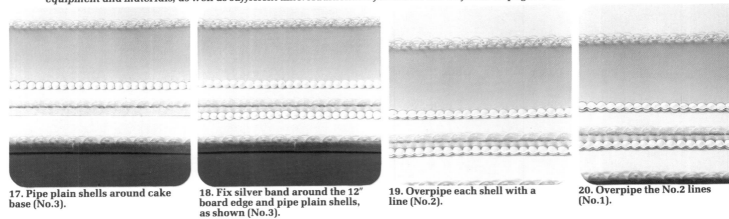

17. Pipe plain shells around cake base (No.3).

18. Fix silver band around the 12″ board edge and pipe plain shells, as shown (No.3).

19. Overpipe each shell with a line (No.2).

20. Overpipe the No.2 lines (No.1).

21. Pipe a branch on each side of the cake, as shown (No.2).

22. Fix lovebirds, as shown.

23. Fix flowers, as shown.

24. Pipe leaves, as shown (Leaf bag).

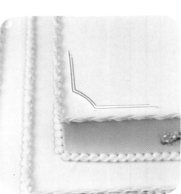

25. Example of lettering to be used for message. (Outline, then flood-in each letter on waxed paper) (L.D. 24 hrs).

26. Fix message on cake top.

27. Pipe a line under each word (No.2), then pipe a line beside each No.2 line (No.1).

28. Pipe a line at each corner except the top right corner (No.2) and then pipe a line beside the No.2 line (No.1).

29. Fix flowers and artificial decorations of choice, as shown.

30. Fix a roll of ribbon at each corner, as shown.

31. Fix flowers in centre of large board.

32. Fix artificial bells to each corner of large board and silver band to board edge.

Petal

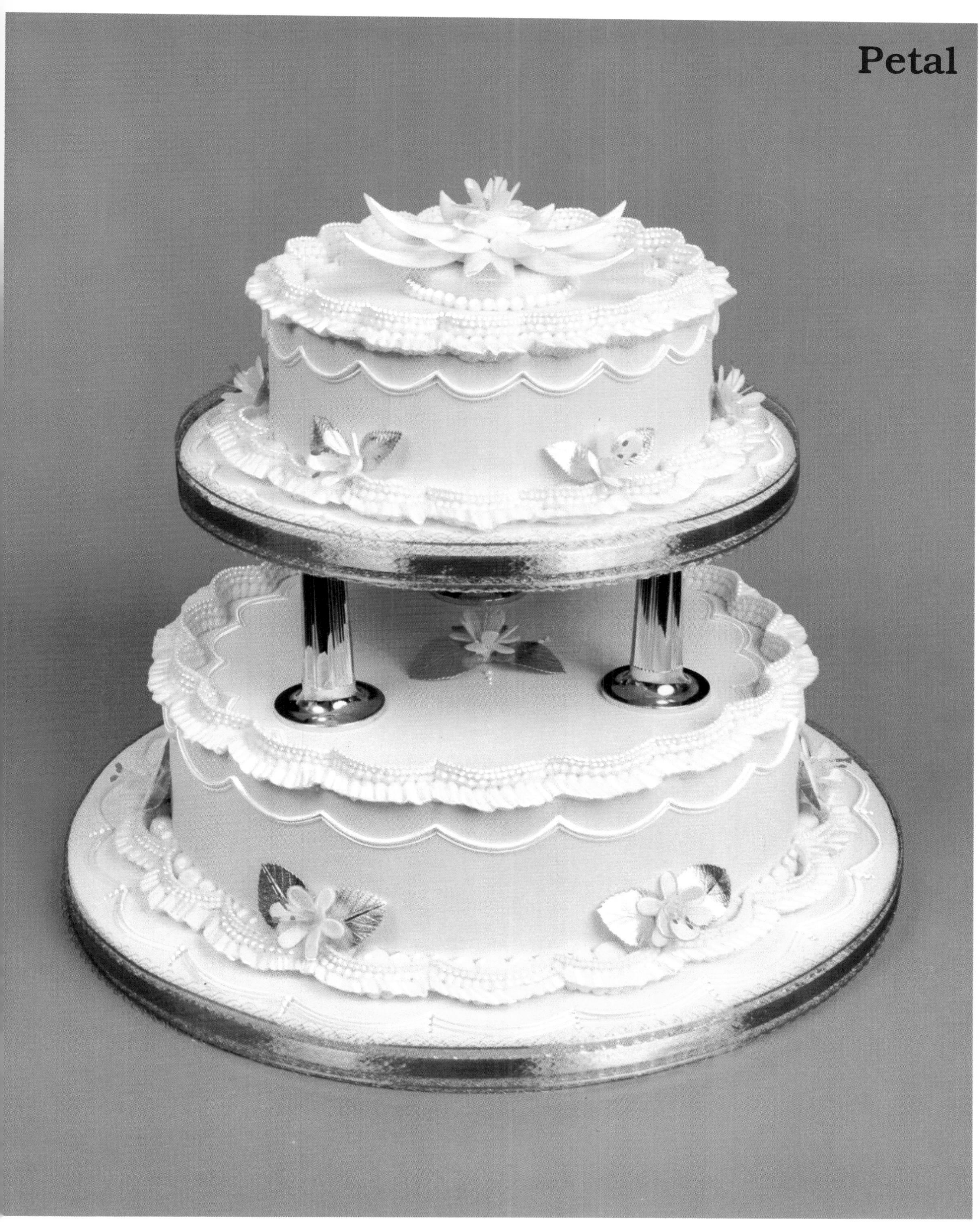

NOTE: *Before attempting to decorate this cake, please study the whole sequence of photographs and notes and ensure you have the proper equipment and materials, as well as sufficient time. Additional information can be found on pages 5–17.*

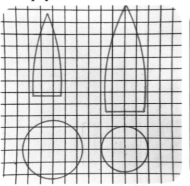

1. Drawing of templates for lily petals and centre. (6 of each petal and 1 of each disc required).

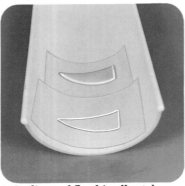

2. Outline and flood-in all petals and discs and place petals in curved mould (L.D. 24 hrs).

3. Mark top of cake into 18 equal spaces with small piped dots (No.1).

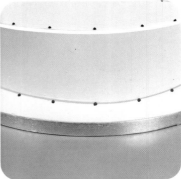

4. Immediately beneath top dots, mark base of cake with piped dots (No.1).

5. Repeat on outer edge of board (No.1).

6. Pipe curved rope mark to mark around top of cake (No.44).

7. Repeat on board (No.44). (Ensure marker dots are hidden).

8. Starting with centre bulb, graduate either side (No.3).

9. Overpipe further rope on 1st rope on top of cake (No.3).

10. Overpipe further rope on base rope (No.3).

11. Pipe a line inside curve of rope on top of cake (No.2).

12. Overpipe further rope on 2nd rope (No.2).

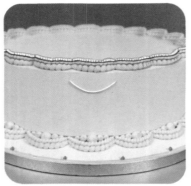

13. Pipe curved line directly below each rope (No.2) (T).

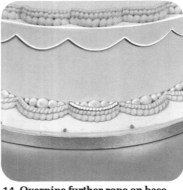

14. Overpipe further rope on base 2nd rope (No.2).

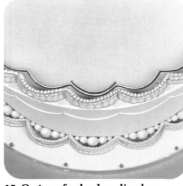

15. On top of cake drop line by side of No.2 (No.1).

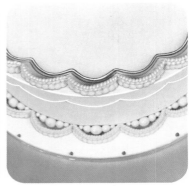

16. Overpipe on top of No.2 (No.1).

22

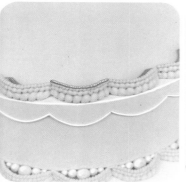

17. Overpipe further rope on 3rd rope (No.1).

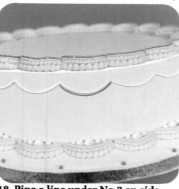

18. Pipe a line under No.2 on side of cake (No.1) (T).

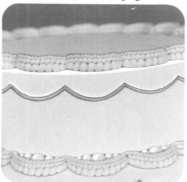

19. Continuing on side of cake, pipe against No.2 (No.1) (T).

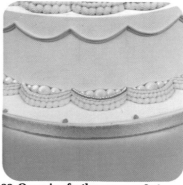

20. Overpipe further rope on 3rd base rope (No.1).

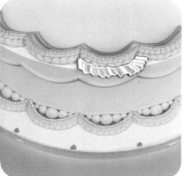

21. Using stiff icing, pipe frill against No.44 using wide end of tube nearest cake. Pipe right to left (No.58).

22. Repeat against base rope (No.58).

23. Pipe a line onto board, following curve of frill (No.2).

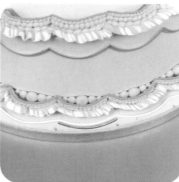

24. Pipe a line beside the No.2 line (No.1). Carefully scrape off marker dots on edge of board.

25. Pipe a line on top of the No.2 line (No.1).

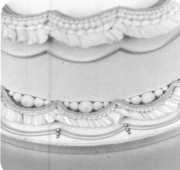

26. Pipe three graduated dots at joins (No.1).

27. Make and secure a sugar paste base to support lily. Pipe plain shells around edge (No.2).

28. Fix larger disc to sugar paste base. Fix 6 large petals around edge. Finish with shells (No.2).

29. Fix smaller petals on top and in between larger petals.

30. Fix smaller disc in centre, hiding base of petals, and pipe small icing spikes between petals (No.1).

31. Pipe small spikes to edge of disc (No.1). Using artificial flowers of choice, fix to centre of lily.

32. Complete cake with matching flowers, silver leaves and silver ribbon.

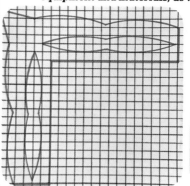

1. Drawing showing template for corner runout pieces.

2. Outline and flood-in on waxed paper 4 corner runout pieces for each tier (L.D. 24 hrs).

3. Outline and flood-in on waxed paper 16 small runout pieces for each tier (L.D. 24 hrs).

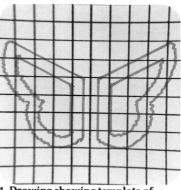

4. Drawing showing template of butterfly wings (4 butterflies required for each tier).

5. Filigree centre of wings on waxed paper (No.1).

6. Pipe-in wing edges, as shown. (No.2) (L.D. 24 hrs).

7. Pipe separate bodies as shown on waxed paper (No.2) (L.D. 24 hrs).

8. Pipe scallops around edges of corner runouts (No.1) (L.D. 12 hrs).

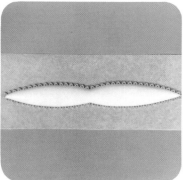

9. Pipe series of 3 dots around edges of small runouts (No.1) (L.D. 12 hrs).

10. Fix a pair of wings to each body, supporting them until dry.

11. Pipe a line around the edge of each corner, as shown (No.3) (L.D. 2 hrs). NOTE: If wedge required, see instructions.

12. Remove small runouts from waxed paper, turn upside-down and pipe a line along length (No.3) (L.D. 30 m).

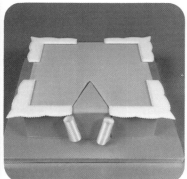

13. Overpipe the cake No.3 lines (No.2) and immediately fix corner runouts into position.

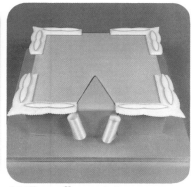

14. Fix small runouts to corner runouts, as shown.

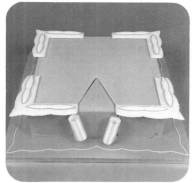

15. Pipe curved line on board so that it matches the runout design (No.2).

16. Flood-in between the board No.2 line and the cake base (L.D. 12 hrs).

25

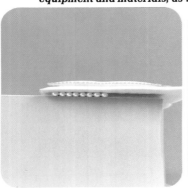

17. Pipe small bulbs beneath the runouts at cake top edge (No.2) (T).

18. Pipe bulbs along cake base (No.2).

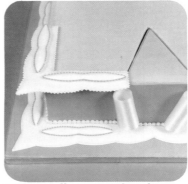

19. Fix small runouts to board runout corners.

20. Pipe a line on the cake top, as shown (No.2).

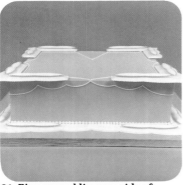

21. Pipe curved lines on side of cake, as shown (No.2) (T).

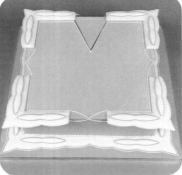

22. Pipe a line beside the board runout design (No.2).

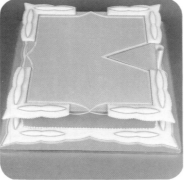

23. Pipe a line beside each No.2 line (No.1) (T as necessary).

24. Overpipe each No. 2 line (No.1) (T as necessary).

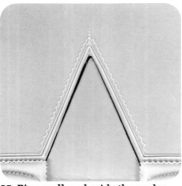

25. Pipe scallops beside the wedge and 3 graduated dots at wedge point (No.1).

26. Pipe angled lines across wedge cut, as shown (No.1).

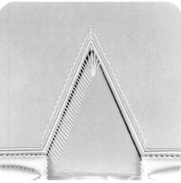

27. Continue piping lines across wedge point, as shown (No.1).

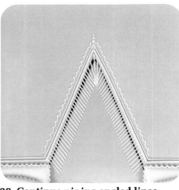

28. Continue piping angled lines across wedge cut, as shown (No.1).

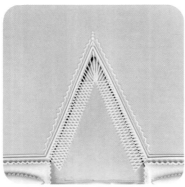

29. Pipe lines over the angled lines, as shown (No.1).

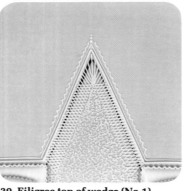

30. Filigree top of wedge (No.1) and then pipe a row of shells along wedge edge (No.1).

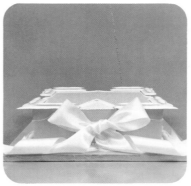

31. Tie the wedge bow.

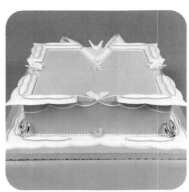

32. Fix butterflies, decorations and ribbon of choice, as shown.

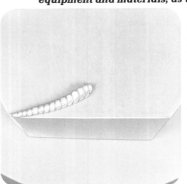

1. Pipe a 'C' scroll from centre of one side to corner, as shown (No.44).

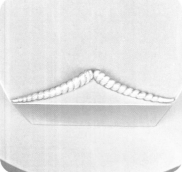

2. Pipe the opposite scroll (No.44).

3. Repeat 1 and 2 on cake top, as shown.

4. Pipe an 'S' scroll from centre top edge to corner (No.44).

5. Pipe the opposite scroll (No.44) then repeat around each top edge.

6. Pipe spiral shells linked by a curved rope along each base (No.44).

7. Pipe bulbs inside the curved rope along cake base (No.3).

8. Overpipe the left 'C' scroll (No.3).

9. Overpipe the right 'C' scroll (No.3) and then repeat 8–9 on all 'C' scrolls.

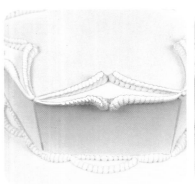

10. Overpipe the left 'S' scroll (No.3).

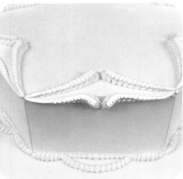

11. Overpipe the right 'S' scroll (No.3) and then repeat 10–11 on all 'S' scrolls.

12. Overpipe each curved rope (No.3).

13. Overpipe each 'C' scroll (No.2).

14. Overpipe each 'S' scroll (No.2).

15. Overpipe each curved rope (No.2).

16. Pipe curved lines on cake side, as shown (No.2) (T).

17. Pipe a line under the No.2 line on cake side (No.1) (T).

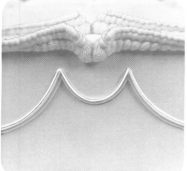

18. Pipe a line against the No.2 line on cake side (No.1) (T).

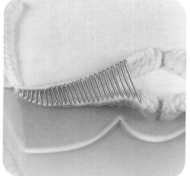

19. Pipe suspended lines across the scrolls, as shown (No.1).

20. Repeat 19 around scrolls on cake top.

21. Pipe lines over the suspended lines to form latticework (No.1).

22. Repeat 21 on all cake top scrolls.

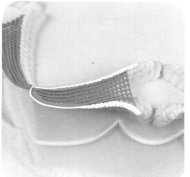

23. Overpipe each scroll (No.1).

24. Picture showing completed latticework.

25. Mark a curved guide line on each side of the cake, as shown (No.1).

26. Pipe suspended lines from the guide line to the rope (No.1).

27. Pipe horizontal lines over the suspended lines to form latticework (No.1).

28. Pipe shells around each latticework (No.2).

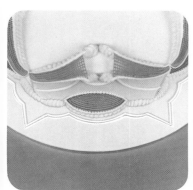

29. Pipe a line on the board, as shown (No.2); then beside the No.2 line (No.1); then overpipe the No.2 line (No.1).

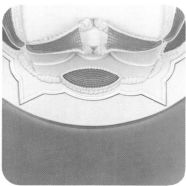

30. Pipe a line on the board beside the No.1 line (No.1).

31. Fix 2 sugar bells on each top corner.

32. Fix artificial slippers, bells and ribbon, as shown.

Andrew

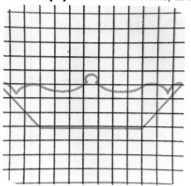

1. Drawing of template for side of CRADLE.

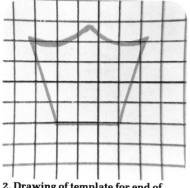

2. Drawing of template for end of CRADLE.

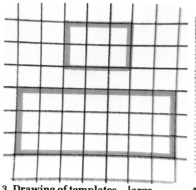

3. Drawing of templates – large oblong, CRADLE BASE and BLANKET – small oblong for PILLOW.

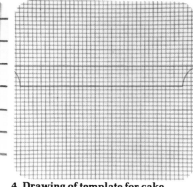

4. Drawing of template for cake top runouts.

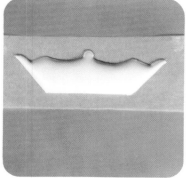

5. Outline and flood-in side of CRADLE (L.D. 24 hrs) (2 required).

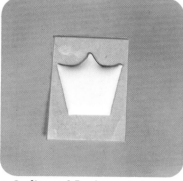

6. Outline and flood-in end of CRADLE (L.D. 24 hrs) (2 required).

7. Outline and flood-in the PILLOW, CRADLE BASE and BLANKET (one of each required) (L.D. 24 hrs).

8. Outline and flood-in the cake top runout (4 required) (L.D. 24 hrs).

9. Decorate the CRADLE sides as shown (No.1).

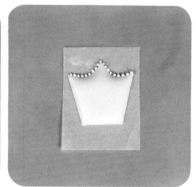

10. Pipe a row of single dots over each CRADLE end top (No.1).

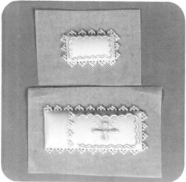

11. Pipe 6-dot sequence and decorate, as shown (No.1) (L.D. 12 hrs).

12. Fix sides and ends to CRADLE BASE.

13. Pipe small shells along inside joins and pipe a line around the top inside of the CRADLE (No.1).

14. Upturn CRADLE and pipe shells along joins. Pipe 2 lines to form rockers (No.1) (L.D. 10 m). Repeat overpiping twice (L.D. 12 hrs).

15. Fix PILLOW, baby-doll and BLANKET into CRADLE.

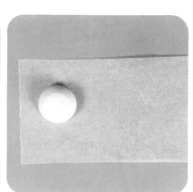

16. Pipe a 3/8″ diameter bulb on to waxed paper to form RATTLE (No.3) (10 required) (L.D. 2 hrs).

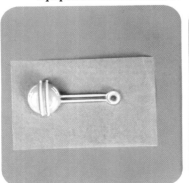

17. Pipe lines and a circle, as shown (No.1) (L.D. 1 hr).

18. Pipe a row of dots between the parallel lines (No.1) (L.D. 1 hr).

19. Pipe a bow on the RATTLE handle (No.1) (L.D. 12 hrs).

20. Fix and align cake top runouts (No.3).

21. Pipe a line on cake board following the cake top runout design (No.2).

22. Flood-in between the No.2 line and cake base (L.D. 12 hrs).

23. Pipe a line on the cake top ⅛" inside the runout (No.2). Pipe a 'V' and two curves on each top runout (No.2).

24. Repeat the 'V's and curves on cake board runouts (No.2).

25. Flood-in between the top two No.2 lines and between the board No.2 line and the cake base (L.D. 12 hrs).

26. Pipe a line of bulbs around the top inside edge of runouts (No.2).

27. Pipe a line of bulbs around the cake base (No.2).

28. Pipe small dots against the No.2 line on top of all runouts (No.1).

29. Pipe names of choice on cake top (No.2).

30. Overpipe the names and lightly pipe the decorative curves (No.1).

31. Fix a pair of RATTLES and the CRADLE to the cake top and decorate with parallel lines (No.1).

32. Fix pairs of RATTLES to cake sides, artificial leaves, flowers to corners and ribbon to board.

Penelope

1. One 9″ diameter sponge cake required.

2. Cut top ⅓rd. of sponge.

3. Divide top ⅓rd. of sponge into 3 pieces (as shown).

4. Turn round the bottom piece.

5. Turn top centre piece of sponge around and then join the outer pieces together in the shape shown.

6. Slice all pieces into two and jam and cream the top of one half of each piece.

7. Rejoin pieces together to form PENELOPE.

8. Cream top and sides of PENELOPE.

9. Roll out a thin sheet of sugar paste and cover the top half of PENELOPE.

10. Roll out and cut two different coloured sheets of sugar paste. Each to be the exact size of the skirt.

11. Place the sugar paste skirts on each other and cut in the shape shown into 12 sections.

12. Fix skirt sections to sponge so they show alternate colours.

13. Roll out a thin strip of sugar paste and cover PENELOPE'S sides.

14. Roll out a thin sheet of sugar paste and cut out and fix the bodice.

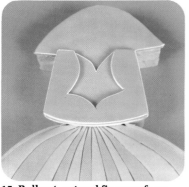

15. Roll out, cut and fix arms from a thin sheet of sugar paste.

16. Roll out, cut and fix a shield-shaped piece of sugar paste to form the face.

17. Pipe PENELOPE'S golden locks (No.3).

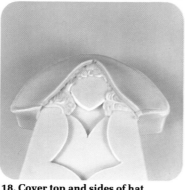

18. Cover top and sides of hat with sugar paste.

19. Paint over face in edible colouring and add a few overlapping locks of hair.

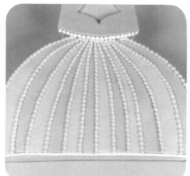

20. Pipe shells down each join of skirt and then at lower arms (No.42).

21. Pipe plain shells along skirt edge (No.3).

22. Pipe plain shells around edges of hat (No.2).

23. Pipe a line at the bodice 'V' (No.2). Pipe a line beneath the No.2 line (No.1). Pipe scallops beside the No.1 line (No.1).

24. Pipe floral pattern (comprising series of 5 outer dots and 1 inner dot) on bodice (No.1).

25. Repeat 24 on each light coloured panel of skirt.

26. Pipe a line over the plain shells on the skirt edge (No.2). Overpipe the No.2 line (No.1).

27. Fix flowers of choice to hat.

28. Pipe flower stems and leaves to cover PENELOPE'S hands (leaf bag).

29. Fix flower of choice to stems and leaves.

30. Pipe a line over the shells around the hat (No.1).

31. Pipe close spikes on the No.1 line on the skirt edge scallops (No.1).

32. Outline, flood-in, decorate and fix a heart-shaped plaque to PENELOPE'S skirt.

35

Johnny

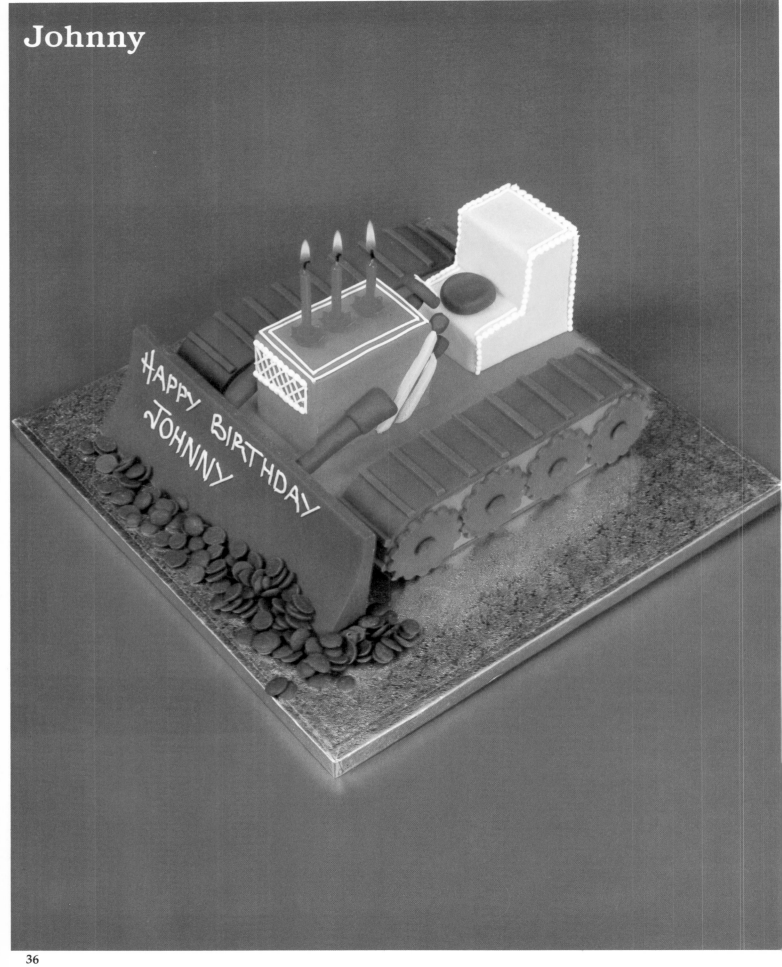

1. Cut a piece of sponge cake – 7″×4″×1″ – to form BASE.

2. Cut 2 pieces of sponge cake – each 3″×2″×1″ – to form ENGINE.

3. Cut 2 pieces of sponge cake
(a) 2½″×2″×1″
(b) 1½″×2″×1″ – to form CHAIR.

4. Cut 2 pieces of sponge cake – each 7″×1½″×1″ – to form WHEELS.

5. Slice the BASE in two and jam the top of one piece.

6. Cream over jam.

7. Join halves together.

8. Cream top and sides.

9. Place BASE on a 14″ square cake board.

10. Roll out a thin sheet of sugar paste and cover top of BASE.

11. Roll out thin sheets of sugar paste and cover sides of BASE.

12. Join ENGINE pieces together with jam and cream. Cream top and sides.

13. Cover ENGINE with thinly rolled-out sugar paste.

14. Place the ENGINE in position on BASE.

15. Join CHAIR pieces together with jam and cream. Cream top and sides.

16. Cover CHAIR in thinly rolled-out sugar paste.

17. Place CHAIR in position on BASE.

18. Slice WHEEL pieces in half and rejoin with jam and cream.

19. Shape the ends of the WHEEL pieces.

20. Cream sides of WHEEL pieces and cover with thinly rolled-out sugar paste.

21. Roll out sugar paste to form WHEEL tracks and fix with cream.

22. Place WHEEL tracks against BASE.

23. Roll and cut out from sugar paste fluted circles to fit into WHEEL tracks and fix.

24. Cut thin strips of sugar paste and fix over tracks.

25. Roll out sugar paste and shape the bulldozer blade (1¾″ high × 7″ wide). (L.D. 2 hrs).

26. Roll out and cut a spacer and place in front of the bulldozer.

27. Fix the bulldozer blade in position against spacer.

28. Shape 2 blade arms and fix to sides of bulldozer ENGINE.

29. Pipe shells on CHAIR and lines and grill on ENGINE (No.1).

30. Make and fix sugar paste items. Add 3 graduated candles as shown.

31. Pipe message of choice on bulldozer blade (No.2).

32. Fix each WHEEL with a chocolate drop hub and place more drops in front of the blade.

38

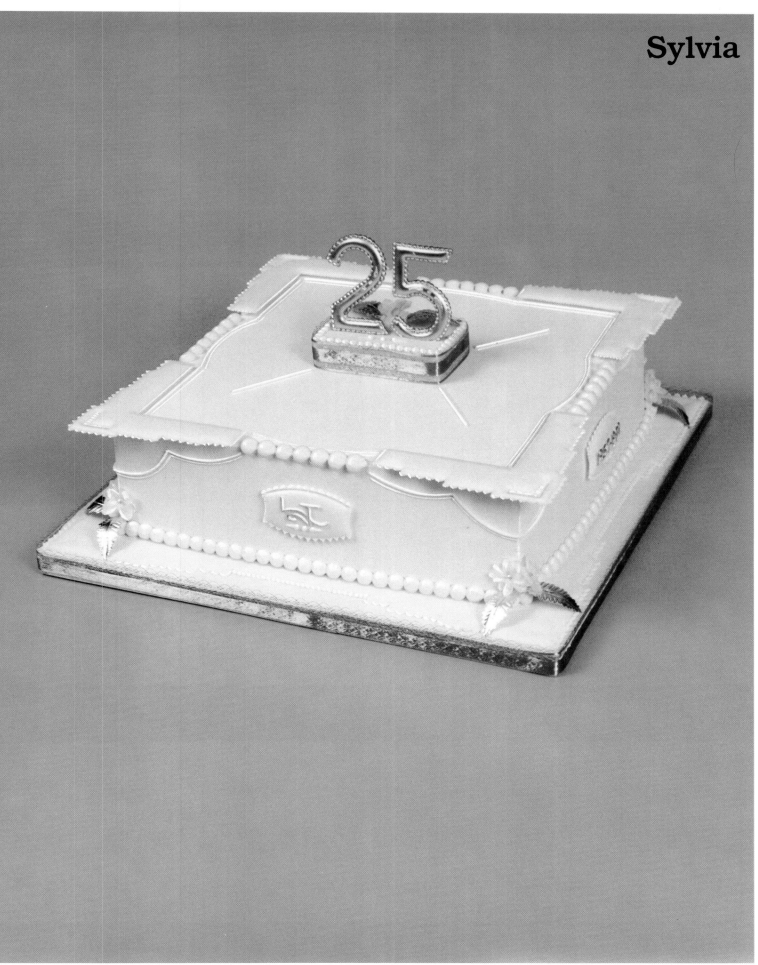

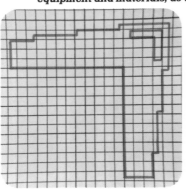

1. Drawing for template of top corner runout (4 required).

2. Using template under waxed paper outline corner runouts (No.1).

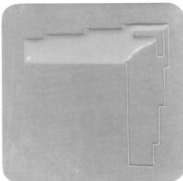

3. Flood-in corner runouts (L.D. 24 hrs).

4. Pipe 6-dot sequence, single dots and filigree, as shown (No.1) (L.D. 12 hrs).

5. Drawing for template of '25'.

6. Using template under waxed paper outline the obverse and reverse of the '25' (No.1).

7. Flood-in the '25' (L.D. 24 hrs).

8. Fix each pair of numerals together. Pipe shells around edges (No.1) (L.D. 12 hrs).

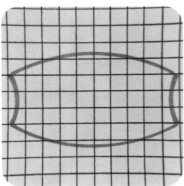

9. Drawing for template of plaque (4 required).

10. Using template under waxed paper outline plaque (No.1).

11. Flood-in plaque. Repeat 10 and 11 for each plaque. (L.D. 24 hrs).

12. Pipe 6-dot sequence and single dots, as shown (No.1) (L.D. 12 hrs).

13. Pipe a line (the length of the runout) on each corner (No.3) (L.D. 2 hrs).

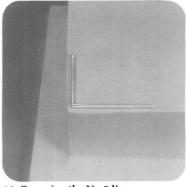

14. Overpipe the No.3 lines (No.2).

15. Immediately fix and align the corner runouts (L.D. 30 m).

16. Pipe small bulbs between runouts and cake top (No.2) (T).

17. Following runout design, pipe a line on cake board (No.2).

18. Flood-in board between the No.2 line and cake base (L.D. 12 hrs).

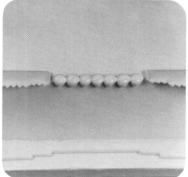

19. Pipe plain shells between corner runouts on top edge of cake (No.3).

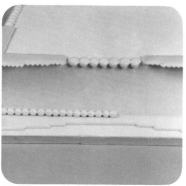

20. Pipe small plain shells around cake base (No.3).

21. Pipe straight corner lines and then pipe curved lines between runouts (No.2).

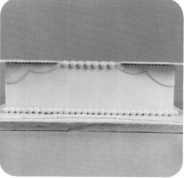

22. Pipe 2 curved lines under each corner runout on sides of cake (No.2) (T).

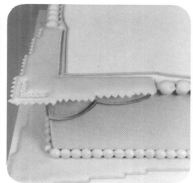

23. Pipe a line beside all No.2 lines, then overpipe all No.2 lines (No.1) (T as necessary).

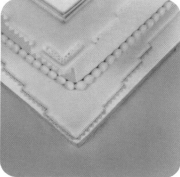

24. Pipe 6-dot sequence around cake board corner runouts (No.1).

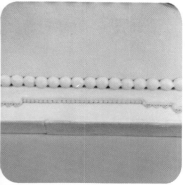

25. Pipe plain shells along each board runout side (No.1).

26. Cut a block of sugar paste 3″ long, 1¾″ wide and 1″ deep (L.D. 2 hrs).

27. Pipe initials of choice on plaque (No.1) and decorate as shown (No.1) (L.D. 2 hrs).

28. Paint '25'. Fix onto block. Pipe shells around top edge (No.1).

29. Fix ribbon around block and decorate with artificial flowers and leaves.

30. Place '25' centrally on cake and pipe 4 diagonal lines (No.2).

31. Pipe a shorter line each side of each diagonal line (No.1) and overpipe each diagonal No.2 line (No.1).

32. Fix plaques to cake sides, artificial flowers and leaves at base corners.

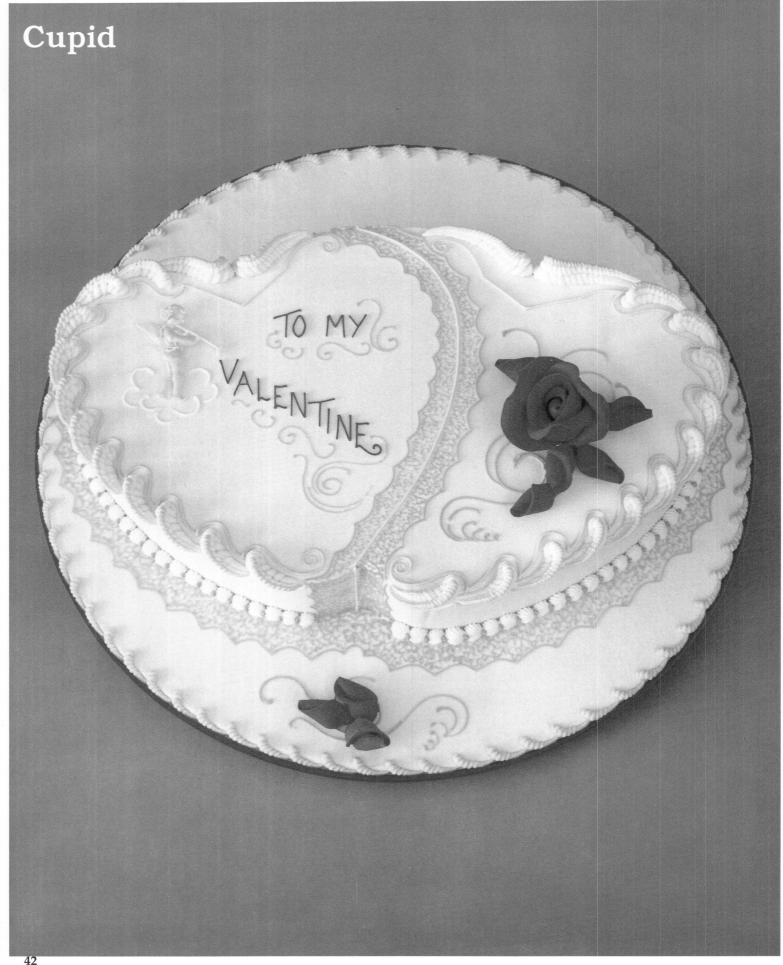

1. 4×8″ heart-shape sponge cakes required.

2. Pair the cakes together.

3. Cut and shape one pair to fit against the other pair, as shown.

4. Jam, marzipan and coat the cake in the normal way.

5. Drawing showing template of Cupid.

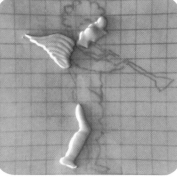

6. Pipe-in areas shown on waxed paper (L.D. 30 m).

7. Pipe further areas shown (L.D. 30 m).

8. Pipe further areas shown (L.D. 30 m).

9. Pipe further areas shown to complete Cupid (L.D. 24 hrs).

10. One large sugar paste rose and 8 small rose-buds required.

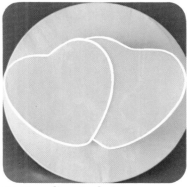

11. Pipe a line at cake join (No.2).

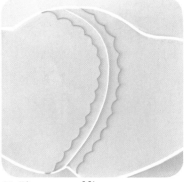

12. Pipe a curved line each side of the No.2 line (No.1).

13. Filigree the areas shown (No.1).

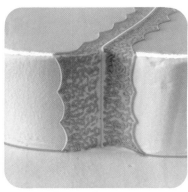

14. Repeat 11–13 down each side of the cake (T).

15. Pipe curved line on cake board, as shown (No.1).

16. Filigree between cake base and curved line (No.1).

43

17. Pipe 2 'S' scrolls at the top of the whole heart, as shown (No.43).

18. Pipe 'C' scrolls on cake-top edge shown (No.43).

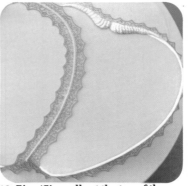

19. Pipe 'S' scrolls at the top of the part heart, as shown (No.43).

20. Pipe 'C' scrolls on cake-top edge shown (No.43).

21. Pipe shells around the base of the cake (No.43).

22. Overpipe each scroll (No.3).

23. Pipe a line beside each scroll, as shown (No.2).

24. Overpipe each scroll (No.2).

25. Pipe a curved line on the cake side beneath each scroll (No.2) (T).

26. Pipe a dot between each shell (No.2).

27. Pipe 'C' scrolls around edge of cake board (No.2).

28. Fix Cupid to the cake top and pipe clouds around his feet, as shown (No.2).

29. Pipe message of choice and curved lines on cake top (No.1).

30. Pipe further lines on the cake top (No.1).

31. Fix the large rose and 5 rose-buds to the lines, as shown.

32. Pipe curved lines on cake board and fix rose-buds. Then fix ribbon to board edge.

44

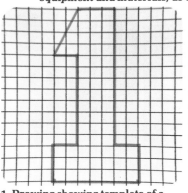

1. Drawing showing template of a figure '1'.

2. Drawing showing template of Teddy.

3. Outline and flood-in on waxed paper the figure '1' (L.D. 24 hrs).

4. Pipe a line around the top edge of the figure '1' (No.1).

5. Pipe the further lines and graduated dots shown (No.1) (L.D. 1 hr).

6. Cover the Teddy template with waxed paper and pipe-in the parts shown (L.D. 30 m).

7. Pipe-in the further parts shown (L.D. 30 m).

8. Pipe-in the further parts shown (L.D. 30 m).

9. Pipe-in the further parts shown (L.D. 24 hrs).

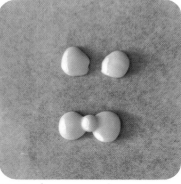

10. Pipe bow on waxed paper in the sequence shown (L.D. 24 hrs).

11. Pipe-in face (No.1) and paint other parts, as shown, with edible colouring.

12. Fix bow to Teddy's neck.

13. Pipe shells along one top edge of the cake (No.7).

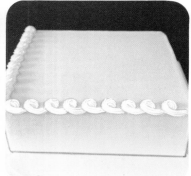

14. Pipe 'C' lines along the adjoining edge (No.7).

15. Pipe shells along the remaining two edges (No.7).

16. Repeat 13–15 at cake base.

17. Pipe shells down each corner (No.7) (T).

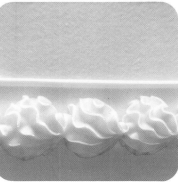

18. Pipe a line beside the top shells (No.3).

19. Pipe a curved line beside the top 'C' line (No.3).

20. Overpipe the top 'C' line (No.3).

21. Overpipe the base 'C' line (No.3).

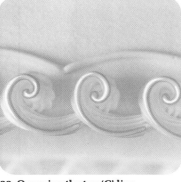

22. Overpipe the top 'C' line (No.2).

23. Pipe a dot between each top shell (No.2).

24. Repeat 22–23 on the base.

25. Fix figure '1' and Teddy to cake top.

26. Pipe message of choice (No.2).

27. Pipe curves, as shown (No.1).

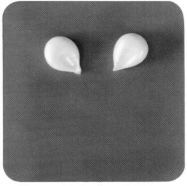

28. Pictures 28–31 show sequence of piping a Teddy on each side of the cake. Pipe ears (No.3).

29. Pipe face (No.3).

30. Pipe body (No.3).

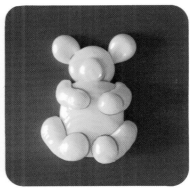

31. Pipe arms and legs (No.3) (L.D. 2 hrs).

32. Paint Teddy's features with edible colouring and fix ribbon to board edge.

47

Petula

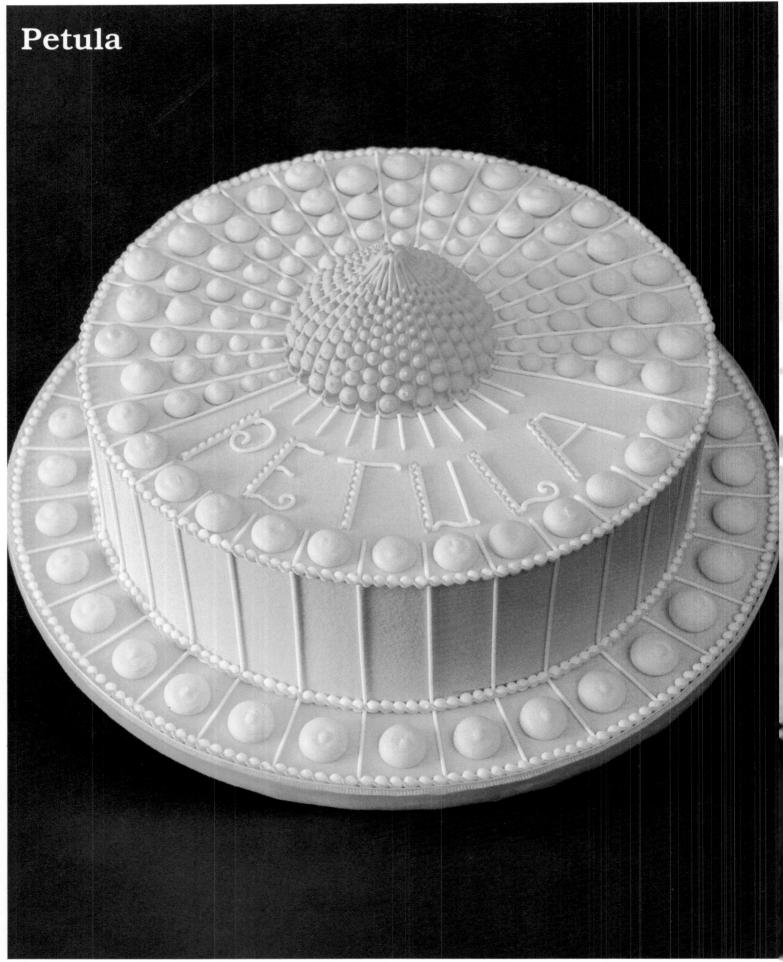

1. Inflate a balloon to a diameter of about 4″ and retain air with a bulldog clip.

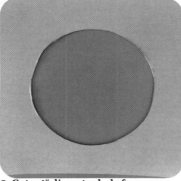

2. Cut a 4″ diameter hole from a piece of card.

3. Push balloon partly through the hole and lightly grease with vegetable fat. Support in a basin, as shown.

4. Pipe 4 lines from the top so as to quarter the balloon (No.2).

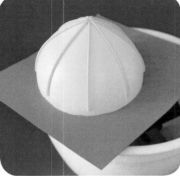

5. Sub-divide with 4 further piped lines (No.2).

6. Sub-divide with 8 further piped lines (No.2).

7. Sub-divide with 16 further piped lines (No.2).

8. Pipe graduated dots between two of the lines, as shown (No.2).

9. Pipe graduated dots between the next pair of lines, as shown (No.2).

10. Repeat 8–9 around balloon (L.D. 24 hrs).

11. Slowly deflate balloon whilst holding the dome in hand.

12. Place dome centrally on cake top.

13. Pipe curved lines on the cake top to join the dome lines (No.2).

14. Pipe name of choice (No.2).

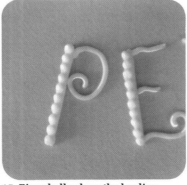

15. Pipe shells along the leading edge of each letter (No.2).

16. Overpipe the shells with a line (No.1).

49

17. Mark the cake-top edge with piped dots into 32 divisions, so that each mark is in line with a dome line.

18. Mark the base of the cake with matching piped dots.

19. Pipe a line from a dome line to the appropriate cake-top edge mark each side of the name, as shown (No.2).

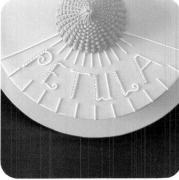

20. Radiate broken lines from dome lines to top edge marks, as shown (No.2).

21. Pipe remaining lines from the dome lines to top edge marks as shown (No.2).

22. Pipe vertical lines (between marks) down the cake side (No.2) (T).

23. Continue piping lines across the cake board (No.2).

24. Pipe graduated bulbs between the first pair of complete lines, as shown (No.4).

25. Continue piping graduated bulbs between alternate pairs of lines, as shown, and single bulbs below the name (No.4).

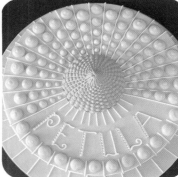

26. Continue piping further graduated bulbs shown (No.4).

27. Pipe plain shells around the top edge of the cake (No.2).

28. Overpipe the shells with a line (No.1).

29. Repeat 27–28 at the base of the cake.

30. Pipe a bulb on each board division (No.4).

31. Repeat 27–28 around the edge of the cake board.

32. Fix ribbon to edge of the board.

Congratulations
on your
Engagement
Claire
and
Robert

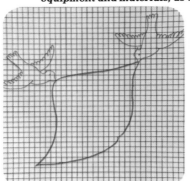

1. Drawing showing template of doves and plaque.

2. Pipe the right wing of the left dove on waxed paper (and keep separate from remainder of dove) (No.1) (L.D. 12 hrs).

3. Pipe the left wing of the right dove on waxed paper (and keep separate from remainder of dove) (No.1) (L.D. 12 hrs).

4. Pipe the left wing of the left dove on waxed paper (No.1).

5. Pipe the head, body and tail of the left dove against the left wing (No.1) (L.D. 24 hrs).

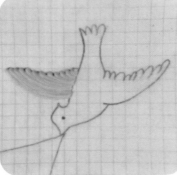

6. Pipe the right wing of the right dove on waxed paper (No.1).

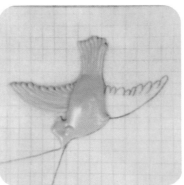

7. Pipe the head, body and tail of the right dove against the right wing (No.1) (L.D. 24 hrs).

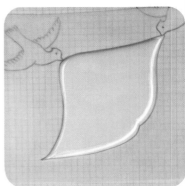

8. Outline and flood-in the plaque on waxed paper (L.D. 24 hrs).

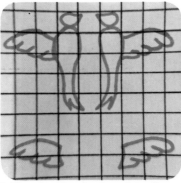

9. Drawing showing template of love-birds (6 love-birds required).

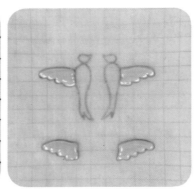

10. Pipe-in the wings on waxed paper, as shown (No.1) (L.D. 12 hrs).

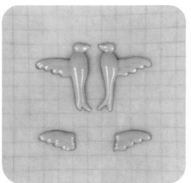

11. Pipe-in heads and bodies on waxed paper, as shown (No.1).

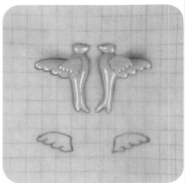

12. Remove love-bird loose wings and fix to bodies, as shown (L.D. 12 hrs).

13. Fix loose doves' wings to bodies at the angle shown (support as necessary) (L.D. 12 hrs).

14. Pipe 'S' scrolls around the edge of the plaque (No.1).

15. Pipe a line along the inside edge of the plaque and pipe sequences of dots to form floral design (No.1).

16. Pipe message of choice in 'flow' of plaque (No.1) (L.D. 12 hrs).

17. Drawing showing template of heart-shape plaques.

18. Outline and flood-in hearts on waxed paper (L.D. 24 hrs). (6 hearts required).

19. Pipe dots around the edge of each heart (No.1).

20. Pipe an initial of choice on each heart (No.1)((L.D. 12 hrs).

21. Pipe shells around top edge and base of cake (No.44).

22. Finish front of base with a long shell (No.44).

23. Overpipe each top shell with a heart design (No.3).

24. Overpipe each base shell with a heart design (No.3).

25. Overpipe each No.3 design (No.2).

26. Overpipe each No.2 design (No.1).

27. Fix plaque and doves to cake top.

28. Fix hearts and supporting love-birds to the front and each side of cake, as shown.

29. Fix artificial flowers and decorations of choice, as shown.

30. Pipe 'S' scrolls around cake board edge (No.2).

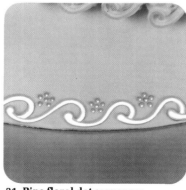

31. Pipe floral dot sequences between each board scroll (No.1).

32. Fix decorative ribbon to board edge.

Lisa

NOTE: *Before attempting to decorate this cake, please study the whole sequence of photographs and notes and ensure you have the proper equipment and materials, as well as sufficient time. Additional information can be found on pages 5–17.*

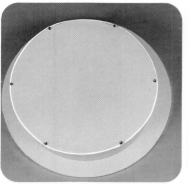

1. Mark top of cake with small piped dots into 6 equal spaces (No.1).

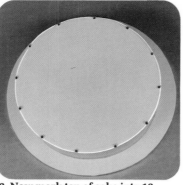

2. Now mark top of cake into 12 equal spaces (No.1).

3. Pipe a line around base of cake (No.44).

4. Immediately beneath each top dot, mark line around base with a piped dot (No.1).

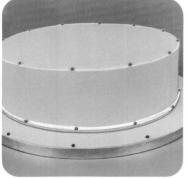

5. Immediately opposite each base dot mark board edge with a piped dot (No.1).

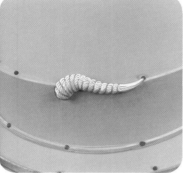

6. Pipe 'S' scroll from left to right between 2 dots on top edge (No.44).

7. Pipe 'S' scroll from right to left between 2 dots on top edge (No.44).

8. Pipe 'C' scroll from left to right inside 'S' scroll (No.44).

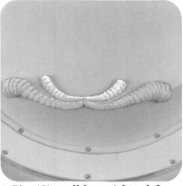

9. Pipe 'C' scroll from right to left inside 'S' scroll (No.44).

10. Repeat scroll designs around top edge of cake.

11. Pipe 'S' scroll between 2 dots on the No.44 line (directly beneath a matching top scroll) (No.44).

12. Pipe 'S' scroll between 2 dots on the No.44 line (directly beneath the next matching top scroll) (No.44).

13. Repeat scroll design around base of cake.

14. Overpipe a top left-to-right 'S' scroll (No.3).

15. Overpipe a top right-to-left 'S' scroll (No.3).

16. Overpipe a top left-to-right 'C' scroll (No.3).

55

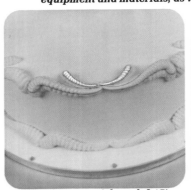

17. Overpipe a top right-to-left 'C' scroll (No.3). Repeat 14–17 around cake top.

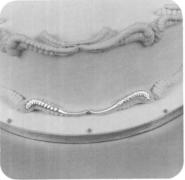

18. Overpipe base scrolls (No.3).

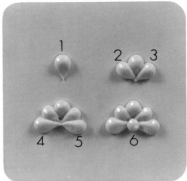

19. Practice flower motif in numerical order (No.3).

20. Pipe flower motif inside each top 'C' scroll (No.3).

21. Overpipe a top left-to-right 'S' scroll (No.2).

22. Overpipe the next top right-to-left 'S' scroll (No.2).

23. Overpipe a top left-to-right 'C' scroll (No.2).

24. Overpipe the next top right-to-left 'C' scroll (No.2). Repeat 21–24 around cake top.

25. Overpipe base scrolls (No.2).

26. Pipe 3 curved lines below scrolls on side of cake (No.2). (T). Continue around cake.

27. Pipe line pattern on board (No.2). Continue around cake and remove marker dots.

28. Pipe line around cake under 1st line (No.1) (T).

29. Pipe a line on board in front of 1st line (No.1).

30. Pipe a line against 1st line around side of cake (T) and on 1st board line (No.1).

31. Overpipe each scroll (No.1). Pipe scallops on side of cake and on board (No.1) (T).

32. Form a central motif with artificial flowers and decorative piping (No.1).

1. Outline and flood-in heart-shape band (inside width at widest point=8½″. Width of band=1½″) (L.D. 24 hrs).

2. Outline and flood-in a 2nd heart-shape band (inside width at widest point=9″. Width of band=1″) (L.D. 24 hrs).

3. Fix 1st runout to an iced heart-shape cake measuring 9″ at the widest point.

4. Pipe a line centrally around 1st runout (No.4) (L.D. 2 hrs).

5. Overpipe the No.4 line (No.4) (L.D. 2 hrs).

6. Overpipe the No.4 line (No.3) (L.D. 2 hrs).

7. Fix 2nd heart-shape runout onto 1st runout (No.3) (L.D. 30 m).

8. Pipe bulbs under 1st runout at cake top edge (No.2) (T).

9. Pipe 18 curved lines around side of cake (No.3) (T).

10. Pipe small plain shells around cake base (No.2).

11. Pipe a line against the curved No.3 lines (No.2) (T).

12. Pipe a suspended line on the inside of the runouts from top to bottom (No.1).

13. Continue piping suspended lines around inside of runouts (No.1).

14. Picture showing the completed sequence of inner suspended lines.

15. Pipe a suspended line on the outside of the runouts from top to bottom (No.1).

16. Continue piping suspended lines around outside of runouts (No.1).

17. Pipe dots along inner bottom edge of runout (No.1).

18. Pipe plain shells along inner top edge of runout (No.2).

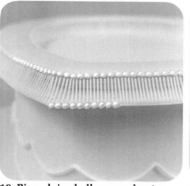

19. Pipe plain shells around outer runout edges (No.2).

20. Pipe 18 curved lines on board (parallel to those on cake side) (No.3).

21. Overpipe the No.3 lines (No.2) (L.D. 30 m).

22. Pipe a suspended line from a side curved line to a board curved line (No.1).

23. Continue piping suspended lines around cake (No.1).

24. Picture showing completed sequence of lines.

25. Pipe plain shells on curved lines on cake side and board (No.2).

26. Pipe a line beside the board No.3 line (No.2), then beside the No.2 line (No.1) and then overpipe the No.2 line (No.1).

27. Picture showing sequence of dots forming a floral pattern.

28. Pipe floral pattern in each curve on cake side (No.1) (T).

29. Pipe 4 floral patterns on top of runout, as shown (No.1).

30. Pipe plain shells around edge of board (No.3).

31. Overpipe the No.3 shells (No.1).

32. Fix artificial leaves and flowers of choice and ribbon, as shown.

1. Mark top of cake into 12 equal spaces with small dots (No.1).

2. Pipe a line around the base of the cake (No.44).

3. Mark the No.44 line with 12 small dots, keeping them immediately beneath the top dots (No.1).

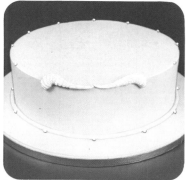

4. Pipe a left-hand scroll between 2 dots and then a right-hand scroll (No.43). Repeat around cake top.

5. Pipe 'C' scrolls around cake top (No.43).

6. Pipe base scrolls to match the top scrolls (No.43).

7. Overpipe all top scrolls (No.3).

8. Overpipe all base scrolls (No.3).

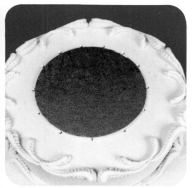

9. Using a disc as a guide, mark top of cake with 12 equally spaced dots (in line with outer edge dots) (No.1).

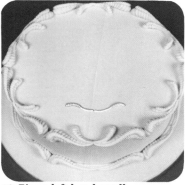

10. Pipe a left-hand scroll between 2 dots and then a right-hand scroll (No.2). Repeat around cake top.

11. Pipe 'C' scrolls around cake top (No.2).

12. Pipe heart-shape motifs inside outer 'C' scrolls (No.2).

13. Pipe flower motif inside each heart-shape (No.1).

14. Outline the inner scrolls with 'V's and curved lines (No.2).

15. Overpipe all top outer scrolls (No.2).

16. Pipe 3 curved lines under each pair of scrolls on side of cake (No.2) (T).

61

17. Overpipe base scrolls (No.2).

18. Pipe 'V's and curved lines on board (keeping pattern symmetrical with cake top pattern) (No.2).

19. Overpipe all cake top inner scrolls (No.1)

20. Pipe a line beside the cake top inner No.2 line and then overpipe the No.2 line (No.1).

21. Overpipe all scrolls (No.1).

22. Pipe a line on side of cake under the No.2 line and then against the No.2 line (No.1) (T).

23. Pipe a line beside the No.2 base line and then overpipe the No.2 line (No.1).

24. Pipe lines across inner scrolls on cake top (No.1).

25. Overpipe cross lines (No.1) and then overpipe the inner scrolls (No.1).

26. Pipe lines across the outer scrolls (working from outer to inner points) (No.1).

27. Pipe curved lines, as shown, overpipe scrolls and then pipe curved lines on cake side (No.1).

28. Pipe lines from the curved lines on the side of the cake to the base scrolls (No.1).

29. Overpipe cross lines with curved lines to centre of lattice (No.1).

30. Overpipe remaining cross lines with curved lines to complete lattice (No.1). Repeat around cake.

31. Pipe plain shells along the top and down the centre of each lattice (No.1).

32. Fix artificial leaves and a rose on cake top.

NOTE: *Before attempting to decorate this cake, please study the whole sequence of photographs and notes and ensure you have the proper equipment and materials, as well as sufficient time. Additional information can be found on pages 5–17.*

1. Template for male figure (4 figures required).

2. Template for female figure (4 figures required).

3. Template for cupid (4 figures required).

4. Template for cherub (4 figures required).

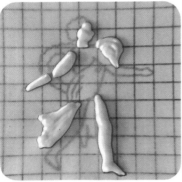

5. Pipe left leg, toga top, face, left arm, and toga back on waxed paper (Template 1) (L.D. 15 m).

6. Pipe hair, garland and toga front (L.D. 15 m).

7. Pipe right leg and back (L.D. 15 m).

8. Pipe right arm and body toga (L.D. 24 hrs).

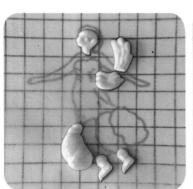

9. Pipe face, feet, flowing waist band and 1st fold of skirt frill on waxed paper (Template 2) (L.D. 15 m).

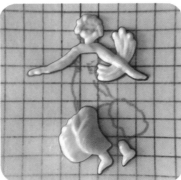

10. Pipe hair, arms, shoulders and 2nd fold of skirt frill (L.D. 15 m).

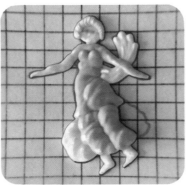

11. Pipe bodice, skirt and 3rd fold of skirt frill (L.D. 15 m).

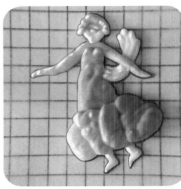

12. Pipe remaining fold of skirt frill (L.D. 24 hrs).

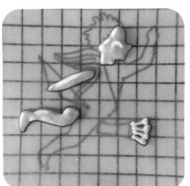

13. Pipe face, left arm, left leg and arrows on waxed paper (Template 3) (L.D. 15 m).

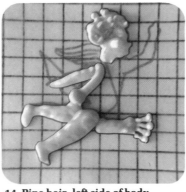

14. Pipe hair, left side of body, quiver and right leg (L.D. 15 m).

15. Pipe right arm, trunk and wing (L.D. 15 m).

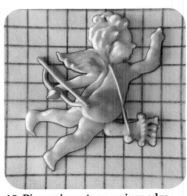

16. Pipe quiver strap, quiver edge and bow (L.D. 24 hrs).

17. Pipe face, wing and left leg on waxed paper (L.D. 15 m).

18. Pipe hair, left arm and right leg. (L.D. 15 m).

19. Pipe trunk and right arm. (L.D. 15 m).

20. Pipe strap and garland. (L.D. 24 hrs).

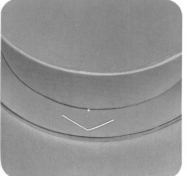

21. Pipe 4 equally spaced 'V's around cake board (No.2).

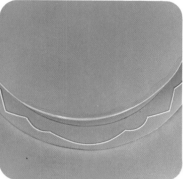

22. Pipe 2 small and 1 large curve between each 'V' (No.2).

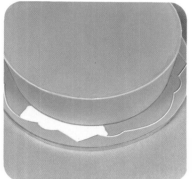

23. Flood-in soft Royal Icing between board line and cake base (L.D. 12 hrs).

24. Pipe large shells around top edge of cake (No.44).

25. Pipe small shells around base of cake (No.43).

26. Pipe a line outside the board runout (No.2).

27. Pipe a line outside the board No.2 line (No.1).

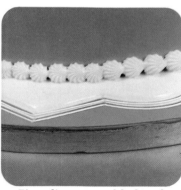

28. Pipe a line on top of the board No.2 line (No.1).

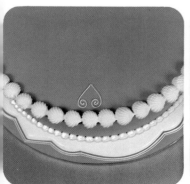

29. Pipe a heart-shape pattern around top edge of cake (No.1).

30. Pipe the floral design shown above each board 'V' on the cake side (No.2) (T).

31. Pipe graduated dots on each side of floral design (No.2).

32. Fix appropriate figures to side of each cake.

Happy Mother's Day

1. An 8″ round cake, marzipanned and coated in the normal way, on an 11″ coated board, required.

2. 9 various sized sugar roses required. (See instructions).

3. Pipe a line in the shape shown in two colours of Royal Icing (No.3).

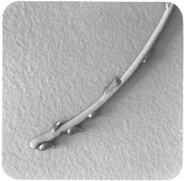

4. Pipe spikes along the line (No.1).

5. Repeat 3–4 three more times to form a spray.

6. 6–9 illustrates the making of a Royal Icing rosebud. Pipe centre of bud, as shown (No.59).

7. Pipe petal, as shown (No.59).

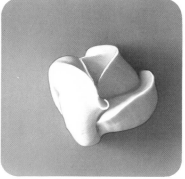

8. Pipe petal, as shown (No.59).

9. Pipe calyx, as shown (No.2).

10. Repeat 7–9 on cake top, as shown.

11. Fix sugar roses on spray, as shown.

12. Pipe-in leaves, as shown (Leaf bag with two colours of Royal Icing).

13. Pipe message of choice (No.2).

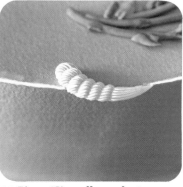

14. Pipe a 'C' scroll on cake-top edge, as shown (No.42).

15. Continue piping 'C' scrolls on the top edge behind the spray (No.42).

16. Pipe shells along the remainder of the top edge (No.3).

17. Picture showing cake top so far.

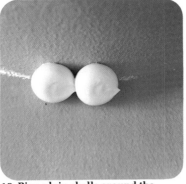

18. Pipe plain shells around the base of the cake (No.3).

19. Picture showing completed circle of base shells.

20. Overpipe each 'C' scroll (No.3).

21. Overpipe each cake-top shell with a line (No.2).

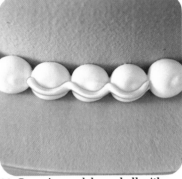

22. Overpipe each base shell with a line (No.3).

23. Overpipe each 'C' scroll line (No.2).

24. Overpipe each cake-top shell line (No.1).

25. Overpipe each base shell line (No.2).

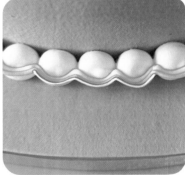

26. Overpipe each base shell line (No.1).

27. Pipe a pair of dots between each cake-top shell (No.1).

28. Pipe wavy lines under the message, as shown (No.1).

29. Pipe curved lines on cake board, as shown (No.3).

30. Pipe spikes to cake-board curved lines (No.1).

31. Pipe rosebuds and fix sugar roses to the board curved lines.

32. Pipe a curved rope line on board edge (No.2) and fix ribbon to board edge.

Claude

69

1. Cut a piece of sponge cake 10″ long×6″ wide×1″ thick.

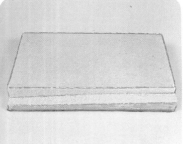

2. Form two wedges by slicing sponge diagonally from top right to bottom left.

3. Jam the top of one wedge.

4. Cream over the jam.

5. Place wedges together – thick end to thick end.

6. Cream top of sponge.

7. Cream sides.

8. Roll out a thin sheet of sugar paste to cover sponge top.

9. Place sugar paste sheet over creamed sponge top.

10. Form another sheet of thin sugar paste. Cut 2 elongated wedges to fit sides of sponge.

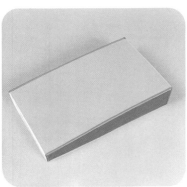

11. Fix wedges to long sides of sponge.

12. Roll out a thin sheet of sugar paste and cut 2 rectangles to cover sponge ends.

13. Fix ends in position.

14. Roll out a thin strip of sugar paste and fix around sponge base.

15. Roll out and fix a thin sheet of sugar paste for calculator window (5″×2″).

16. Roll out and cut a sheet of sugar paste (3¾″×3¾″×¼″). Then cut it into 25 equal squares (each ¾″×¾″).

17. Cut and slope opposite sides of each square.

18. Cut and slope remaining sides of each square.

19. Fix 25 squares on sponge top.

20. Example of lettering on squares.

21. Pipe lettering on squares in 1st row (No.1).

22. Pipe lettering on squares in 2nd row (No.1).

23. Pipe lettering on squares in 3rd row (No.1).

24. Pipe lettering on squares in 4th row (No.1).

25. Pipe lettering on squares in 5th row (No.1).

26. Diagramatic photograph of complete calculator keyboard.

27. Pipe a line ½″ inside the window edge (No.1).

28. Pipe numbers in window (No.1).

29. Make 2 sugar paste squares and fix to top right side of sponge. Pipe the "ON" and "OFF" (No.1).

30. Pipe message on top left side of sponge cake (No.1).

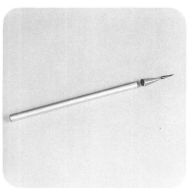

31. Roll out 3 different coloured pieces of sugar paste and fix together to form pencil.

32. Cut out 2 different coloured wedges of sugar paste and fix together to form the rubber.

1. A round cake and board coated in the normal way required.

2. A second board of the same size required.

3. Cover the second board with waxed paper.

4. Divide perimeter of waxed paper into 16 equal portions with piped dots (No.2).

5. Pipe a curved line between each pair of dots, as shown (No.2).

6. Upturn cake onto waxed paper and flood-in as shown (L.D. 24 hrs).

7. Upturn the cake and remove the waxed paper.

8. Pipe matching curved lines on the cake board (No.2).

9. Flood-in base of cake to the No.2 line (L.D. 12 hrs).

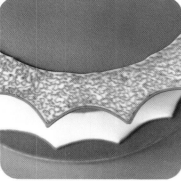

10. Filigree the top runout (No.1).

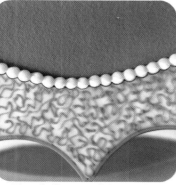

11. Pipe shells around the inside edge of the top runout (No.2).

12. Pipe shells around base of cake (No.3).

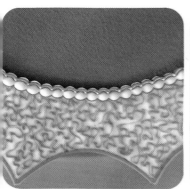

13. Overpipe the top edge shells with a line (No.1).

14. Pipe parallel lines on cake top, as shown (No.2).

15. Pipe a curved line on cake top, as shown (No.2).

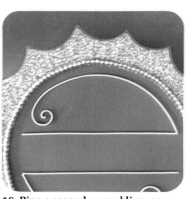

16. Pipe a second curved line, as shown (No.2).

17. Pipe a line beside each No.2 line (No.1).

18. Pipe scallops beside each No.1 line (No.1).

19. Pipe curved lines around the middle of the cake, as shown (No.2) (T).

20. Pipe a line under the cake-side No.2 line (No.1) and then pipe a line against the No.2 line (No.1) (T).

21. Pipe the vertical lines shown (No.1) (T).

22. Overpipe the base shells with a line (No.2).

23. Pipe a line beside the base runout (No.2).

24. Overpipe the base shell No.2 line (No.1).

25. Pipe a line beside the board No.2 line (No.1) and then overpipe the board No.2 line (No.1).

26. Pipe a 6-dot motif at each board runout point (No.1).

27. Pipe a 6-dot motif above each cake-side line curve (No.1).

28. Fix candle holders to cake top and pipe the lines shown (No.1).

29. Pipe message of choice (No.1).

30. Pipe the 6-dot motifs shown (No.1).

31. Fix artificial flowers and pipe the lines shown (No.1).

32. Fix candles to holders and ribbon to the board edge.

74

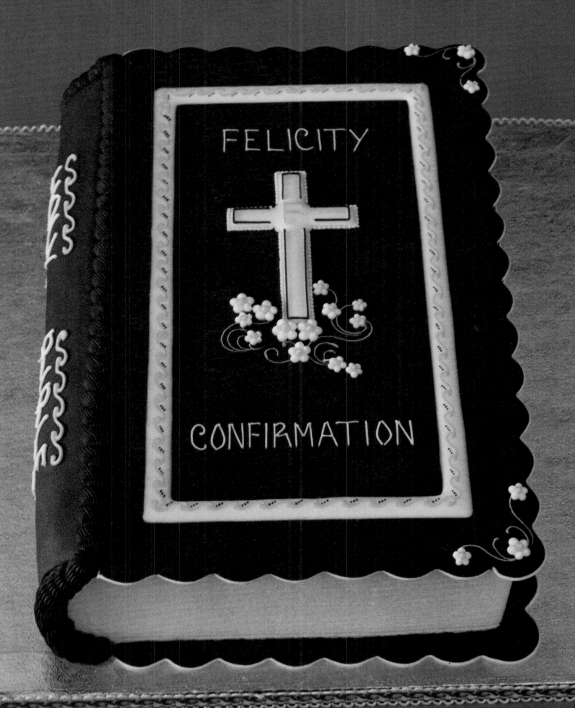

1. 8″×8″ square cake required.

2. Cut off a 2″ slice.

3. Fix slice to end of cake and remove surplus.

4. Trim left side of cake to form book spine.

5. Marzipan and coat cake in normal way on board.

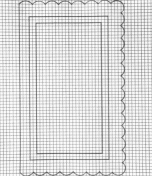

6. Drawing showing template of book cover – 11″×6¼″.

7. Outline the book cover areas shown on waxed paper (No.2).

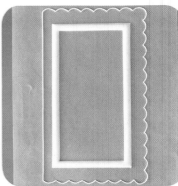

8. Flood-in the white frame shown (L.D. 6 hrs).

9. Flood-in remaining areas in black, as shown (L.D. 24 hrs).

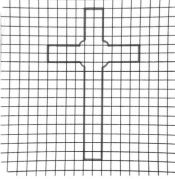

10. Drawing showing template of Cross – 3¼″ high.

11. Outline and flood-in the Cross on waxed paper (L.D. 24 hrs).

12. Drawing showing floral dot sequence to be piped on waxed paper (No.2) (L.D. 1 hr).

13. Complete the flower with a piped dot centre (No.2) (L.D. 12 hrs) (20 flowers of various sizes required).

14. Pipe shells around the Cross edges (No.2).

15. Pipe lines on the Cross, as shown (No.2) and then overpipe the No.2 lines (No.1).

16. Pipe initial of choice at centre of Cross (No.1) (L.D. 12 hrs).

17. Roll out a thin sheet of sugar paste and fix to the spine of the 'book'.

18. Coat sides of cake using a (sterilised) fine toothed comb to create a page effect (L.D. 4 hrs).

19. Pipe a curved line on the board to match the top cover template (No.2).

20. Flood-in in black between the cake base and the No.2 line.

21. Fix the Cross centrally to the top cover.

22. Pipe curved lines at the base of the Cross, as shown (No.1).

23. Fix flowers to the curved lines, as shown.

24. Pipe inscription of choice on cover (No.1).

25. Pipe 'S' pattern on the white frame, as shown (No.1).

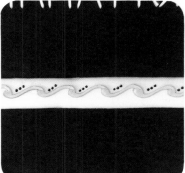

26. Pipe dots beside each 'S' pattern, as shown (No.1).

27. Pipe curved lines on the top and bottom right-hand corners of the top cover (No.1).

28. Fix flowers to the curved lines, as shown.

29. Fix cover to the cake.

30. Pipe rope lines to spine, as shown (No.44).

31. Pipe inscription of choice to spine (No.2).

32. Pipe a matching 'S' pattern each side of the inscription (No.2) and fix ribbon to board edge.

77

1. Two round cakes required – each 7″ in diameter × 1½″ thick.

2. Jam and marzipan each cake top in the normal way and fix together.

3. Cut a cake plastic scraper to form a bowl outline design.

4. Shape the cake (using the scraper as a guide).

5. Roll out a thin strip of marzipan to cover the bottom half of the cake and fix in the normal way.

6. Repeat 5 for top half of cake (L.D. for about 3 days).

7. Coat the cake side with Royal Icing using the shaped scraper. (L.D. 24 hrs).

8. Coat top of cake with Royal Icing (L.D. 24 hrs).

9. Flat-pipe lines around cake from dark green base to pale green. Finish with blue top edge.

10. Whilst still wet, smooth Royal Icing with the shaped scraper (L.D. 24 hrs).

11. Obtain a real polyanthus leaf and fix it with cow gum to a piece of waxed paper.

12. Form a circular ¾″ high wall of sugar paste around the leaf.

13. Mix a small amount of plaster-of-paris and pour it into the circular mould so the leaf is covered (L.D. 2 hrs).

14. Turn mould over and remove waxed paper.

15. Carefully remove leaf. (Leave mould to dry for 2 hours).

16. Lightly dust the mould with icing sugar. Press a knob of sugar paste into the mould so that the leaf is fully covered.

17. Remove the sugar paste immediately from the mould and curve it slightly (L.D. 24 hrs) (30 leaves required).

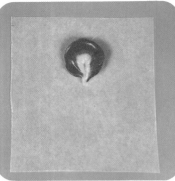

18. Pipe a petal using two colours of Royal Icing in bag (No.59).

19. Continue piping 4 remaining petals (60 flowers required) (L.D. 24 hrs).

20. Lightly brush food colouring onto centre of each flower.

21. Pipe flower stamens (No.1) (L.D. 2 hrs).

22. Upturn each flower. Pipe calyx, as shown (No.4) (L.D. 6 hrs).

23. Pipe (from top of calyx to flowers) 6 sepals around each calyx (L.D. 24 hrs).

24. Coat top of cake with pale blue Royal Icing (L.D. 12 hrs).

25. Pipe bulbs around top edge of cake (No.4) (L.D. 2 hrs).

26. Overpipe the bulbs with a line (No.2) (L.D. 1 hr).

27. Fix some leaves, as shown, to cake top.

28. Fix more leaves, as shown, to overlap cake top edge.

29. Fix different coloured groups of flowers around cake top.

30. Fix more leaves at cake top centre.

31. Fix more groups of flowers at cake top centre.

32. Remove cake board and place POLLY onto a tray. Then lay some flowers and a leaf at the base of the cake.

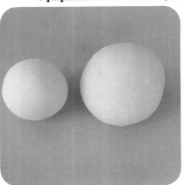

1. Form two balls of marzipan, as shown.

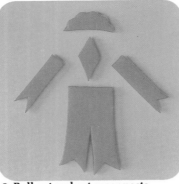

2. Roll out and cut sugar paste wings, feet, comb and beak.

3. Fix balls together with melted chocolate and fix beak to head in shape shown.

4. Fix feet and wings (and add other decorations, as required).

5. Picture of complete father chick (one required).

6. Picture of complete mother chick (one required).

7. Picture of a complete child chick (4 required).

8. Picture of a complete baby chick (2 required).

9. Pipe a narcissus petal on waxed paper (No.58) (see instructions).

10. Pipe another petal, as shown (No.58).

11. Repeat 10.

12. Repeat 10.

13. Repeat 10 to complete the petals.

14. Pipe a ring at the flower centre (No.1).

15. Pipe-in stamens (No.1).

16. Overpipe the ring (No.1) (L.D. 24 hrs) (12 required).

NOTE: Before attempting to decorate this cake, please study the whole sequence of photographs and notes and ensure you have the proper equipment and materials, as well as sufficient time. Additional information can be found on pages 5–17.

17. Place an 8″ square cake to the back of a 12″ board, then marzipan and coat in the normal way.

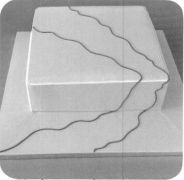

18. Pipe lines on cake and board, as shown (No.2) (T as necessary).

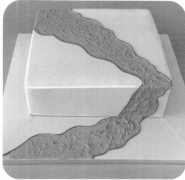

19. Stipple-in between the lines to form a path.

20. Pipe an 'S' scroll on the top corner shown (No.44).

21. Pipe another 'S' scroll, as shown (No.44).

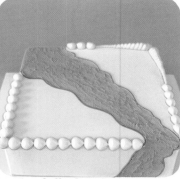

22. Pipe shells along the parts of the top edge shown (No.4).

23. Pipe shells around the cake base – except the path (No.4).

24. Pipe curved lines beside the scrolls (No.3).

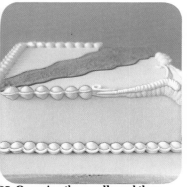

25. Overpipe the scrolls and then overpipe each shell with a line (No.3).

26. Overpipe the scrolls and then overpipe each shell No.3 line (No.2).

27. Pipe curved lines on the cake top, as shown (No.2).

28. Fix narcissi to curved lines.

29. Pipe message of choice to cake top (No.2) and then overpipe twice (No.1).

30. Fix family of chicks to cake.

31. Repeat 27–28 on cake-board front.

32. Repeat 27–28 on cake-board back. Fix ribbon to board edge.

83

Pearl

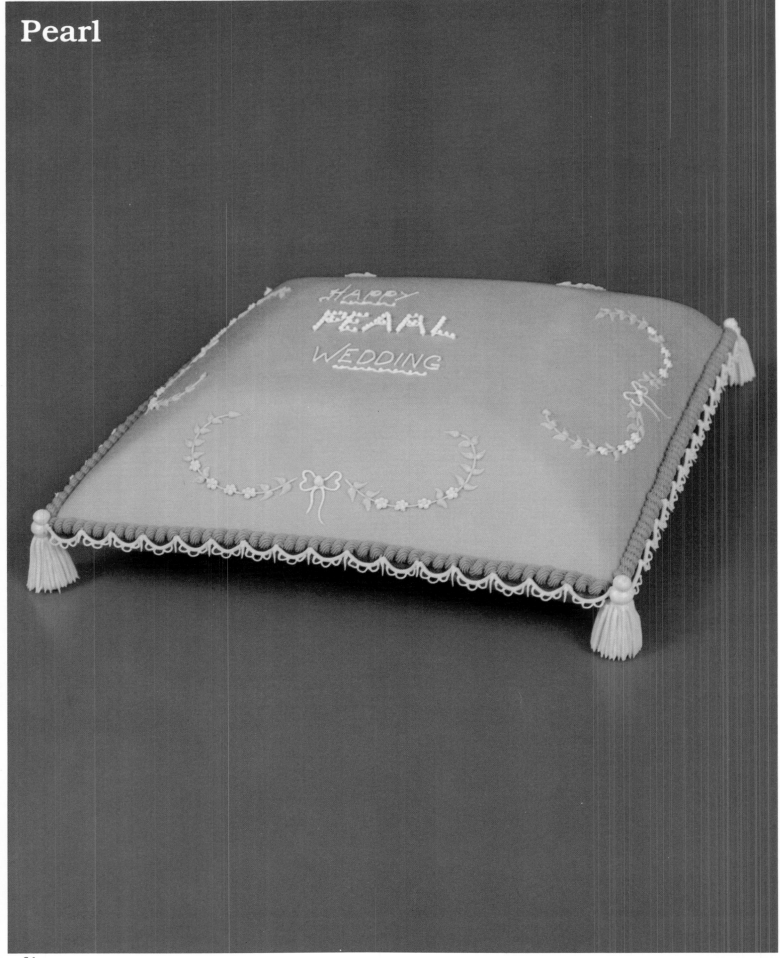

NOTE: Before attempting to decorate this cake, please study the whole sequence of photographs and notes and ensure you have the proper equipment and materials, as well as sufficient time. Additional information can be found on pages 5–17.

1. Two pieces of sponge cake required – each piece 8″×8″×1″.

2. Jam top of one piece.

3. Cream over the jam.

4. Join pieces together.

5. Cut and place a 4″ square of paper to centre of top of cake.

6. Trim a curve from the paper to the outer left edge of top half of cake.

7. Trim a curve from the paper to the outer right edge of top half of cake.

8. Repeat 6 and 7 to the front and back of the top half of the cake.

9. Remove paper and turn cake over. Repeat trimming sequence to form the cushion slope.

10. Cream over the top.

11. Cover top with a thin sheet of sugar paste and trim edges.

12. Turn cake over and cream top.

13. Cover top with a thin sheet of sugar paste so that both edges neatly meet – trim as necessary.

14. Pipe a rope around the CUSHION edge (No.42) (L.D. 1 hr).

15. Pipe 4 cones – each ¾″ high – onto waxed paper (No.4) (L.D. 24 hrs).

16. Pipe 16 loops against the side of the rope. Repeat on each side (No.2) (L.D. 1 hr).

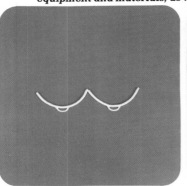

17. Pipe a small loop beneath each large loop (No.1).

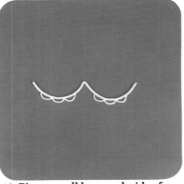

18. Pipe a small loop each side of 17 (No.1).

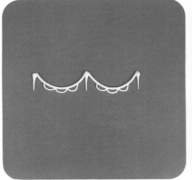

19. Pipe a spike at each large loop join (No.1).

20. Repeat 17–19 around cake.

21. Remove the 4 cones from waxed paper and mount each cone on a sugar paste stem.

22. Pipe lines from the top to the base around each cone (No.2) (L.D. 2 hrs). Repeat 3 times around each cone to create tassels.

23. Pipe 2 curved lines on each CUSHION top slope (No.1).

24. Pipe leaves on to the No.1 lines, as shown, using a cut paper leaf-bag.

25. Pipe flowers – each comprising 5 outer and 1 central dot – on to the No.1 lines (No.1).

26. Pipe a bow to join each pair of No.1 lines (No.1).

27. Pipe inscription on CUSHION top (No.1).

28. Pipe small dots on the word 'Pearl' (No.2).

29. Pipe decorative lines under 'Happy' and 'Wedding' (No.1).

30. Remove tassels from sugar paste stems and place at CUSHION corners.

31. Pipe a bulb at each corner fixing a tassel to the CUSHION (No.2) (L.D. 20 m).

32. Pipe a small bulb on each tassel bulb (No.1). (L.D. 12 hrs).

1. 80–100 rose-buds need to be made for each tier – see instructions.

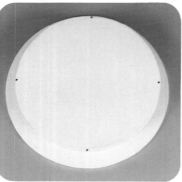

2. Mark top of cake into 4 equal divisions with piped dots.

3. Pipe a curved line, as shown, between each dot (No.2).

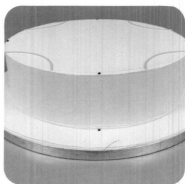

4. Mark base of cake (beneath top dots) into 4 equal divisions with piped dots.

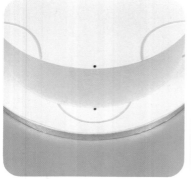

5. Pipe curved line on cake board around each base dot, as shown (No.2).

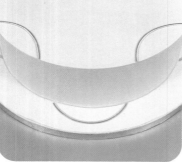

6. Pipe a line inside each No.2 top line and outside each No.2 board line (No.1).

7. Overpipe all No.2 lines (No.1).

8. Pipe plain shells inside all No.2 lines and on parts of the cake edge shown (No.2).

9. Pipe scallops outside all No.1 lines (No.1) and then inside all shells (No.1).

10. Pipe 4 spiral shells on top edge between each design (No.43).

11. Repeat 10 on cake board (No.43).

12. Overpipe all spiral shells with a rope (No.3).

13. Pipe a curved rope inside cake-top spiral shells (No.2).

14. Pipe a curved rope beneath cake-top spiral shells (No.2) (T).

15. Pipe a curved rope over base spiral shells (No.2) (T).

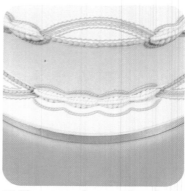

16. Pipe a curved rope on board around base spiral shells (No.2).

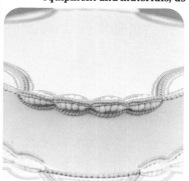

17. Overpipe all top spiral shell ropes (No.2).

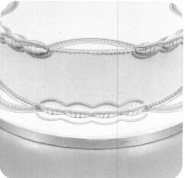

18. Overpipe all base spiral shell ropes (No.2).

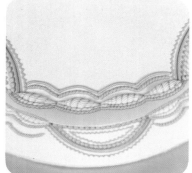

19. Pipe a line inside each cake top No.2 rope (No.2).

20. Pipe a line on the cake side under each top rope (No.2) (T).

21. Pipe a line over each base No.2 rope (No.2) (T) and then pipe a line outside each board No.2 rope (No.2).

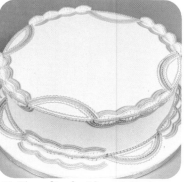

22. Pipe a line beside each No.2 line (No.1) (T as necessary).

23. Overpipe each No.2 line (No.1) and then pipe a line against each No.2 line (No.1) (T as necessary).

24. Overpipe all top and base spiral shell ropes (No.1).

25. Pipe 2 bird heads on cake side, as shown, under the 1st pair of spiral shells (No.1).

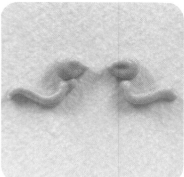

26. Pipe bird bodies (No.1).

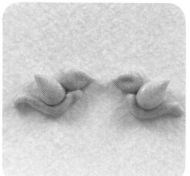

27. Pipe bird wings (No.1).

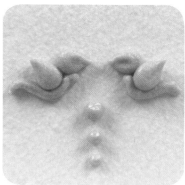

28. Pipe 3 graduated dots beneath each bird (No.1).

29. Fix 3 sugar rose-buds and artificial leaves as shown.

30. Fix, as shown, further rose-buds down cake side.

31. Finish spray with smaller rose-buds and artificial leaves.

32. Pipe leaves with leaf shaped piping bag. Repeat 29–32 three more times around cake.

Daisy

NOTE: *Before attempting to decorate this cake, please study the whole sequence of photographs and notes and ensure you have the proper equipment and materials, as well as sufficient time. Additional information can be found on pages 5–17.*

1. Pipe 1st petal of a daisy on waxed paper (No.57).

2. Continue piping tight petals in clockwise direction.

3. Continue piping tight petals.

4. Complete circle of petals.

5. Complete daisy with yellow centre (No.2) (135 daisies required) (L.D. 24 hrs).

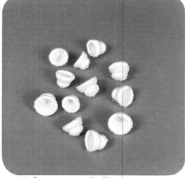

6. Make 12 sugar bells (No.3) (see instructions).

7. Pipe 4 dots at points on diagonal line (corner to corner).

8. Divide top of cake into 3 and pipe 2 dots between existing dots but closer to cake centre.

9. Pipe 2 further dots on cake board. (They must be in line with the 2 middle dots on cake top). Repeat around cake.

10. Pipe curved lines from outer dots to inner dots (No.3).

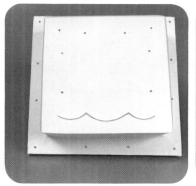

11. Join the outer lines with central curved line (No.3).

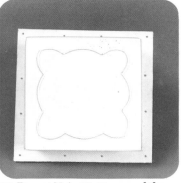

12. Repeat No's.10–11 around the top of the cake (No.3).

13. Pipe equal curves on each side around the cake board (No.3).

14. Pipe a line inside the No.3 line around the cake top (No.2).

15. Overpipe the No.3 line around the top of cake (No.2).

16. Pipe a line outside the No.3 line around the board and then pipe a line on top of the No.3 line (No.2).

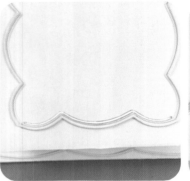

17. Pipe a line inside the No.2 line on top of the cake (No.1).

18. Pipe a line on top of the middle line on top of the cake (No.1).

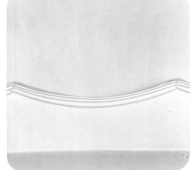

19. Pipe a line on top of outer line on cake top (No.1).

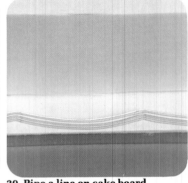

20. Pipe a line on cake board outside the No.2 line and then overpipe both No.2 lines (No.1).

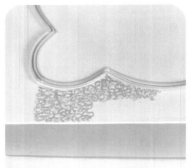

21. Filigree outer edge of top of cake (No.1).

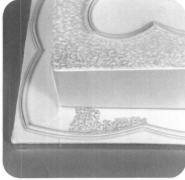

22. Filigree inside pattern on cake board (No.1).

23. Pipe plain shells around top edge of cake (No.4).

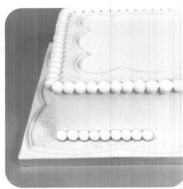

24. Pipe plain shells around base of cake (No.4).

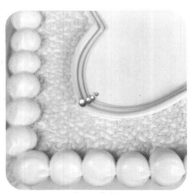

25. Pipe 4 graduated dots at each pattern corner, both on cake top and board (No.1).

26. Fix 4 equally spaced daisies on each side of cake.

27. Join each central daisy pair with a curve of daisies.

28. Join further daisy curves to form chain around the cake.

29. Fix 3 daisies to centre top of cake.

30. Fix bells on top of cake at pattern corners.

31. Fix single daisies at cake base.

32. Fix artificial wishbone at each base corner.

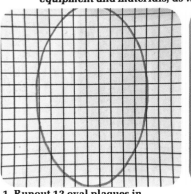

1. Runout 12 oval plaques in proportion to cake sizes (see full cake photograph). (L.D. 24 hrs).

2. Pipe 4 marker dots on cake top (No.1).

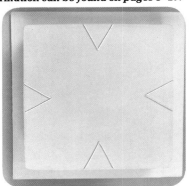

3. Pipe lines to form 'V's on each cake top edge (No.2).

4. Follow 'V' lines down cake sides (No.2). (T).

5. Pipe 'V's on board to form pattern (No.2).

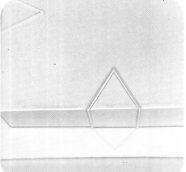

6. Pipe a line beside the No.2 lines on cake top (No.1).

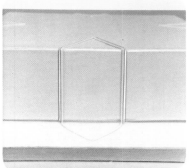

7. Continue lines down cake sides (No.1) (T).

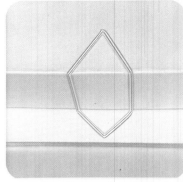

8. Continue lines on board (No.1).

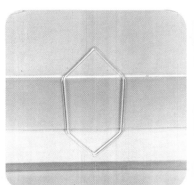

9. Overpipe a line on all No.2 lines (No.1) (T as necessary).

10. Pipe a scallop beside all the No.1 lines and finish 'V's with 3 graduated dots (No.1) (T as necessary).

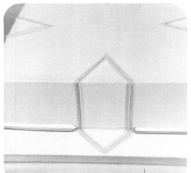

11. Pipe a line around cake base, excluding 'V's (No.44).

12. Pipe a scroll from 'V' to right-hand corner (No.44).

13. Pipe a 'C' scroll to right-hand cake corner (No.44).

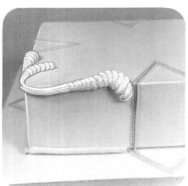

14. Pipe a scroll from 'V' to left-hand corner (No.44).

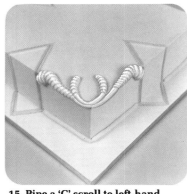

15. Pipe a 'C' scroll to left-hand cake corner (No.44).

16. Pipe left and right-handed scrolls to base corner (No.44). (Repeat 12–16 at each corner).

17. Overpipe each cake-top scroll (No.3).

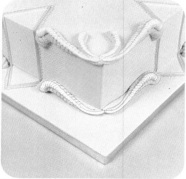

18. Overpipe each base scroll (No.3).

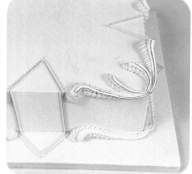

19. Overpipe each No.3 cake-top scroll (No.2).

20. Overpipe each No.3 base scroll (No.2).

21. Overpipe each No.2 cake-top scroll (No.1).

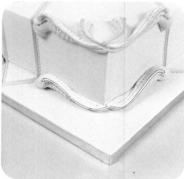

22. Overpipe each No.2 base scroll (No.1).

23. Pipe curved lines under each scroll on cake side (No.2) (T).

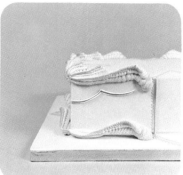

24. Pipe a line under and then pipe a line against each No.2 line on cake side (No.1) (T).

25. Pipe a 'V' and then a curved line on each corner of board (No.2).

26. Pipe a line on the board beside each No.2 line and then overpipe each No.2 line (No.1).

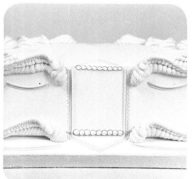

27. Pipe small plain shells on cake-top edge and base (No.2).

28. Pipe small plain shells and initials on each plaque (No.1) (L.D. 12 hrs).

29. Overpipe the shells and initials in coloured Royal Icing (No.1) (L.D. 2 hrs).

30. Fix plaque to each side of cake and finish with decorative dots.

31. Pipe corner motif with coloured Royal Icing (No.1) and then overpipe shells (No.1).

32. Pipe a scallop at each corner 'V' (No.1) and then fix decoration of choice.

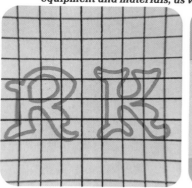

1. Template for style of lettering. (Use initials of choice).

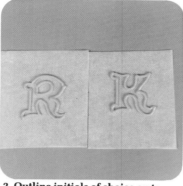

2. Outline initials of choice on to waxed paper (9 sets required) (No.1) (L.D. 30 m).

3. Flood-in with soft Royal Icing (L.D. 24 hrs).

4. Pipe part of a circle on cake top at each corner (No.2).

5. Pipe part of a circle on cake board at each corner (No.2).

6. Pipe a line beside each No.2 line on cake top (No.1).

7. Pipe a line beside each No.2 line on cake board (No.1).

8. Overpipe each No.2 line on cake top (No.1).

9. Overpipe each No.2 line on cake board (No.1).

10. Pipe scallops around each No.1 line on cake top (No.1).

11. Pipe scallops around each No.1 line on cake board (No.1).

12. Filigree inside each cake top circle (No.1).

13. Filigree inside each cake board circle (No.1).

14. Pipe plain shells along each top and base corner edge (No.2).

15. Pipe a bulb at the centre of a top edge (No.4).

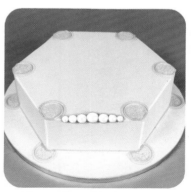

16. Pipe graduated bulbs each side of the central bulb (No.4). Repeat 15 & 16 along each top edge.

17. Repeat 15 & 16 around cake base (No.4).

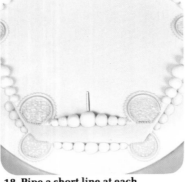

18. Pipe a short line at each central bulb on cake top (No.2).

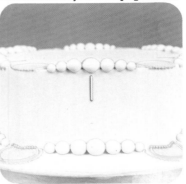

19. Pipe a short line at each central bulb on 3 alternate panels on cake side (No.2) (T).

20. Repeat 18 on cake board (No.2).

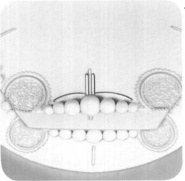

21. Pipe a shorter line and a curve each side of the No.2 line on cake top (No.2).

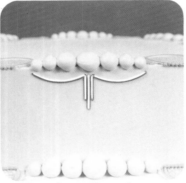

22. Pipe a shorter line and a curve on each side of each No.2 line on the 3 cake sides (No.2) (T).

23. Repeat 21 on cake board (No.2).

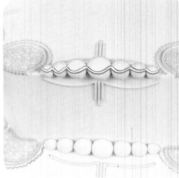

24. Overpipe all bulbs on the cake top with a line (No.2).

25. Overpipe all bulbs on cake base with a line (No.2).

26. Overpipe each central No.2 line on cake top (No.1).

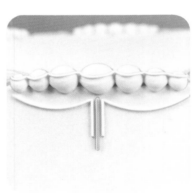

27. Repeat 26 on cake side (No.1) (T).

28. Repeat 26 on cake board (No.1).

29. Overpipe the No.2 line on top edge bulbs (No.1).

30. Repeat 29 on base bulbs (No.1).

31. Fix artificial decoration to each corner.

32. Fix initials to plain sides and ribbon to board edge.

NOTE: *Before attempting to decorate this cake, please study the whole sequence of photographs and notes and ensure you have the proper equipment and materials, as well as sufficient time. Additional information can be found on pages 5–17.*

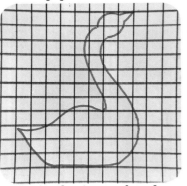

1. Drawing showing template of swan's body.

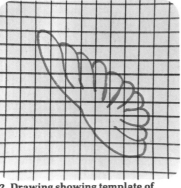

2. Drawing showing template of swan's wing.

3. Outline and flood-in on waxed paper 6 swan's bodies (L.D. 24 hrs).

4. Pipe on waxed paper the part of the wing shown (No.3).

5. Pipe-in the remaining wing sections (No.3).

6. Repeat 3–5 in opposite direction.

7. Whilst wet, place wings over a dowel or tube 1" in diameter (L.D. 24 hrs) (6 of each wing required).

8. Outline and flood-in 6×1¼" high heart plaques on waxed paper (L.D. 24 hrs).

9. Outline and flood-in – 4×2¼" high and 4×1¾" high – oval plaques (L.D. 24 hrs).

10. Fix swan's left and right facing bodies together and mount on the heart plaques (L.D. 2 hrs).

11. Fix wings (L.D. 2 hrs).

12. Paint beak and eyes with edible colouring.

13. Pipe scallops around the edge of each oval plaque (No.1).

14. Pipe a spike between each scallop (No.1), then pipe name of choice on each large plaque (No.1) (L.D. 12 hrs).

15. Pipe name of choice on small plaque as shown (No.1) (L.D. 12 hrs).

16. A 6" diameter coated round cake and a 10" square coated cake and board required.

17. Place 6" thin cake board onto the square cake and mount the round cake centrally.

18. Pipe shells around the base of each cake (No.44) and fix plaques as shown.

19. Pipe shells around top edge of the round cake (No.44).

20. Pipe shells on the edge above each square cake plaque (No.44).

21. Pipe an 'S' scroll on each side of the square cake top edge shells (No.44).

22. Overpipe all base shells with a line (No.2).

23. Pipe a decorative line on each cake top corner, as shown (No.2).

24. Overpipe each scroll (No.2).

25. Pipe a line on the cake board, as shown (No.2).

26. Overpipe the round cake base No.2 line (No.1) and pipe a dot between each round cake-top shell (No.1).

27. Overpipe the square cake base No.2 line (No.1) and pipe a dot between each square cake-top shell (No.1).

28. Fix an artificial baby to the back of each of 2 swans and an artificial flower of choice to the back of each of 4 swans.

29. Pipe reins from beak to baby's hands (No.1).

30. Fix swans in the positions shown and add matching artificial flowers.

31. Pipe a 'V' line beside each corner 'V' on board (No.1).

32. Fix artificial flowers and leaves and ribbon of choice, as shown.

1. Cut 2 pieces of sponge cake. Each piece to be 7″×4″×1″.

2. Slice each piece in two.

3. Jam top of 2 pieces.

4. Cream over the jam.

5. Sandwich pieces together, as shown. The uncreamed piece will form the SEAT BACKS.

6. Cream top and sides of BODY.

7. Cover top and sides of BODY in sugar paste.

8. Cut 2 further pieces of sponge cake. Each piece to be 3″×2½″×1″ (to form the CAR ENGINE).

9. Jam and cream the ENGINE pieces and sandwich together.

10. Cut 3 further pieces of sponge cake. Each piece to be 4″×1¼″×1″.

11. Cut one of the pieces diagonally and place on the ENGINE (to form angled bonnet). (Remaining 2 pieces will form SEATS).

12. Cut SEAT BACK into 3 equal pieces and then discard one piece.

13. Join the SEATS and SEAT BACKS together with jam and cream.

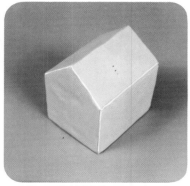

14. Cover ENGINE in sugar paste.

15. Cut and fix triangular arm rests from sponge and then cover the SEAT backs and fronts in sugar paste.

16. Cover the SEAT insides with sugar paste and mark lines with back of knife. Roll out and fix sugar paste arm rests.

17. Fix VINTAGE CAR BODY, ENGINE and SEATS to cake board.

18. Cover SEAT sides with sugar paste. Cut 4 DOORS (L.D. 2 hrs). Assemble.

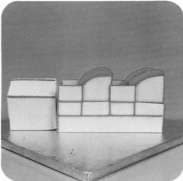

19. Pipe small plain shells around all edges of VINTAGE CAR (No.2).

20. Cut out a 1″ diameter disc of sugar paste. Cut 6 spokes for each WHEEL and fix to disc. (5 WHEELS required).

21. Roll out and fix black coloured sugar paste tyre to each WHEEL (L.D. 2 hrs).

22. Cut and fix sugar paste white tyre circles and hubs and then fix WHEELS to CAR.

23. Roll out sugar paste and cut FASCIA BOARD (L.D. 2 hrs). Fix between ENGINE and BODY.

24. Fix a narrow strip of sugar paste around front of ENGINE.

25. Cut, mark and fix a RADIATOR GRILL to front of ENGINE and small ball as RADIATOR CAP.

26. Cut 2 pieces of sugar paste to form running boards.

27. Roll out and cut 4 sugar paste mudguards and place over WHEELS.

28. Make and fix a variety of sugar paste CAR lamps.

29. Make a sugar paste steering wheel and fix on to a cocktail stick.

30. Make and fix number plates from sugar paste. Pipe registration number of choice (No.1).

31. Pipe handles, mudguard surrounds and running board grip lines (No.1).

32. Decorate sugar paste plaque with message of choice and fix plaque to the VINTAGE CAR cake board.

1. Drawing showing template of Peter.

2. Pipe-in on waxed paper the parts shown (L.D. 20 m).

3. Pipe-in the further parts shown (L.D. 20 m).

4. Pipe-in the further parts shown (L.D. 20 m).

5. Pipe-in the further parts shown (L.D. 20 m).

6. Pipe-in the further parts shown to complete Peter (L.D. 20 m).

7. Pipe a line and dot to form fishing rod, as shown (No.2) (L.D. 24 hrs).

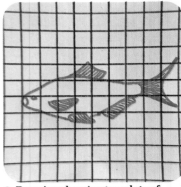

8. Drawing showing template of fish.

9. Pipe-in on waxed paper the parts of the fish shown (L.D. 20 m).

10. Pipe-in the further parts shown (L.D. 20 m).

11. Pipe-in the further parts shown to complete fish (L.D. 24 hrs). Remove waxed paper, upturn repeat 9–11.

12. Paint fish, as shown, with edible colouring (18 whole fish required).

13. Repeat 9–12 but leave a gap, as shown (3 required).

14. Remove Peter and rod from waxed paper, upturn and then repeat 2–7.

15. Picture showing coated square cake.

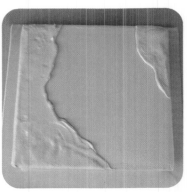

16. Cover the areas shown in Royal Icing to form river banks.

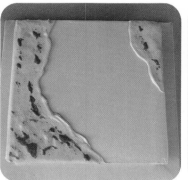

17. Stipple-in coloured Royal Icing to form ground effect.

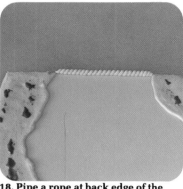

18. Pipe a rope at back edge of the cake to represent a weir (No.43).

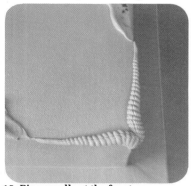

19. Pipe scrolls at the front corner of the cake to represent a waterfall (No.43).

20. Pipe a rope around the base of the cake (No.43).

21. Pipe plain shells along the parts of the cake-top edge shown (No.4).

22. Fix 2 whole fish and all heads and bodies to river, as shown.

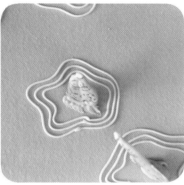

23. Pipe water ripples around each fish, as shown (No.1).

24. Fix Peter, as shown.

25. Fix the rod and then pipe a line, as shown (No.1).

26. Fix 4 whole fish in the positions shown to each side of the cake.

27. Pipe ripples and bubbles on each cake side (No.1).

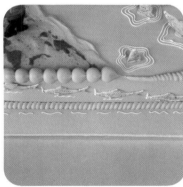

28. Pipe ripples on the cake board (No.1).

29. Pipe message of choice on the cake board (No.2).

30. Overpipe the message (No.1).

31. Make 4 sugar paste fishing basket sets, as shown.

32. Fix a basket to each cake-board corner, decorate as shown (No.1) and fix ribbon to board edge.

107

Courtney

1. Roll out and cut black coloured sugar paste strips to cover bottom half of each side of cake.

2. Roll out and cut white sugar paste strips to cover top half of each side of cake.

3. Roll out and leave on icing sugared table top, a thin sheet of white sugar paste the exact size of the cake top.

4. Mark and score the sheet of sugar paste into 12 equal vertical widths.

5. Mark and score the sheet of sugar paste into 12 equal horizontal widths.

6. Cut through the scores on the sugar paste, thus obtaining 144 equally sized squares (L.D. 2 hrs).

7. Roll out a sheet of sugar paste to make 36 squares, but in black.

8. Mark, score and cut sugar paste sheet into 36 squares (L.D. 2 hrs).

9. Align and fix the first 5 squares (in the order shown) with the top left edge of the cake.

10. Finish the first line.

11. Fix squares in the order shown for the next 3 lines. (A ruler edge may be used to straighten-up the lines).

12. Fix squares in the order shown for the next 4 lines (8 lines are now completed).

13. Complete fixing the squares over the cake top in the order shown.

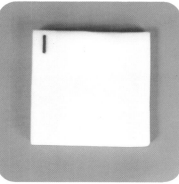

14. Indication of the size of numerals in comparison to size of a square.

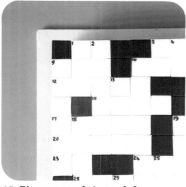

15. Pipe numerals in top left corner of cake, as shown, in black coloured Royal Icing (No.1).

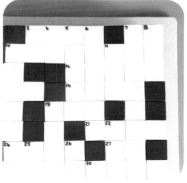

16. Pipe numerals in top right corner of cake, as shown, in black coloured Royal Icing (No.1).

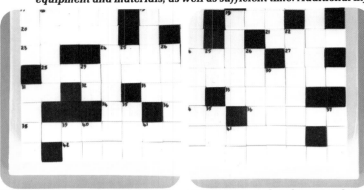

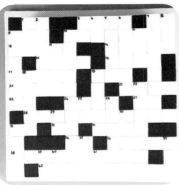

17. Pipe numerals in bottom left corner of cake, as shown, in black coloured Royal Icing (No.1).

18. Pipe numerals in bottom right corner of cake, as shown, in black coloured Royal Icing (No.1).

19. This photograph shows the top of the cake complete with numerals.

20. Indication of the size of letters in comparison to size of a square.

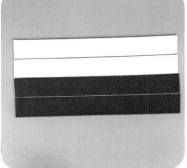

21. Pipe lettering, as shown, in first line (No.1).

22. Complete lettering, as shown, on cake top (No.1).

23. Roll out and cut 2 white and 2 black sugar paste strips to cover the length and width of the cake board border.

24. Mark and cut the 4 strips into 48 equal pieces.

25. Fix, as shown, 1 black piece.

26. Fix, as shown, 1 white piece.

27. Continue alternating colours to length of cake.

28. Leaving corners of board blank, repeat 27 on the 3 remaining board borders.

29. Mark and diagonally cut 2 black and 2 white squares to fit, each board corner, as shown.

30. Fix the triangular pieces to corners, as shown.

31. Fix artificial flowers of choice to each side of cake.

32. Fix velvet ribbon to edge of cake board.

NOTE: Before attempting to decorate this cake, please study the whole sequence of photographs and notes and ensure you have the proper equipment and materials, as well as sufficient time. Additional information can be found on pages 5–17.

1. Drawing showing template of runout pieces.

2. Outline and flood-in on waxed paper a blue scalloped disc (L.D. 24 hrs).

3. Outline and flood-in on waxed paper the numerals in blue icing (L.D. 24 hrs).

4. Outline and flood-in on waxed paper a white scalloped disc (L.D. 24 hrs).

5. Outline and flood-in on waxed paper a white disc (L.D. 24 hrs).

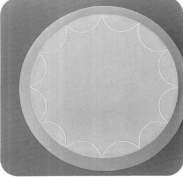

6. Mark the top of the cake into 16 divisions and pipe a curved line between marks, as shown (No.1).

7. Pipe opposite curved lines on cake side, as shown (No.1) (T).

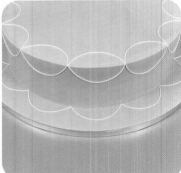

8. Pipe matching curved lines on board (No.1).

9. Pipe a diagonal central line inside one cake top oval pattern (No.2).

10. Pipe parallel lines to the left of the central line (No.2).

11. Pipe parallel lines to the right of the central line (No.2).

12. Repeat 9–11 around top of cake.

13. Pipe a central diagonal line across the lines of one oval, as shown (No.2).

14. Complete piping diagonal lines in one oval, as shown (No.2).

15. Repeat 13–14 around cake top.

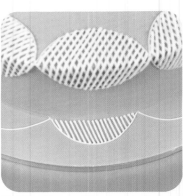

16. Pipe diagonal lines around cake board pattern, as shown (No.2).

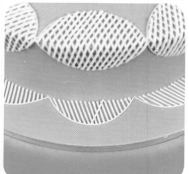

17. Pipe a diagonal line in opposite direction, as shown (No.2).

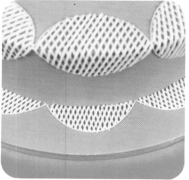

18. Complete piping diagonal lines around cake board, as shown (No.2).

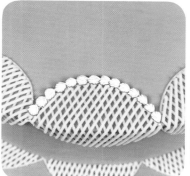

19. Pipe shells around each cake top No.1 curved line (No.42).

20. Pipe shells around each cake side No.1 curved line (No.42) (T).

21. Pipe shells around cake base (No.42).

22. Pipe shells around each curved No.1 line on cake board (No.42).

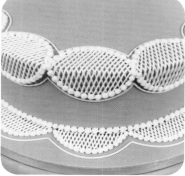

23. Pipe a line beside each curved line (No.2) (T as necessary).

24. Pipe a line beside each No.2 line (No.1) and then overpipe each No.2 line (No.1) (T as necessary).

25. Fix numerals on the white disc.

26. Fix the white disc to the blue disc.

27. Pipe shells around the white disc (No.1).

28. Pipe names of choice on the blue disc (No.1) (L.D. 2 hrs).

29. Pipe small dots and spikes around the white scalloped disc, as shown (No.1).

30. Pipe message of choice on white scalloped disc (No.1) (L.D. 12 hrs).

31. Fix artificial leaves, flowers and ribbon of choice; support the '25' in angled position on top tier.

32. Fix matching artificial leaves, flowers and ribbon to bottom tier and fix the white scalloped disc centrally.

Pedro

1. Pipe a flag outline on waxed paper to a cocktail stick (No.2).

2. Flood-in the flag (L.D. 24 hrs).

3. Pipe message of choice on flag (No.1) (L.D. 2 hrs).

4. Make a cone of waxed paper.

5. Pipe four 2″ lines down cone, as shown (No.2).

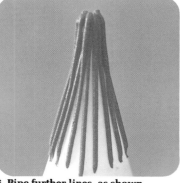

6. Pipe further lines, as shown (No.2).

7. Pipe further lines, as shown (No.2).

8. Pipe a bulb at top of cone (No.2) to complete a tassel (4 required) (L.D. 12 hrs).

9. A cake baked in a 2pt. pudding basin and upturned on a 16″ round board required.

10. Marzipan and coat the cake in the normal way.

11. Coat the board with Royal Icing.

12. Pipe a line along the edge of the board (No.32) (L.D. 2 hrs).

13. Overpipe the No.32 line in the manner shown (No.32) (L.D. 2 hrs).

14. Overpipe the No.32 line in the manner shown (No.32) (L.D. 2 hrs).

15. Pipe short lines around the crown of the sombrero, as shown (No.22).

16. Pipe a line across each of the No.22 lines (No.22).

17. Pipe the further lines shown (No.22).

18. Pipe the further lines shown in colour (No.22).

19. Pipe the further lines shown (No.22).

20. Pipe the further lines shown (No.22).

21. Repeat 7–10 once and then 7–12 once.

22. Continue piping 7–10 in one colour (No.22).

23. Pipe crossed lines in colour, as shown (No.22).

24. Continue piping rows in the manner shown (No.22).

25. Continue piping rows in the manner shown (No.22).

26. Continue piping crossed lines over the sombrero brim (No.22).

27. Pipe lines on the sombrero crown, as shown (No.22).

28. Pipe further lines on the crown, as shown (No.22).

29. Pipe bulbs around the sombrero rim, as shown (No.2).

30. Pipe suspended lines from each bulb and finish tassel with a top bulb (No.2).

31. Fix the 4 cone tassels to the cake base with a piped rope (No.2).

32. Fix the flag to the crown of Pedro's sombrero.

116

NOTE: *Before attempting to decorate this cake, please study the whole sequence of photographs and notes and ensure you have the proper equipment and materials, as well as sufficient time. Additional information can be found on pages 5–17.*

1. Marzipan and coat a 9" square cake in the normal way.

2. A serrated scraper required.

3. Coat each side of cake with two colours of Royal Icing.

4. Whilst wet, comb each side with the scraper to obtain effect shown (L.D. 12 hrs).

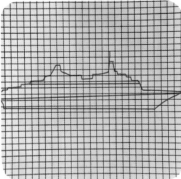

5. Drawing showing template of ship.

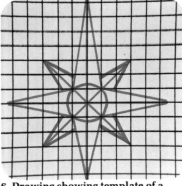

6. Drawing showing template of a compass.

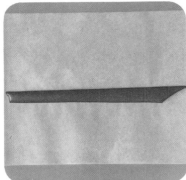

7. Outline and flood-in on waxed paper the ship's hull (L.D. 2 hrs).

8. Outline and flood-in on waxed paper the parts of the compass shown (L.D. 2 hrs).

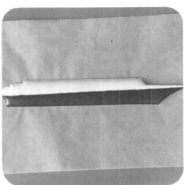

9. Outline and flood-in the further parts of the boat shown (L.D. 2 hrs).

10. Outline and flood-in the further parts of the compass shown (L.D. 24 hrs).

11. Outline and flood-in the further parts of the boat shown (L.D. 24 hrs).

12. Paint the centre of the compass in edible colouring.

13. Decorate the ship with piped lines and dots, as shown (No.1) (L.D. 2 hrs).

14. Coat the cake board and divide each cake-top edge into 6 portions with piped dots.

15. Pipe an 'S' scroll on the top edge the length of 2 dots, as shown (No.7).

16. Pipe a further scroll, starting at the first dot, as shown (No.7).

NOTE: *Before attempting to decorate this cake, please study the whole sequence of photographs and notes and ensure you have the proper equipment and materials, as well as sufficient time. Additional information can be found on pages 5–17.*

17. Continue piping 'S' scrolls along each top edge (No.7).

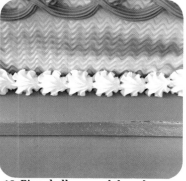

18. Pipe shells around the cake base (No.7).

19. Pipe a curved line beside each scroll (No.3).

20. Complete the curved lines with a curl at each corner (No.3).

21. Overpipe the first 'S' scroll (No.3).

22. Continue overpiping each 'S' scroll (No.3).

23. Pipe an 'S' scroll over two base shells, as shown (No.3).

24. Continue piping 'S' scrolls over the shells around the base (No.3).

25. Overpipe each cake-top scroll (No.2).

26. Overpipe each cake-base scroll (No.2).

27. Overpipe each cake-top scroll (No.1).

28. Overpipe each cake-base scroll (No.1).

29. Fix ship to cake top and pipe wavy lines and clouds, as shown (No.1).

30. Fix compass to cake top and pipe 'N' as shown (No.2).

31. Pipe message of choice to cake top (No.2).

32. Pipe 'S' scrolls on board edge, as shown (No.2) and fix ribbon to board edge.

119

Anne

1. Mark top of cake into 4 equal spaces with small dots (No.1).

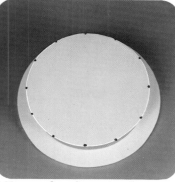

2. Now mark each quarter of cake-top into 3 equal spaces (dividing top edge into 12) (No.1).

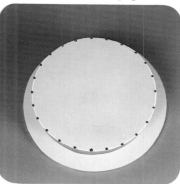

3. Now halve and mark each division (creating 24 divisions in all) (No.1).

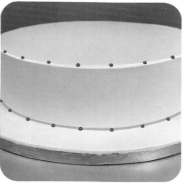

4. Repeat on base of cake, keeping marks immediately beneath the top marks (No.1).

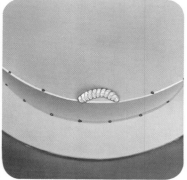

5. Pipe a curved rope between 2 dots (No.43).

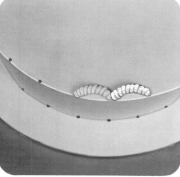

6. Pipe a 2nd curved rope between dots (No.43).

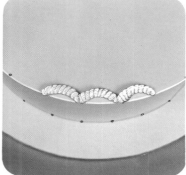

7. Continue piping *uniform* curved ropes around top of cake (No.43).

8. Pipe a curved rope against the side of the cake, linking ends with previous curves (No.43).

9. Pipe a 2nd curved rope between dots (No.43).

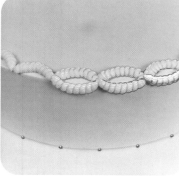

10. Continue piping *uniform* curved ropes around side of cake (No.43).

11. Pipe a spiral shell between 2 dots on base (No.43).

12. Pipe 2nd spiral shell between dots on base (No.43).

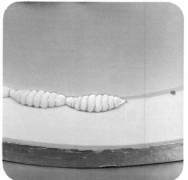

13. Continue piping *uniform* spiral shells around base of cake (No.43).

14. Overpipe a top rope (No.3).

15. Overpipe the next top rope (No.3).

16. Continue *uniform* overpiping of top ropes (No.3).

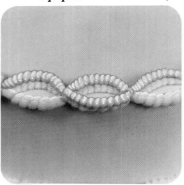

17. Overpipe a rope on side of cake (No.3).

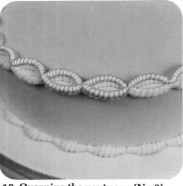

18. Overpipe the next rope (No.3).

19. Continue overpiping the side ropes (No.3).

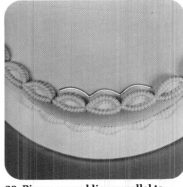

20. Pipe a curved line parallel to ropes on top of cake (No.2).

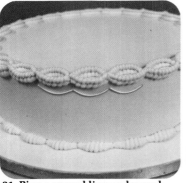

21. Pipe a curved line under each rope around side of cake (No.2) (T).

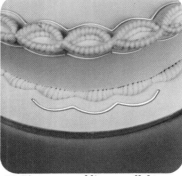

22. Pipe a curved line parallel to each spiral shell on board (No.2).

23. Overpipe the top ropes (No.2).

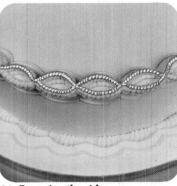

24. Overpipe the side ropes (No.2).

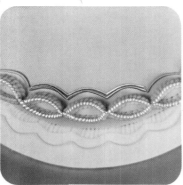

25. Pipe a line inside the No.2 line on cake top and then overpipe the No.2 line (No.1).

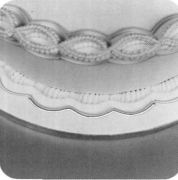

26. Pipe a line on board outside the No.2 line and then overpipe the No.2 line (No.1).

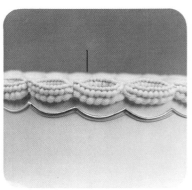

27. Pipe a line under the No.2 line on cake side and then pipe a line against the No.2 line (No.1) (T).

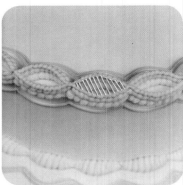

28. Pipe diagonal lines – from left to right – across rope pattern with coloured icing (No.1). (Repeat around cake).

29. Overpipe diagonal lines – from right to left – on rope pattern with coloured icing (No.1). (Repeat around cake).

30. Overpipe lattice ends with plain shells (No.2).

31. Fix hand-made rosebuds and artificial leaves at 4 equally spaced points around base of cake.

32. Fix top decoration of hand-made rosebuds and roses. (See instructions for making flowers).

1. Diagram of template of heart – 4¼″ high approx.

2. Using template under waxed paper outline heart shape (No.2).

3. Flood-in with soft Royal Icing (L.D. 24 hrs).

4. When dry, peel off waxed paper and turn heart over. Outline (No.2).

5. Flood-in with soft Royal Icing (L.D. 24 hrs).

6. Pipe plain shells around edge of heart (No.2) (L.D. 2 hrs).

7. Overpipe top of shells (No.1).

8. Overpipe side of shells (No.1).

9. Pipe thin rope inside shells (No.1).

10. Overpipe the side of shells (No.1).

11. Overpipe the side of shells with deeper pink (No.0) (L.D. 12 hrs).

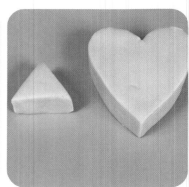

12. Cut out a sugar paste heart 2″ long × ½″ thick and a triangle to form the back support.

13. Fix triangle on sugar paste heart.

14. Press the runout heart onto the sugar paste heart and fix artificial decoration of choice (L.D. 12 hrs).

15. Pipe plain bulbs around top left edge of cake (No.4).

16. Pipe plain bulbs around top right edge of cake (No.4).

124

17. Repeat 15 and 16 on base (L.D. 2 hrs).

18. Overpipe all top edge bulbs with a line (No.3).

19. Pipe a line on the side of all top edge bulbs (No.3).

20. Repeat 18 and 19 on base bulbs.

21. Overpipe the inner No.3 line on cake top (No.2).

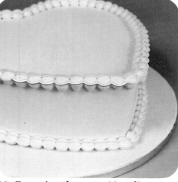

22. Overpipe the outer No.3 line on cake top (No.2).

23. Repeat 21 and 22 on cake base bulbs.

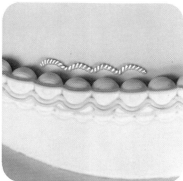

24. Pipe a curved rope around each bulb on cake top (No.2).

25. Pipe a curved rope under each top bulb and then repeat above the base bulbs (No.2) (T).

26. Pipe a curved rope around the cake board ensuring it is always centrally on board (No.2).

27. Overpipe the inner No.2 line on cake top (No.1).

28. Overpipe the outer No.2 line on cake top (No.1).

29. Repeat 27 and 28 on base bulbs.

30. Overpipe the outer No.1 line with deeper pink (No.1).

31. Repeat 30 on base bulbs.

32. Fix decorations of choice and ribbon to board edge.

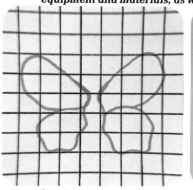

1. Template for butterfly (12 butterflies required for 2 tier cake).

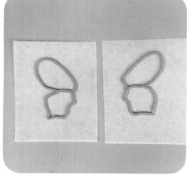

2. Using template under waxed paper pipe outline of wings (No.1).

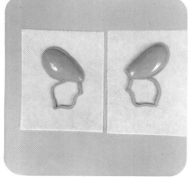

3. Flood-in top section of wings (L.D. 30 m).

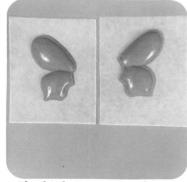

4. Flood-in bottom section of wings (L.D. 24 hrs).

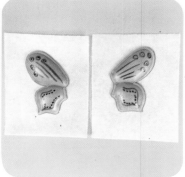

5. Using edible colouring, paint design on wing with fine brush (L.D. 30 m).

6. Pipe a butterfly body on waxed paper (No.2).

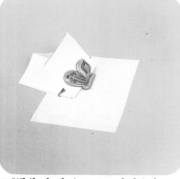

7. Whilst body is wet push dried wing into place and support with folded piece of waxed paper.

8. Repeat 2–8 for opposite wing. (Ensure both wings are set at same angle) (L.D. 12 hrs).

9. Mark top of cake into 4 equal spaces with small dots (No.1).

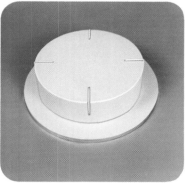

10. Pipe a line to each dot and down side of cake, as shown (No.3).

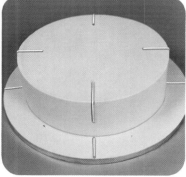

11. Pipe a line the full width of the cake board. (This should be directly under each vertical line) (No.3).

12. Pipe a slightly shorter line on each side of the No.3 lines on the top and side of cake (No.2).

13. Pipe a slightly shorter line on each side of the No.3 lines on the cake board (No.2).

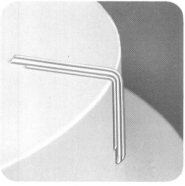

14. Overpipe the top and side No.3 lines with slightly shorter lines (No.2).

15. Overpipe the No.3 lines on cake board with slightly shorter lines (No.2).

16. Pipe a slightly shorter line on each side of the No.2 lines on the top and side of cake (No.1).

127

17. Pipe a slightly shorter line on each side of the No.2 lines on the cake board (No.1).

18. Overpipe all No.2 lines with slightly shorter lines (No.1).

19. Pipe 3 curved lines on cake top between each existing pattern (No.2).

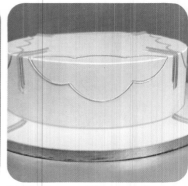

20. Pipe 3 curved lines on cake side between each existing pattern (No.2) (T).

21. Pipe 3 curved lines on cake board between each pattern (No.2).

22. Pipe filigree inside curved lines on cake top, side and board (No.1).

23. Pipe a line outside each curved line on cake top (No.1).

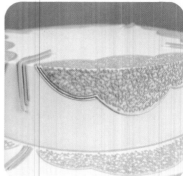

24. Pipe a line below each curved line on cake side (No.1) (T).

25. Pipe a line outside each curved line on cake board (No.1).

26. Overpipe the No.2 lines on cake top (No.1).

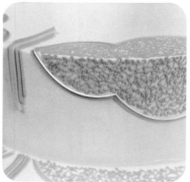

27. Pipe against the No.2 lines around the cake side (No.1) (T).

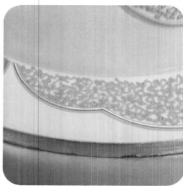

28. Overpipe the No.2 lines on cake board (No.1).

29. Pipe bulbs around cake base on filigree (No.3).

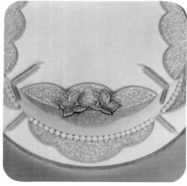

30. Fix butterflies in position on top of cake.

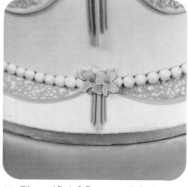

31. Fix artificial flowers of choice to cake base.

32. Fix velvet ribbon around board edge.

Sarah

129

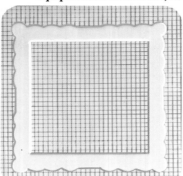

1. Outline and flood-in on waxed paper 2 runouts in the shape shown. Sizes as required (L.D. 24 hrs).

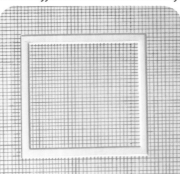

2. Outline and flood-in on waxed paper 2 runouts in the shape shown. Sizes as required (L.D. 24 hrs).

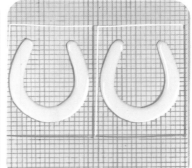

3. Outline and flood-in on waxed paper 2 horseshoes=each 3¾" high (L.D. 24 hrs).

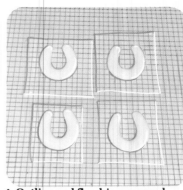

4. Outline and flood-in on waxed paper 8 horseshoes=each 1¼" high (L.D. 24 hrs).

5. Make 18 piped doves and 9 piped bells.

6. Sequence showing how to make a 4-leaf clover (No.1 on waxed paper) (L.D. 24 hrs) (21 required).

7. Pipe a single row of dots against each 'corner' of the large runout (No.1).

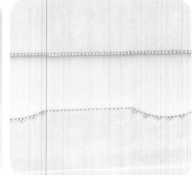

8. Pipe 6-dot sequence against curves and single dots against straight edges of large runout (No.1) (L.D. 12hrs).

9. Pipe a single row of dots against each inner and outer edge of the small runout (No.1) (L.D. 12 hrs).

10. Pipe a single row of dots against each small horseshoe edge and larger 'nail' dots on top (No.1).

11. Pipe a bow across each small horseshoe (No.1) (L.D. 12 hrs).

12. Fix the 2 large horseshoes together (back to back) and pipe shells against the edge (No.2) (L.D. 12 hrs).

13. Overpipe the shells (No.1) and pipe 'nail' dots on top of the horseshoe (No.2).

14. Pipe a line along top edge of cake (No.3) (L.D. 2 hrs).

15. Overpipe the No.3 line (No.2) and immediately fix the large runout in position.

16. Pipe a line on the inside edge of the large runout (No.3) (L.D. 2 hrs).

17. Overpipe the No.3 line (No.2) and immediately fix the small runout in place.

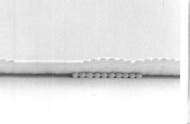

18. Pipe small bulbs under the large runout along the cake-top edge (No.2) (T).

19. Outline the shape of the large runout on the cake board (No.2).

20. Flood-in between the No.2 line and base of cake (L.D. 12 hrs).

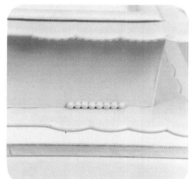

21. Pipe bulbs along base of cake (No.3).

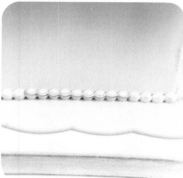

22. Overpipe the bulbs (No.1).

23. Fix a small horseshoe centrally to each side of the cake.

24. Pipe curved lines along each side of the cake (No.2) (T).

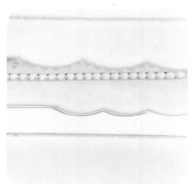

25. Pipe a line beside the board runout (No.2).

26. Pipe a line under the cake-side No.2 lines and then against the No.2 lines (No.1) (T).

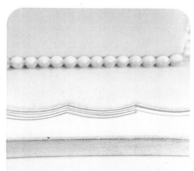

27. Pipe a line beside the board No.2 lines and then overpipe the No.2 lines (No.1).

28. Fix a clover on each corner of the board and top runouts.

29. Fix a bell to each small horseshoe.

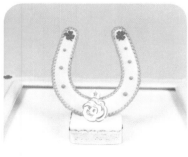

30. Fix the large horseshoe onto a sugar paste base and decorate with ribbon, an artificial rose and 2 clovers.

31. Fix doves to top runout and large horseshoe. (L.D. 24 hrs).

32. Fix a matching artificial rose – with leaves – to each base corner.

Many hoppy returns to our Twins

1. Cut 3 pieces of sponge cake – each piece = 7″×5″×1″.

2. Slice each sponge in two and jam the 3 tops.

3. Cream over the jam.

4. Rejoin the pieces.

5. Jam and cream the top of one piece.

6. Place the 2nd piece on top to form the TREASURE CHEST.

7. Cut each of 2 cake cards into 7″×5″ oblongs.

8. Place the CHEST on to one of the cards and then cream top and sides.

9. Place the 3rd piece of sponge – which forms the CHEST LID – on the other card. Cut narrow ends to form curves.

10. Cream top and sides of LID.

11. Cover the CHEST top with a thin sheet of sugar paste.

12. Cut 1lb of sugar paste into 3 graduated sizes and colour each piece a different shade of brown.

13. Roll sugar paste pieces into 18″ lengths.

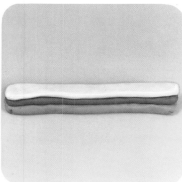

14. Sandwich the 3 pieces together.

15. Flatten out sugar paste to a width of 4″.

16. Fold sugar paste into 3.

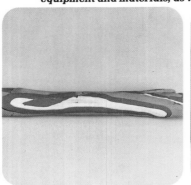

17. Roll out sugar paste to a length of 18″.

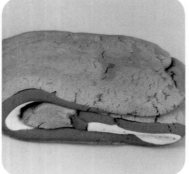

18. Flatten out to width of 4″ and fold into 3.

19. Continue the process of rolling and folding the sugar paste until a woodgrain effect is achieved.

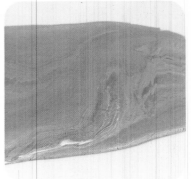

20. Now roll out the sugar paste to form a thin sheet.

21. Cut the sugar paste and cover the sides of the CHEST.

22. Cover the LID with remaining sugar paste.

23. Cut thin strips of sugar paste to line the outer edge and corners of CHEST.

24. Cut thin strips of sugar paste to line the outer edge of LID.

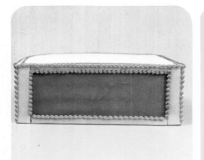

25. Pipe plain shells on all inner and outer CHEST and LID edges (No.42).

26. Model 2 handles, a padlock, latch and clasp from sugar paste (L.D. 2 hrs).

27. Decorate CHEST edges with scrolls (No.2).

28. Decorate LID edges with scrolls and write message of choice (No.1).

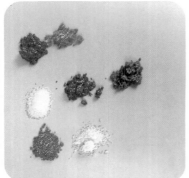

29. Coloured granulated sugar required (see Instructions).

30. Pipe top edge and front (No.4) and at once sprinkle with coloured sugar.

31. Repeat 30 along the top front and side edges (L.D. 2 hrs). Place TREASURE CHEST LID in position.

32. Fix the 'ironmongery' to the front and sides of CHEST.

134

1. A marzipanned and coated cake in the shape of a '5' required on a round board.

2. Roll out of a strip of sugar paste to cover the sides of the '5'.

3. Fix the sugar paste to the sides of the '5'.

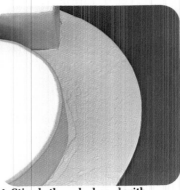

4. Stipple the cake board with Royal Icing.

5. Roll out and cut from sugar paste 5×¾" diameter discs.

6. Moisten two discs and place on waxed paper, as shown.

7. Moisten and add a third disc, as shown.

8. Moisten and add a fourth disc, as shown.

9. Moisten and add a fifth disc, as shown.

10. Form a sugar paste dome, moisten and fix to centre of discs.

11. Shape discs to form petals (L.D. 12 hrs).

12. Repeat 5–11 in various colours to make 10 flowers.

13. Pipe a rope over the part of the dome shown (No.2).

14. Pipe eyes, as shown (No.2).

15. Pipe nose and mouth, as shown (No.2).

16. Pipe eyelids, as shown (No.2) (Repeat 13–16 on each flower). (L.D. 2 hrs).

136

17. Pipe rosettes around cake-top edge (No.7).

18. Pipe rosettes around cake base (No.7).

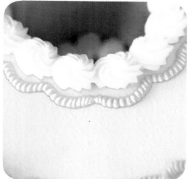

19. Pipe a curved rope beside each cake-top rosette (No.2).

20. Pipe a curved rope beside each base rosette (No.2).

21. Pipe a dot at the centre of each rosette (No.2).

22. Pipe part of the message of choice on cake top, as shown (No.2).

23. Pipe another part of the message of choice, as shown (No.2).

24. Complete message of choice, as shown (No.2).

25. Overpipe message (No.1).

26. Pipe rosettes on board, as shown (No.7).

27. Pipe rosettes on board, as shown (No.7).

28. Fix a flower to each board rosette.

29. Repeat 28 on other side of the '5'.

30. Pipe curved lines on board (No.3); pipe a rosette centrally (No.7) and finish with a piped dot (No.2).

31. Pipe 5 shaped rings on cake top, as shown (No.2).

32. Fix a candle holder and candle in each ring and ribbon to the board edge.

137

Laura

138

NOTE: *Before attempting to decorate this cake, please study the whole sequence of photographs and notes and ensure you have the proper equipment and materials, as well as sufficient time. Additional information can be found on pages 5–17.*

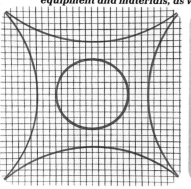

1. Drawing showing template for central plaque.

2. Outline and flood-in plaque on waxed paper (L.D. 24 hrs).

3. Pipe 4 equally spaced curved lines on side of cake, as shown (No.1) (T).

4. Pipe a vertical line inside a curve, as shown (No.44) (T).

5. Fill each curve with vertical lines, as shown (No.44) (T) (L.D. 1 hr).

6. Pipe further vertical lines between the No.44 lines (No.44) (T) (L.D. 1 hr).

7. Repeat 6 to form side basket.

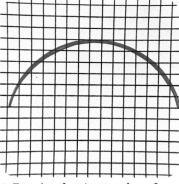

8. Drawing showing template of handle.

9. Pipe rope on waxed paper to form handle (No.42) (L.D. 12 hrs) (8 required).

10. Fix pairs of handles together (L.D. 12 hrs).

11. Coat the top of each side basket.

12. Pipe horizontal lines across alternate vertical lines, as shown (No.1).

13. Continue piping horizontal lines, as shown (No.1).

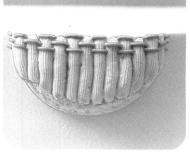

14. Continue piping horizontal lines, as shown (No.1).

15. Continue piping horizontal lines to complete basket weave, as shown (No.1).

16. Pipe shells around each basket edge and at base, as shown (No.42).

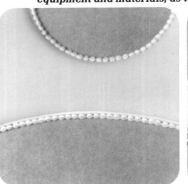

17. Pipe small shells around plaque edges (No.1).

18. Pipe scallops around outer plaque edges (No.1).

19. Pipe a dot in each scallop curve (N0.1) (L.D. 12 hrs).

20. Pipe curved lines on cake top between ends of each basket, as shown (No.1).

21. Filigree each basket top (No.1).

22. Pipe plain shells around each basket top (No.2).

23. Pipe scallops along the outside of the inner basket edge (No.1).

24. Make 40 small sugar paste rosebuds and one large rose (See instructions).

25. Upturn the plaque and pipe a line, as shown (No.4), then overpipe the No.4 line (No.4) (L.D. 2 hrs).

26. Pipe plain shells on top edge between each basket and around the base of the cake (No.3).

27. Fix plaque to top of cake in position shown.

28. Fix rosebuds, fern, handles and the rose, as shown.

29. Overpipe base shells with a line (No.2).

30. Overpipe the No.2 line (No.1).

31. Fix a rosebud and fern on cake base between each basket.

32. Fix velvet ribbon to board edge.

140

1. An 8″ square cake required.

2. Cut a section from one end.

3. Trim cut section and fix to cake, as shown.

4. Cut and trim cake to form an open book.

5. Marzipan and coat the cake on a 14″ square board in the normal way.

6. Cut a template from card to match the cake top size.

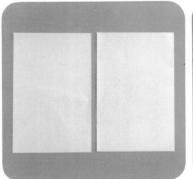

7. Cut the template in half and then cut two matching sheets of waxed paper.

8. Place a bent straw on top of the cake, as shown.

9. Place one template on top of the straw and cake, as shown.

10. Coat one piece of waxed paper in Royal Icing.

11. Lay coated waxed paper on cake-top template (L.D. 24 hrs).

12. Repeat 8–11 but fix a cocktail stick to corner to form a curved page, as shown.

13. Drawing showing template of a flower.

14. Outline and flood-in on waxed paper the part of the flower shown (L.D. 30m).

15. Outline and flood-in the further parts shown (L.D. 30m).

16. Outline and flood-in the further parts shown (L.D. 30m).

142

17. Pipe a bulb in the centre of the flower (L.D. 24 hrs) then paint as shown in edible colouring.

18. Remove top pages and coat each side of the book using a fine comb.

19. Coat top and bottom ends of half the book using a fine comb.

20. Coat top and bottom ends of half the book using a fine comb.

21. Pipe a line on the board in the shape shown (No.2).

22. Flood-in between the line and the base of the cake (L.D. 12 hrs).

23. Pipe shells around base of cake (No.42).

24. Peel off waxed paper from pages.

25. Fix flower in the position shown and then pipe the lines, as shown (No.1).

26. Picture showing page-edge decoration.

27. Pipe the decoration as shown.

28. Pipe message of choice and decorative lines (No.1).

29. Pipe message of choice, decorative lines and page-edge decoration (No.1).

30. Fix pages to the top of the cake.

31. Pipe lines along the edge of the board runout (No.1).

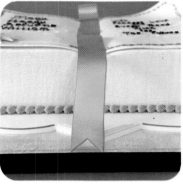

32. Fix bookmark and ribbon around the edge of the board.

143

Katrina

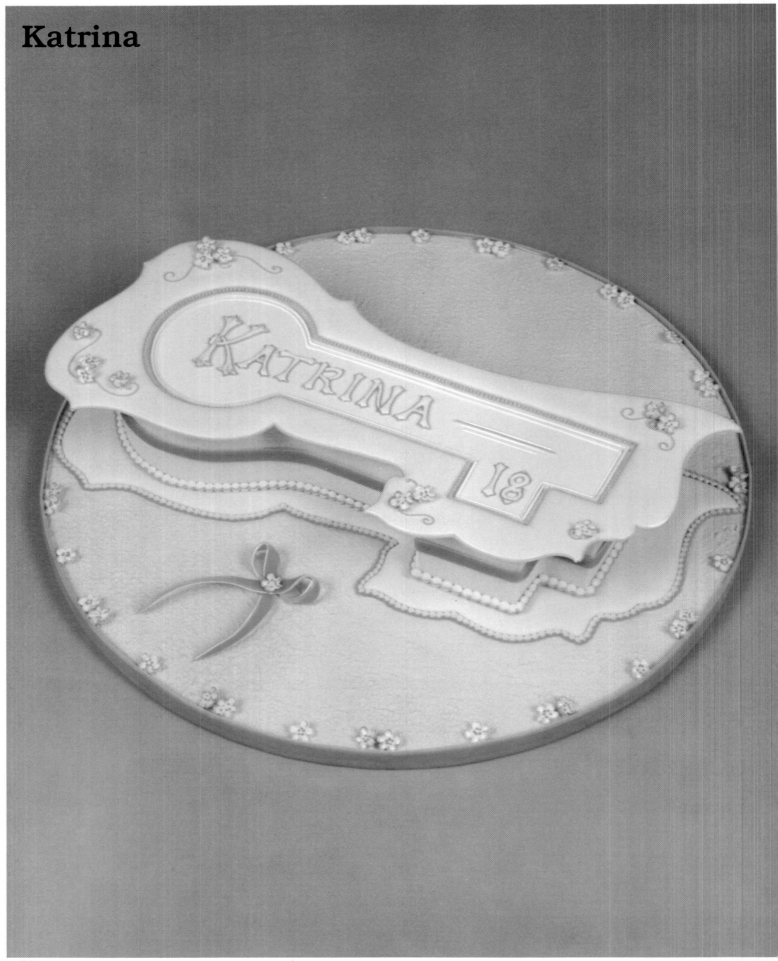

1. One 4″ round and one 4″ square fruit cake required.

2. Cut the square cake in half.

3. Cut 1″ off the end of one of the halves.

4. Place cakes in position, as shown, to form KEY.

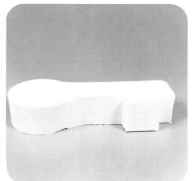

5. Marzipan and coat KEY in normal way.

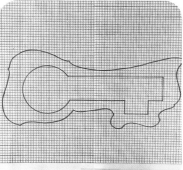

6. Drawing showing template of runout for KEY.

7. Outline and flood-in runout on waxed paper (L.D. 24 hrs).

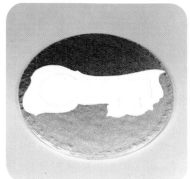

8. Using the same template, cut a card to shape and place on a 15″ round board.

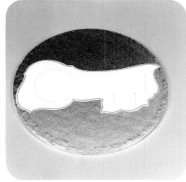

9. Outline template (No.2).

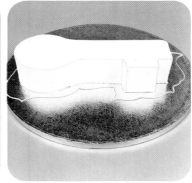

10. Remove template and place cake on centre of board.

11. Flood-in between outline and cake base. (L.D. 12 hrs).

12. Coat and stipple the board in Royal Icing (L.D. 2 hrs).

13. Pipe a line around the top edge of cake (No.3) (L.D. 2 hrs).

14. Pipe dots along inside of the top runout (No.1) (L.D. 12 hrs).

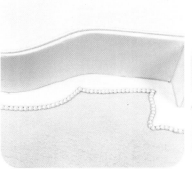

15. Pipe plain shells outside the board runout (No.2).

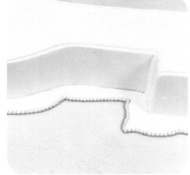

16. Overpipe the shells (No.1).

17. Pipe plain shells around base of cake (No.3).

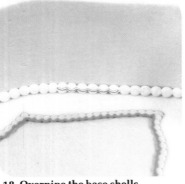

18. Overpipe the base shells (No.1).

19. Overpipe the No.3 line (No.2) and fix KEY runout to it.

20. Pipe plain shells under top runout at cake top (No.2).

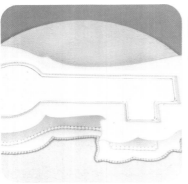

21. Pipe a line inside the top runout (No.2).

22. Pipe a line beside the No.2 line and then overpipe the No.2 line (No.1).

23. Plain runout showing style of writing of name of choice. (Outline on waxed paper and flood-in letters and age) (L.D. 24 hrs).

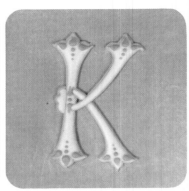

24. Decorate first letter (No.1) (L.D. 2 hrs).

25. Fix runout name letters and age to KEY.

26. Pipe flower stems (No.1).

27. Fix flowers of choice to stems.

28. Repeat 26 at KEY end.

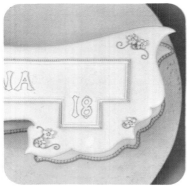

29. Repeat 27 at KEY end.

30. Pipe 3 parallel lines at end of name, then overpipe the centre line (No.1).

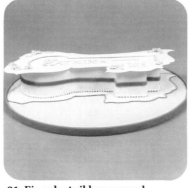

31. Fix velvet ribbon around board and side of cake.

32. Fix a bow and flowers of choice around edge of board.

146

1. Serrated scraper required.

2. On final coating use serrated scraper to form pattern around cake.

3. Drawing showing template of the British Isles.

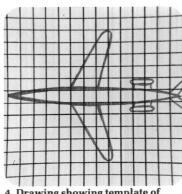

4. Drawing showing template of an aeroplane.

5. Outline the British Isles on waxed paper (No.2).

6. Flood-in the British Isles (L.D. 24 hrs).

7. Outline and flood-in on waxed paper the parts of the aeroplane shown (L.D. 1 hr).

8. Flood-in remaining parts of the aeroplane and a separate tail, as shown (L.D. 24 hrs).

9. Pipe shells around edge of cake top (No.4).

10. Pipe shells around base of cake (No.4) (L.D. 2 hrs).

11. Overpipe each top shell with a curved line (No.3).

12. Overpipe each base shell with a curved line (No.3).

13. Overpipe each No.3 top line (No.2).

14. Overpipe each No.3 base line (No.2).

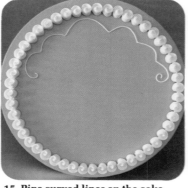

15. Pipe curved lines on the cake top, as shown (No.2).

16. Pipe further curved lines on the cake top, as shown (No.2).

17. Pipe short curved lines on cake top, as shown (No.1).

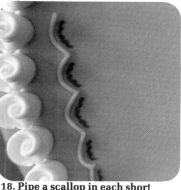

18. Pipe a scallop in each short curved line on the cake top (No.1).

19. Decorate the British Isles with edible colouring, as shown.

20. Fix tail to aeroplane.

21. Decorate aeroplane with piped lines and dots, as shown (No.1).

22. Fix British Isles and aeroplane to cake top.

23. Pipe message of choice (No.1).

24. Complete message of choice (No.2)

25. Pipe lines beside message (No's 1 & 2).

26. Pipe seagulls around message (No.1).

27. Pipe seagulls around British Isles (No.1).

28. Overpipe the top shell curved lines (No.1).

29. Overpipe the base shell curved lines (No.1).

30. Pipe curved lines around the cake board, as shown (No.2).

31. Pipe scallops and dots on board, as shown (No.1).

32. Fix artificial flowers to cake base and ribbon to board edge.

149

April Cottage

NOTE: *Before attempting to decorate this cake, please study the whole sequence of photographs and notes and ensure you have the proper equipment and materials, as well as sufficient time. Additional information can be found on pages 5–17.*

1. 3 pieces of sponge cake required to form COTTAGE FRONT – each piece 6½″×4″×1″.

2. 3 pieces of sponge cake required to form FRONT ROOF – each piece 6½″×2″×1″.

3. 3 pieces of sponge cake required to form COTTAGE REAR – each piece 4″×4″×1″.

4. 2 pieces of sponge cake required to form REAR ROOF – each piece 5″×2″×1″.

5. Jam and cream the 3 COTTAGE FRONT pieces together.

6. Jam and cream the 3 FRONT ROOF pieces together.

7. Cut FRONT ROOF diagonally in two.

8. Fix FRONT ROOF to COTTAGE FRONT with jam and cream.

9. Repeat 5–8 but using the pieces of sponge specified in 3 and 4 (COTTAGE REAR and REAR ROOF).

10. Shape 9 to fit against 8.

11. Cover a 12″ cake board with green stippled Royal Icing (L.D. 2 hrs).

12. Place complete cottage on board and cream all over.

13. Shape and cream 4 pieces of sponge cake to form the dormer windows.

14. Fix dormer windows to roofs.

15. Make various sized windows and frames from sugar paste (L.D. 2 hrs).

16. Decorate windows with glazing bars, hinges and handles (No.1) (L.D. 2 hrs).

17. Make sugar paste doors (marking panels with back of knife) (L.D. 2 hrs).

18. Make and/or fix sugar paste doors, windows and frames. Decorate (No.1).

19. COTTAGE REAR showing side door.

20. Partially mix colouring into 1lb of sugar paste and form into a roll.

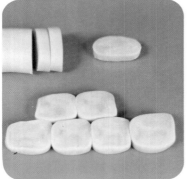

21. Reduce diameter of roll to ½″ and cut into thin discs.

22. Fix discs to cottage wall and squeeze each one to form rugged stonework shape.

23. COTTAGE SIDE showing stonework.

24. Roll out a thin sheet of sugar paste and draw a sterilised comb against its edge to create straw effect.

25. Cut and fix strips of straw on to roof starting from the eaves and working up to ridge.

26. COTTAGE SIDE showing thatched roof and end overhang.

27. Cut, shape and fix chimney from sugar paste.

28. Pipe the words 'APRIL COTTAGE' on the door lintel (No.1).

29. Colour and roll out 5 separate thin strips of sugar paste. Freely mount the strips on each other.

30. Cut layers in the shapes shown to create crazy paving.

31. Using the coloured paving in rotation (one from each layer) lay path around APRIL COTTAGE.

32. Mix spare sugar paste pieces together and colour brown to make flower pots. Decorate. Pipe ivy over walls (No.2).

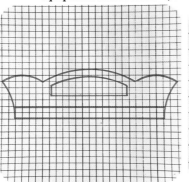

1. Drawing showing template of runouts. (N.B. All runouts to be made on waxed paper).

2. Drawing showing template of swan runout.

3. Drawing showing template of cygnet runout.

4. Drawing showing template of swan's wing.

5. Outline and flood-in 6 wide top runouts and 6 narrow base runouts for each cake (L.D. 24 hrs).

6. Outline and flood-in 14 facing pairs of swan bodies (L.D. 24 hrs).

7. Outline and flood-in 6 facing pairs of cygnet bodies (L.D. 24 hrs).

8. Pipe on waxed paper 14 facing pairs of swan wings (left wing shown) (No.3) (L.D. 24 hrs).

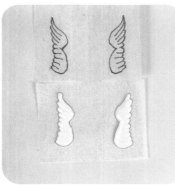

9. Pipe cygnet wings on waxed paper 1″ long as shown (No.1) (L.D. 24 hrs) (6 pairs required).

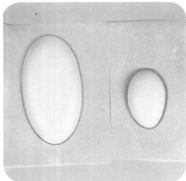

10. Outline and flood-in on waxed paper 14 ovals – 1¼″ high – and 6 ovals – ¾″ high (L.D. 24 hrs).

11. Fix half swans together and fix to ovals (L.D. 2 hrs).

12. Fix wings to bodies as shown (L.D. 12 hrs).

13. Paint swan's eyes and beaks in edible colouring.

14. Fold two pieces of ribbon and fix into swan, as shown.

15. Repeat 11–13 for cygnets.

16. Pipe 6-dot triangular sequences along outer edge and single dots along ends of each runout (No.1) (L.D. 12 hrs).

154

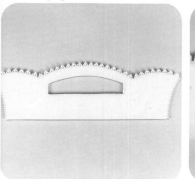

17. Remove waxed paper from runouts and turn upside-down.

18. Pipe lines across runout 'windows', as shown (No.1) (L.D. 2 hrs).

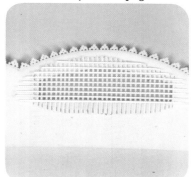

19. Overpipe the No.1 lines to form latticework (No.1) (L.D. 12 hrs).

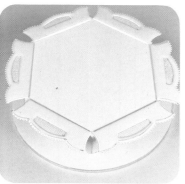

20. Fix wide runouts to cake top (L.D. 2 hrs).

21. Pipe a line around the base of the cake (No.3) (L.D. 2 hrs).

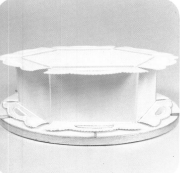

22. Overpipe No.3 line (No.2). Fix narrow runouts to board-support (L.D. 2 hrs).

23. Pipe bulbs along inside edge of top runouts (No.2).

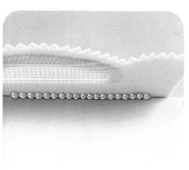

24. Pipe bulbs under each top runout along cake top edge (No.2) (T).

25. Pipe a line beside the No.2 top inner edge bulbs (No.2).

26. Pipe a line beside the No.2 line and then overpipe the No.2 line (No.1).

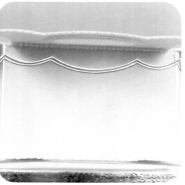

27. Pipe curved lines against each side (No.2), then under No.2, then against No.2 (No.1) (T).

28. Pipe bulbs along base of cake (No.2).

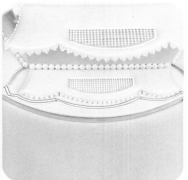

29. Pipe a line beside board runouts (No.2), then a line beside the No.2 and then overpipe the No.1).

30. Fix artificial flowers, leaves, ribbon and swans (cygnets on 3rd tier).

31. Roll out and cut sugar paste plinth and fix ribbon around its edge.

32. Fix swans and matching artificial flowers to plinth (L.D. 12 hrs) and place centrally on top tier.

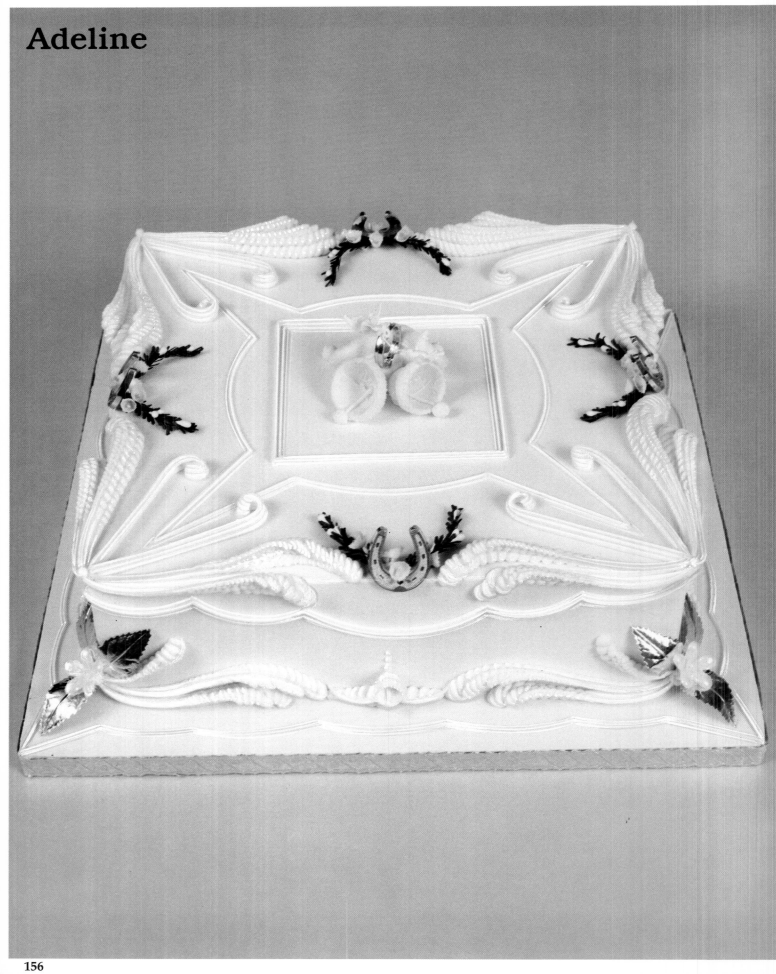

1. Cut a square of paper exactly ⅓rd the length and width of the cake and place on top.

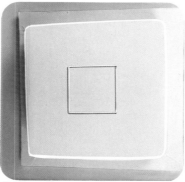

2. Pipe a line around the paper square (No.1) remove the paper.

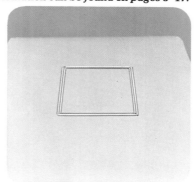

3. Pipe a line outside the No.1 line (No.2).

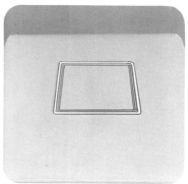

4. Pipe a line outside the No.2 line (No.3).

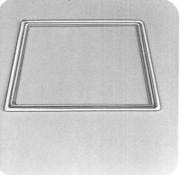

5. Overpipe the No.2 line (No.1).

6. Overpipe the No.3 line (No.2).

7. Overpipe the No.2 line (No.1).

8. Pipe a 'V', as shown, from each corner of the central square (No.2).

9. Pipe a curved line to connect each 'V' (No.2).

10. Pipe a line beside the No.2 line and then overpipe the No.2 line (No.1).

11. Pipe an elongated heart shape at each cake top corner (No.4).

12. Overpipe each heart shape (No.3).

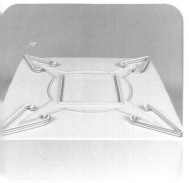

13. Overpipe each heart shape (No.2) and then overpipe each heart shape (No.1).

14. Pipe 'S' scrolls, as shown, around top edges of cake (No.4).

15. Beneath each scroll pipe a shorter 'S' scroll (No.4).

16. Pipe 'S' scrolls, as shown, around cake base (No.4) (T).

157

17. Pipe 'S' scrolls, as shown, on cake board (No.4) (T).

18. Pipe 'C' scrolls at each cake-side corner (No.4) (T).

19. Pipe a spiral shell between base scrolls (No.4).

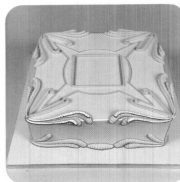

20. Overpipe each top scroll (No.3).

21. Overpipe each base scroll (No.3).

22. Overpipe each spiral shell with 2 curved lines (No.3).

23. Pipe 5 curved lines around each side of cake, as shown (No.3) (T).

24. Overpipe each top scroll (No.2).

25. Overpipe each base scroll and spiral shell (No.2).

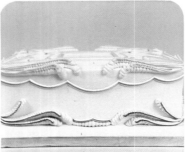

26. Pipe a line under each No.3 curved line on cake sides (No.2) and then against each No.3 line (No.2) (T).

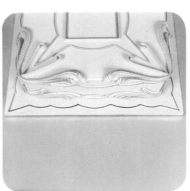

27. Pipe, as shown, a series of curved lines and 'V's on cake board (No.2).

28. Overpipe each top scroll, base scroll and spiral shell (No.1).

29. Pipe a line under each No.2 line on the cake side and then against each No.2 line (No.1) (T).

30. Pipe a line beside each No.2 line on the board and then overpipe each No.2 line (No.1).

31. Fix 4 sugar bells and decorations of choice at centre top of cake.

32. Fix decorations of choice to cake, as shown.

158

NOTE: Before attempting to decorate this cake, please study the whole sequence of photographs and notes and ensure you have the proper equipment and materials, as well as sufficient time. Additional information can be found on pages 5–17.

About 80 roses and buds of various sizes required – see instructions.

1. 10" round cake, 13" round cake board and 16" round cake board required. Mount as shown and coat in normal way.

2. Place an 8" round cake card centrally on cake top.

3. Place an 8" round cake on the cake card.

4. Place a 6" cake card centrally on cake top.

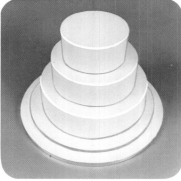

5. Place a 6" round cake on the cake card.

6. Pipe icing into the spaces between cakes (No.4). Fix a gold band to each board edge.

7. Fix 4 roses to base of cake.

8. Trail off to the left of the cake with more roses.

9. Offset sets of roses on each step.

10. Fill in space on side of bottom tier with roses.

11. Fill in space on side of middle tier with roses.

12. Fill in space on side of top tier with roses.

13. Shape and place a bulb of sugar paste in the centre of the top tier.

14. Fix a large rose to the top of the bulb.

15. Arrange and fix various sized roses around top tier edge.

16. Fix roses to the top tier to completely cover the bulb.

17. Fix artificial leaves amongst the roses on the bottom and middle tiers.

18. Fix artificial leaves amongst the roses on the side of the top tier.

19. Fix artificial leaves amongst the roses on top of the cake.

20. Fix a spray of roses and artificial leaves, as shown, on each tier at the back of the cake.

21. Pipe small bulbs around the base of each tier and around the edge of the 13″ cake board (No.3).

22. Pipe bulbs around the edges of the bottom and middle tiers (No.4) (L.D. 4 hrs).

23. Pipe a loop from the 3rd bulb to the 5th bulb (No.2) (L.D. 10 m).

24. Pipe a loop from the 2nd bulb to the 4th bulb (No.2).

25. Pipe a loop from the 4th bulb to the 6th bulb (No.2) (L.D. 10 m).

26. Pipe a loop from the 1st bulb to the 4th bulb (No.2).

27. Pipe a loop from the 4th to the 7th bulb (No.2).

28. Repeat the pattern described in 23–27 around the top edges of the bottom and middle tiers.

29. Repeat the pattern described in 23–27 against the top edge of the top tier.

30. Pipe a series of curved lines on the 16″ board (No.2).

31. Pipe a series of curved lines on the 13″ board (No.2). (Parallel to 30) as shown.

32. Repeat 31 on the top of both the bottom and middle tiers (No.2).

Heather

NOTE: *Before attempting to decorate this cake, please study the whole sequence of photographs and notes and ensure you have the proper equipment and materials, as well as sufficient time. Additional information can be found on pages 5–17.*

1. Pipe 4 dots at points on diagonal line (corner to corner).

2. Pipe straight lines from dots to edge of cake (No.2).

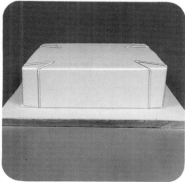

3. Continue lines down side of cake (No.2) (T).

4. Continue lines to corner of board (No.2). Repeat at each corner.

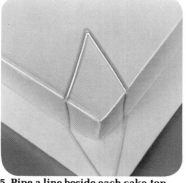

5. Pipe a line beside each cake-top No.2 line (No.1).

6. Pipe a line beside each cake-side No.2 line (No.1).

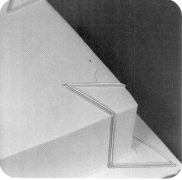

7. Pipe a line beside each board No.2 line (No.1).

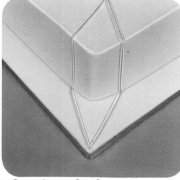

8. Overpipe each cake-top No.2 line (No.1).

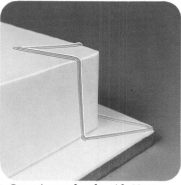

9. Overpipe each cake-side No.2 line (No.1).

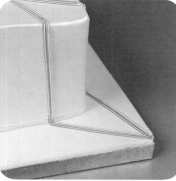

10. Overpipe each board No.2 line (No.1).

11. Pipe scallops beside the lines on each corner (No.1).

12. Filigree each corner (No.1).

13. Pipe 3 graduated dots on top of cake to complete each corner design (No.1).

14. Pipe plain shells along top edges of cake (No.4).

15. Pipe plain shells around base of cake (No.4).

16. Overpipe top and base shells (No.3).

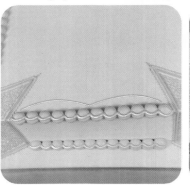

17. Pipe 2 equal curves between each corner design (No.2).

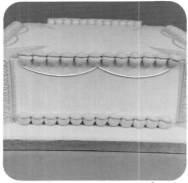

18. Repeat curves against each side of cake (No.2) (T).

19. Repeat curves on cake board (No.2).

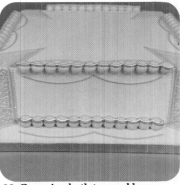

20. Overpipe both top and base shells (No.2).

21. Pipe a line beside the top curved line (No.1).

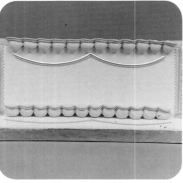

22. Pipe a line under side curved line (No.1) (T).

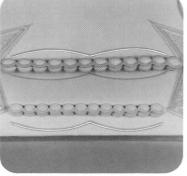

23. Pipe a line beside the base curved line (No.1).

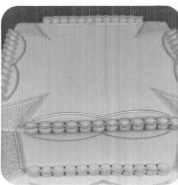

24. Overpipe 1st curved line on cake top (No.1).

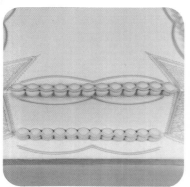

25. Pipe a line against 1st curved line on side of cake (No.1) (T).

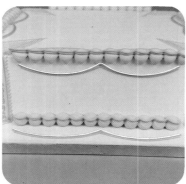

26. Overpipe 1st curved line on base (No.1).

27. Overpipe top and base shells with coloured Royal Icing (No.1).

28. Curve 4 artificial silver leaves and fix centrally.

29. Using artificial flower of choice, fix to centre of leaves.

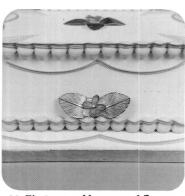

30. Fix 2 curved leaves and flower on centre of each side.

31. Fix silver shoe (or other motif of choice) with matching flowers to each corner.

32. Finish top corners with hand-made sugar doves.

164

GOLDEN
51
YEARS

1. Drawing showing template for cake top.

2. Outline and flood-in on waxed paper the outer runout (L.D. 24 hrs).

3. Outline and flood-in on waxed paper the central plaque (L.D. 24 hrs).

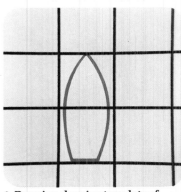

4. Drawing showing template of water lily petal.

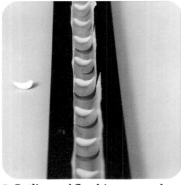

5. Outline and flood-in on waxed paper 60 petals (L.D. 24 hrs) in curved position.

6. Turn the outer runout upside-down and remove waxed paper. Pipe lines as shown (No.1) (L.D. 2 hrs).

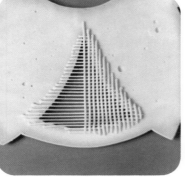

7. Pipe central line and then pipe lines, as shown (No.1).

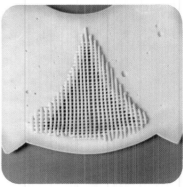

8. Continue piping lines, as shown (No.1) (L.D. 12 hrs).

9. Join 5 petals together with a piped dot to form flower (No.1) (12 flowers required).

10. Pipe stamens at centre of each flower (No.1) (L.D. 12 hrs).

11. Pipe single dots against number edges and then 6-dot triangular sequence against the plaque edge (No.1) (L.D. 12 hrs).

12. Upturn the outer runout and place on cake top.

13. Pipe a dot at each inner point to secure runout to cake top (No.1).

14. Fix central plaque to cake top.

15. Pipe a line beside the outer runout, as shown (No.2).

16. Pipe wording of choice on cake top (No.2).

166

17. Overpipe wording (No.1).

18. Pipe a line beside the No.2 line (No.1).

19. Overpipe the No.2 line (No.1).

20. Fix lilies, as shown.

21. Pipe 2 curved lines on cake side between each cake top 'V' (No.2) (T).

22. Pipe a line under the cake-side No.2 line (No.1) (T).

23. Pipe a line against the cake-side No.2 line (No.1) (T).

24. Pipe bulbs around base of cake (No.3).

25. Overpipe the bulbs with a line (No.2).

26. Pipe a spike between each bulb on the No.2 line (No.1).

27. Pipe curved lines on board so they match the cake-side No.2 line (No.2).

28. Pipe a line beside the board No.2 line (No.1) and then overpipe the No.2 line (No.1).

29. Overpipe the board No.1 line (No.1).

30. Pipe a suspended line, as shown (No.1).

31. Continue piping suspended lines around cake (No.1).

32. Pipe 3 graduated dots at each board suspended line join (No.1).

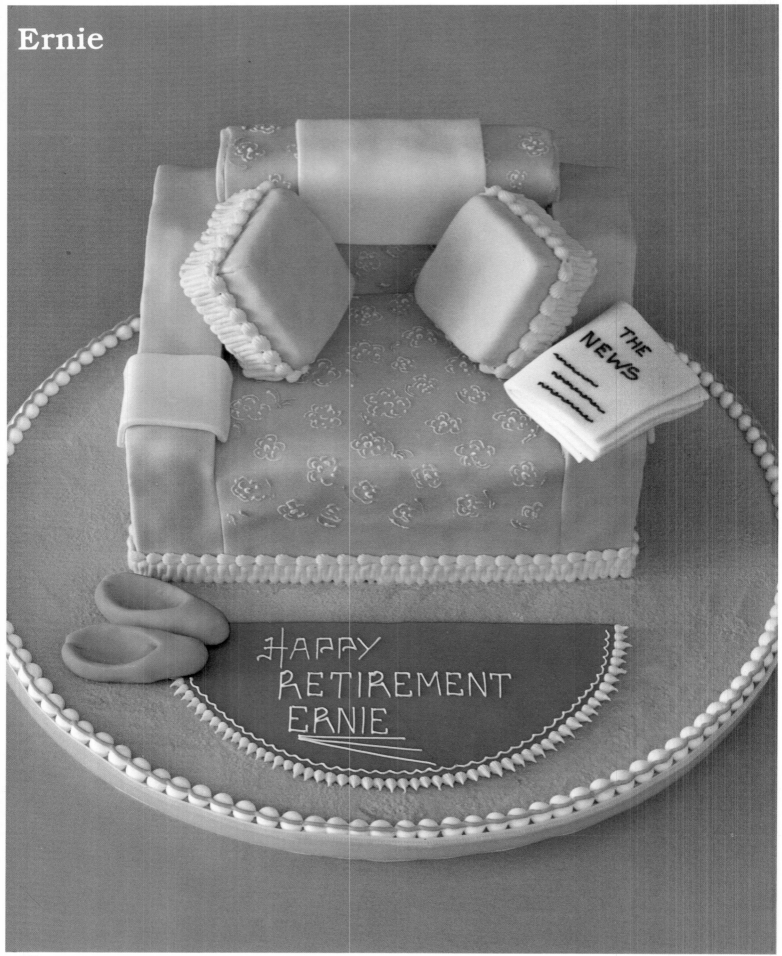

1. One sponge cake – 6″×8″×1″ – required for the chair arms.

2. Two sponge cakes – each 5″×4″×1″ – required for the seat.

3. One sponge cake – 5″×5″×1″ – required for the chair back.

4. Two sponge cakes – each 2″×2″×1″ – required for cushions.

5. Cut 'arms' sponge in shaped half, as shown.

6. Jam and cream the seat sponges together.

7. Fix the chair back to the seat with jam and cream.

8. Fix the arms in position with jam and cream.

9. Place the chair on a 14″ round cake board and cover with cream.

10. Roll out, cut and place a sugar paste cover over the seat and back, as shown.

11. Roll out, cut and place sugar paste covers over the inside and outside of the arms.

12. Roll out, cut and place sugar paste covers over the remaining areas.

13. Roll out, cut and place sugar paste covers over the two cushions, fixing with cream.

14. Picture showing antique floral design for chair covering.

15. Pipe floral design over the area shown (No.1).

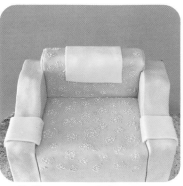

16. Roll out, cut and place sugar paste chair covers, as shown.

169

17. Stipple the board with Royal Icing to create carpet effect.

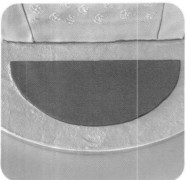

18. Roll out, cut and place sugar paste mat on board.

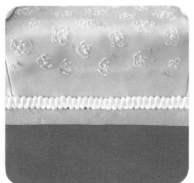

19. Pipe fringe around chair base (No.42).

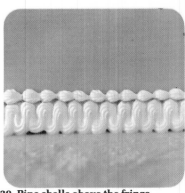

20. Pipe shells above the fringe (No.42).

21. Pipe fringe around the base of each cushion (No.42).

22. Pipe shells above each cushion fringe (No.42).

23. Pipe spikes around the curved edge of the mat (No.42).

24. Roll out and cut two pieces of sugar paste – each 2″×3½″.

25. Place the two pieces together and fold to form newspaper.

26. Pipe wording and imitation print on the newspaper (No.1).

27. Form a pair of slippers from sugar paste.

28. Position cushions, newspaper and slippers.

29. Pipe message of choice on the mat (No.1).

30. Pipe lines under message and scallops around mat, as shown (No.1).

31. Pipe shells around top edge of cake board (No.3).

32. Overpipe the board shells with a line (No.1) and fix ribbon to board edge.

TRACY
5
TO-DAY

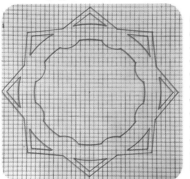

1. Drawing showing template of cake-top runout.

2. Drawing of Tracy.

3. Drawing of bird carrying parcel.

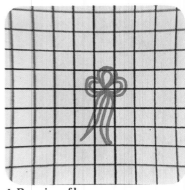

4. Drawing of bow.

5. Outline and flood-in the runout on waxed paper (L.D. 24 hrs).

6. Pipe-in the parts of Tracy shown on waxed paper (L.D. 30 m).

7. Pipe-in the further parts of Tracy shown (L.D. 30 m).

8. Pipe-in the further parts of Tracy shown (L.D. 30 m).

9. Pipe-in the further parts of Tracy shown (L.D. 30 m).

10. Pipe-in the further parts of Tracy shown (L.D. 30 m).

11. Complete the piping of Tracy and then decorate, as shown (L.D. 24 hrs).

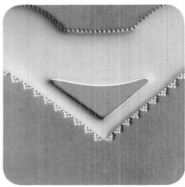

12. Pipe single dots along inside edge and 6-dot sequences along outer pattern edge (No.1) (L.D. 12 hrs).

13. Pipe-in bird's right wing and tail on waxed paper (No.1) (L.D. 10 m) (5 birds required).

14. Pipe-in bird's body using two colours (No.1) (L.D. 10 m).

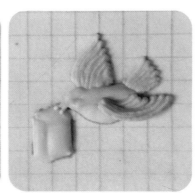

15. Pipe-in left wing and parcel (No.1) (L.D. 24 hrs).

16. Decorate bird and parcel, as shown.

17. Pipe a flower motif in each runout triangular space (No.1) (L.D. 12 hrs).

18. Pipe a line around the top edge of the cake (No.3) (L.D. 1 hr).

19. Overpipe the No.3 line (No.2) and immediately fix runout to cake top.

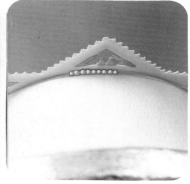

20. Pipe bulbs under runout at top edge of the cake (No.2) (T).

21. Pipe a line on the cake board to match the runout outline (No.2).

22. Flood-in between the board No.2 line and cake base (L.D. 12 hrs).

23. Pipe the bow on waxed paper (No.1) (L.D. 2 hrs) (8 required).

24. Pipe bulbs around the base of the cake (No.2).

25. Pipe a line beside the board runout (No.2).

26. Pipe a line beside the No.2 line (No.1) and then overpipe the No.2 line (No.1).

27. Fix Tracy to the cake top.

28. Fix a bird and parcel to cake top and then join parcel to beak with a piped bow (No.1).

29. Pipe ground beneath Tracy's feet (No.1).

30. Pipe message of choice (No.1) and then overpipe the message (No.1).

31. Fix 4 remaining bird sets around cake side.

32. Fix bows and ribbon of choice around cake board.

Brian

HAPPY BIRTHDAY

BRIAN

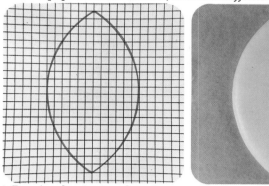

1. Drawing showing template of cake-top plaque (approximately 4½" high).

2. Outline and flood-in the plaque on waxed paper (L.D. 24 hrs).

3. Drawing showing template of capital letter design.

4. Outline and flood-in letter (L.D. 24 hrs).

5. Pipe shells around one-third of the cake-top edge (No.32).

6. Pipe 'C' scrolls around remainder of top edge (No.32).

7. Pipe shells around cake base (No.32).

8. Overpipe all shells with a line (No.3).

9. Overpipe all scrolls (No.3).

10. Pipe a line inside each scroll, as shown (No.2).

11. Pipe a rope inside the cake-top shells, as shown (No.2).

12. Overpipe the scrolls (2).

13. Overpipe the shell No.3 line (No.2).

14. Overpipe the scrolls (No.1).

15. Overpipe the shell No.2 line (No.1).

16. Pipe graduated dots beside each scroll line (No.1).

17. Pipe a rope under each cake-top shell (No.2) (T).

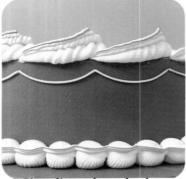

18. Pipe a line under each cake-top scroll (No.2) (T).

19. Pipe a rope above and below each base shell, as shown (No.2).

20. Pipe graduated dots at each base rope join, as shown (No.1).

21. Pipe a line on the plaque, as shown (No.1).

22. Pipe a further line on the plaque, as shown (No.1).

23. Pipe a further line on the plaque, as shown (No.1).

24. Fix letter to plaque.

25. Pipe a sequence of 'S's along the right edge of the plaque (No.1).

26. Pipe plain shells along the left edge of the plaque (No.1) (L.D. 12 hrs).

27. Fix plaque to cake top.

28. Pipe message of choice to the left of the plaque (No.1).

29. Pipe remainder of name in manner shown (No.2).

30. Overpipe the name No.2 lines (No.1).

31. Pipe a line above and below the name, as shown (No.2).

32. Pipe a line beside each No.2 line (No.1) and fix ribbon to board edge.

1. A fruit cake baked in a 2 pint pudding basin and turned upside-down required.

2. Fix marzipan to form dome.

3. Cover whole cake with a thin sheet of marzipan.

4. Coat with thin layer of Royal Icing (L.D. 24 hrs).

5. Cover a 10″ round cake board with sugar paste. (L.D. 12 hrs).

6. Place cake in centre of board.

7. Roll out, cut and fix a sugar paste underskirt to front of cake.

8. Pipe curved lines on board, as shown (No.2).

9. Flood-in between curved line and cake base (L.D. 12 hrs).

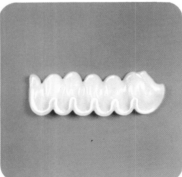

10. Picture showing pattern for overskirt frill.

11. Pipe overskirt frill at cake base (No.57).

12. Overpipe frill (No.57).

13. Picture showing enlarged bow.

14. Pipe small bows on the underskirt (No.1).

15. Cut crimped discs from a thin sheet of sugar paste.

16. Fix a single row of crimped discs around the base of the cake.

178

17. Fix another row of crimped discs between the 1st row.

18. Continue over-lapping rows of discs to cake top.

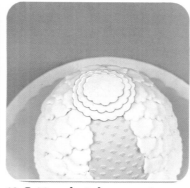

19. Cut 3 graduated sugar paste crimped discs and fix to cake top, as shown.

20. Fix doll bust to top.

21.Pipe a curved line on each disc (No.1).

22. Picture showing dot sequence to be piped on each curved line.

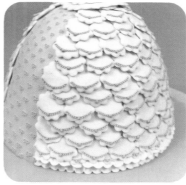

23. Pipe dots on all curved No.1 lines (No.1).

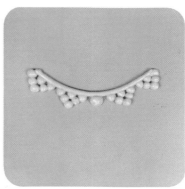

24. Picture showing completed dot sequence.

25. Pipe complete dot sequence on all curved lines (No.1).

26. Decorate the top 3 graduated discs as shown (No.1).

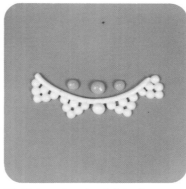

27. Picture showing 3 dots above a curved line.

28. Pipe 3 dots above each curved line to complete the overskirt decoration.

29. Complete piping decorations on the top 3 graduated discs, as shown (No.1).

30. Pipe name of choice on cake board runout. (No.1).

31. Make and fix a ribbon bow at back.

32. Fix velvet ribbon around edge of board.

179

1. Two pieces of sponge cake required – each 9″×2½″×1″ (to form BASE).

2. Two pieces of sponge cake required – each 4″×2″×1″ (to form BOILER).

3. Two pieces of sponge cake required – each 2″×2″×1″ (to form FIREBOX).

4. Jam and cream each pair of cakes together.

5. Trim, as shown, the BOILER edges.

6. Cover all cakes in thin sugar paste except one end of the BOILER.

7. Fix the 3 cakes in the position shown to form the ENGINE.

8. Cut, form and fix a domed disc of sugar paste to front of BOILER.

9. Cover a 13″×6″ cake board with a thin sheet of sugar paste.

10. Roll out a thin sheet of sugar paste and cut into thin strips. Chop the strips to form gravel.

11. Roll out and fix strips of sugar paste 3½″×¼″ (to form SLEEPERS).

12. Sprinkle the gravel over the board.

13. Place the ENGINE on the board.

14. Cut 6×2½″ diameter discs of sugar paste (to form WHEELS).

15. Pipe a circle on each disc. Add a centre bulb and then pipe spokes from bulb to rim (No.3) (L.D. 12 hrs).

16. Pipe 2×6½″ parallel lines on waxed paper (No.4) (L.D. 12 hrs). (to form HANDRAILS).

181

NOTE: Before attempting to decorate this cake, please study the whole sequence of photographs and notes and ensure you have the proper equipment and materials, as well as sufficient time. Additional information can be found on pages 5–17.

17. Pipe two pairs of parallel lines 6½" long onto waxed paper (No.3) (L.D. 12 hrs). (to form WHEEL RODS).

18. Pipe lines, as shown, over the BOILER and FIREBOX (No.2).

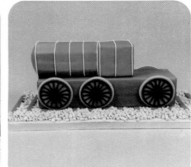

19. Fix WHEELS to ENGINE.

20. Roll out and cut 2 thin strips of sugar paste to form RAILS. Fix in position.

21. Roll out a strip of sugar paste to cover the WHEELS. Fix in position, as shown.

22. Roll out a strip of sugar paste to encase the upper part of the WHEELS, as shown. Fix in position.

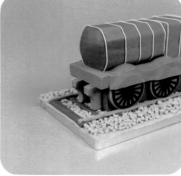

23. Roll out, cut and fix sugar paste pieces for the ENGINE front.

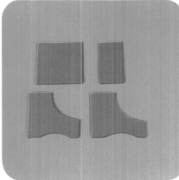

24. Roll out and cut sugar paste pieces for the front, sides and top of the CABIN, as shown (L.D. 2 hrs).

25. Cut out windows and fix cabin front. Decorate as shown.

26. Pipe a line around each outer-side-edge of the CABIN. Fix CABIN sides and roof in position (No.2).

27. Fix HANDRAILS to side of ENGINE.

28. Form and fix ENGINE WHISTLE, DOME, CHIMNEY and VALVE.

29. Decorate the WHEEL guards and CABIN with piped markings.

30. Decorate the ENGINE front, as shown.

31. Pipe message of choice on CABIN side (No.2). Make sugar paste hand lanterns and fix in position.

32. Fix WHEEL RODS in position.

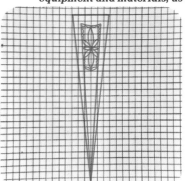

1. Drawing showing template of a section of fan.

2. Drawing showing template of the fan tassel.

3. Drawing showing part of the word 'Mother'.

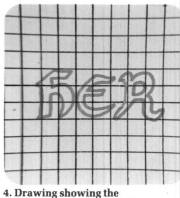

4. Drawing showing the remaining part of the word 'Mother'.

5. Outline and flood-in on waxed paper the area of the fan section shown (L.D. 3 hrs) (8 required).

6. Filigree, pipe curved lines and 6-dot sequences as shown (No.1) (L.D. 2 hrs).

7. Pipe the floral motif shown (No.1) (L.D. 24 hrs).

8. Pipe tassel ropes on waxed paper, as shown (No.2).

9. Pipe further ropes, as shown (No.2).

10. Pipe remaining ropes, tassel and tassel bulb, as shown (No.2) (L.D. 12 hrs).

11. Outline each letter on waxed paper (No.1) (L.D. 1 hr).

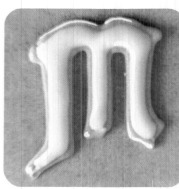

12. Flood-in letters (L.D. 24 hrs).

13. Fix a fan section to the cake top and support it at an angle until dry (L.D. 1 hr).

14. Fix and support next section, as shown (L.D. 1 hr).

15. Continue fixing and supporting sections to the left (L.D. each section 1 hr).

16. Repeat 15 to the right.

17. Pipe a ring at the fan end, as shown (L.D. 2 hrs).

18. Pipe a rope link to corner of cake, as shown (No.2).

19. Pipe curved ropes along the two top edges shown (No.42).

20. Pipe matching curved ropes around the whole of the cake base (No.42).

21. Pipe plain shells along the remaining two top edges (No.2).

22. Pipe graduated bulbs in each base curve (No.2).

23. Pipe a line beside the top ropes, as shown (No.2).

24. Fix letters to the cake top.

25. Pipe a floral decoration to the cake top corner shown (No.1).

26. Pipe dots against the No.2 line, as shown (No.1).

27. Pipe a floral decoration on each side of the cake (No.2) (T).

28. Pipe curved line and dots on each side of the cake, as shown (No.2) (T).

29. Pipe curved lines around the board, as shown (No.2).

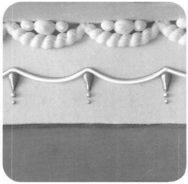

30. Pipe the decorations shown against the curved board lines (No.1).

31. Fix the tassel to the cake in the position shown.

32. Fix ribbon to edge of board.

185

Carmen

1. Pipe 10 bulbs of ¼" diameter and 10 bulbs ⅜" diameter on waxed paper (No.2) (L.D. 2 hrs).

2. Pipe a series of spikes (using colour of choice) around each bulb (No.1) (L.D. 30m).

3. Pipe 2 further rows of spikes around each bulb (No.1) (L.D. 30m).

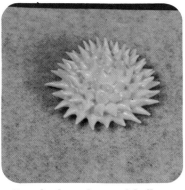

4. Completely enclose each bulb with spikes (No.1) (L.D. 4 hrs).

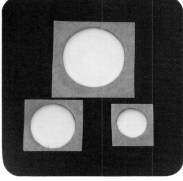

5. Outline and flood-in on waxed paper, 3 discs=one at 1", one at 1¼" and one at 2½". (L.D. 24 hrs).

6. Fix middle sized disc to large disc.

7. Fix the small disc to the middle sized disc.

8. Fix flower to small disc.

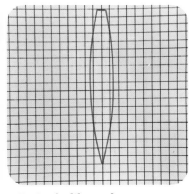

9. Design for lily petal (height=3¾") (6 petals required).

10. Using template under waxed paper outline a petal (No.1).

11. Flood-in the petal.

12. Whilst petal is still wet, place on curved piece of tin. Repeat 10, 11 and 12 for each petal. (L.D. 24 hrs).

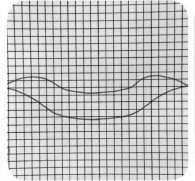

13. Design for cake top runout template (4 required for each cake).

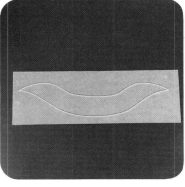

14. Using template under waxed paper, pipe shape outline (No.1).

15. Flood-in the runout (L.D. 24 hrs). Repeat 14 and 15 for each shape.

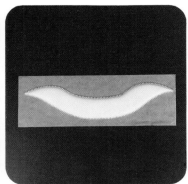

16. Pipe single dots around edge of runouts (No.1) (L.D. 12 hrs).

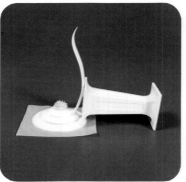

17. Fix and support 1 petal to base of small disc.

18. Repeat 17 on opposite side (L.D. 2 hrs).

19. Fix and support 2 more petals.

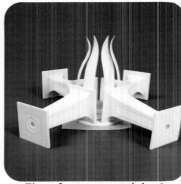

20. Fix and support remaining 2 petals (L.D. 12 hrs then remove supports).

21. Fix the 4 runouts around cake top (No.3).

22. Pipe curved line on board following contours of each top runout shape (No.2).

23. Flood-in board between the No.2 line and cake base (L.D. 12 hrs).

24. Pipe plain bulbs on flooded-in areas against cake base (No.3).

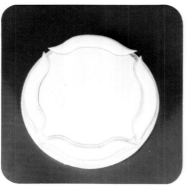

25. Pipe a line along shape of cake-top and board runouts (No.2).

26. Pipe 3 curved lines on cake side under each runout (No.2) (T).

27. Pipe a line beside all the No.2 lines (No.1). (T as necessary).

28. Overpipe all No.2 lines (No.1). (T as necessary).

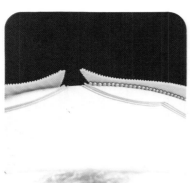

29. Pipe small bulbs under the top runouts (No.2) (T).

30. Pipe tiny bulbs between base of petals and around edge of middle disc (No.1).

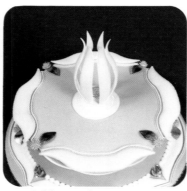

31. Fix lily on cake top. Decorate with flowers, artificial leaves and horseshoes.

32. Pipe tiny bulbs around large disc and then pipe coloured spikes at base of each petal (No.1).

1. Mark the top of a square cake with 4 dots (in the positions shown).

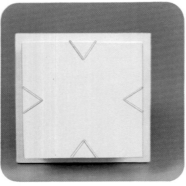

2. Pipe lines from each dot to form triangles at cake top edges (No.2).

3. Pipe a curved line on each side of the cake to meet the top triangular lines (No.2) (T).

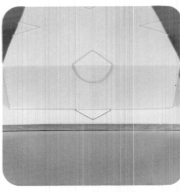

4. Pipe a 'V' centrally on cake board. Repeat on each side (No.2).

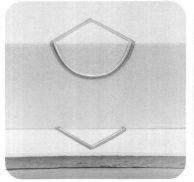

5. Pipe a line beside each No.2 line (No.1) (T as necessary).

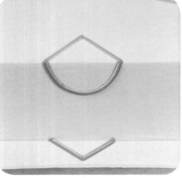

6. Overpipe all No.2 lines (No.1) and then pipe a line against each No.2 line (No.1) (T as necessary).

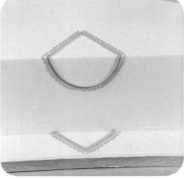

7. Pipe scallops around all the No.1 lines (No.1) (T as necessary).

8. Pipe 3 graduated dots at each cake top triangular point (No.1).

9. Filigree each pattern (No.1).

10. Pipe a line around each base corner to meet each 'V' (No.44).

11. Pipe an 'S' scroll from left to right on cake top edge (No.44).

12. Pipe an 'S' scroll from right to left on cake top edge (No.44).

13. Pipe a 'C' scroll inside each 'S' scroll (No.44).

14. Repeat 11–13 around cake top edge.

15. Pipe an 'S' scroll at each cake base corner (No.44).

16. Overpipe each cake top 'S' scroll (No.3).

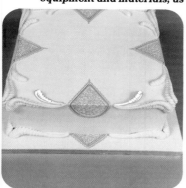

17. Overpipe each cake top 'C' scroll (No.3).

18. Overpipe each cake base 'S' scroll (No.3).

19. Pipe plain shells between 'S' scrolls at cake base (No.3).

20. Overpipe each 'S' scroll on cake top (No.2).

21. Overpipe each 'C' scroll on cake top (No.2).

22. Overpipe each 'S' scroll at cake base (No.2).

23. Pipe 2 curved lines on cake side under each top 'S' scroll (No.2)(T).

24. Pipe 2 curved lines and a 'V' at each cake board corner (No.2).

25. Pipe a line under each cake side No.2 line and then against each cake side No.2 line (No.1)(T).

26. Pipe a line beside each cake board No.2 line (No.1) and then overpipe each cake board No.2 line (No.1).

27. Pipe lines from the 'C' to the 'S' scrolls on cake top (No.1).

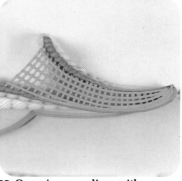

28. Overpipe cross lines with curved ones (to form latticework) and then overpipe each scroll (No.1)

29. Pipe a curved line above each base scroll (No.1) and then pipe lines from each curved line to each scroll (No.1).

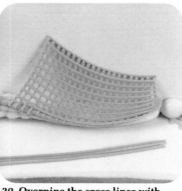

30. Overpipe the cross lines with curved ones (to form latticework) (No.1).

31. Pipe shells along each curved line and then overpipe each base scroll. Overpipe the shells with a line (all No.1).

32. Fix artificial flowers and decorations of choice at triangle centres and cake base corners.

Sandra

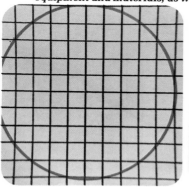

1. Drawing showing template of a 2″ diameter circle.

2. Pipe a 2″ diameter circle on waxed paper (No.3) (L.D. 10 m) (2 required).

3. Overpipe each circle but with a slightly reduced diameter as shown (No.3) (L.D. 10 m).

4. Continue overpiping 3 more times – with 10 m interval between each – to give a conical effect (No.3) (L.D. 1 hr).

5. Continue overpiping 3 more times – with 10 m interval between each – to form cones (No.3) (L.D. 12 hrs).

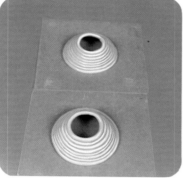

6. Picture showing completed cones.

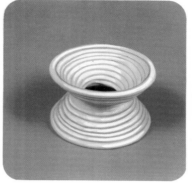

7. Fix cones together to form bird ornament (L.D. 12 hrs).

8. Drawing showing template of a large and small heart shape.

9. Pipe a large heart shape on waxed paper (No.2) (32 required) and then a small heart shape (No.1) (16 required) (L.D. 1 hr).

10. Pipe a floral pattern inside each large heart shape, as shown (No.1) (L.D. 12 hrs).

11. Prepare cake and boards, as shown, then mark cake-top edge into 16 portions with piped dots.

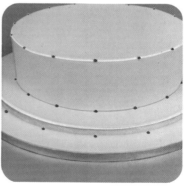

12. Mark base of cake and small board with parallel dots, as shown.

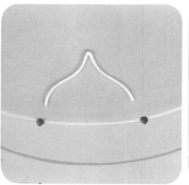

13. Pipe curved line pattern on cake top, as shown (No.2).

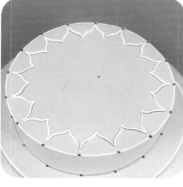

14. Continue piping pattern around cake top.

15. Remove the top edge marker dots and pipe a line around the top edge of cake (No.2).

16. Repeat 13–14 on cake board but in reverse, as shown.

17. Flood-in cake-top and board pattern. (L.D. 12 hrs).

18. Pipe a line beside each pattern line (No.2).

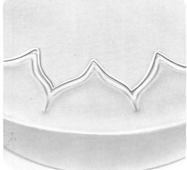

19. Pipe a line beside each No.2 line (No.1) and then overpipe each No.2 line (No.1).

20. Pipe 'S' scrolls in the position shown and then repeat around top edge of cake (No.2).

21. Pipe shells around base of cake (No.2).

22. Fix large hearts to top edge and board, as shown. (Support until dry).

23. Fix ribbon to small board edge. Pipe curved line on large board and then around board edge (No.2).

24. Remove marker dots and flood-in outer edge of large board, as shown.

25. Pipe shells around edge of small board (No.2).

26. Overpipe board runout with curved lines and floral designs, as shown (No.1).

27. Pipe plain shells around top edge of bird ornament (No.1).

28. Pipe small suspended loops and dots around top edge of ornament (No.1) and fix sugar rose in centre.

29. Fix small hearts around base of ornament.

30. Pipe a line linking the small hearts (No.1) (L.D. 12 hrs).

31. Fix sugar birds to edge of ornament and then fix ornament to top centre of cake.

32. Pipe shells around edge of the large board (No.1) and fix ribbon around edge.

194

1. Drawing showing heart-shape template.

2. Outline heart on waxed paper (No.1) (4 of same size required for one tier. Size to reduce as upper tiers reduce).

3. Flood-in each heart (L.D. 24 hrs).

4. Pipe scallops around edge of each heart (No.1).

5. Pipe names or message of choice onto hearts (No.1) (L.D. 12 hrs).

6. Place paper heart-shape template centrally over top edge of cake.

7. Outline top half of heart-shape template (No.2).

8. Outline bottom half of template (No.2) (T).

9. Remove paper template and repeat 6–8 on each top edge of cake.

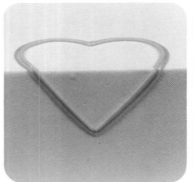

10. Pipe a line beside each No.2 line (No.1) (T as necessary).

11. Overpipe each No.2 line (No.1) (T as necessary).

12. Pipe curved lines across the top of each corner (No.3).

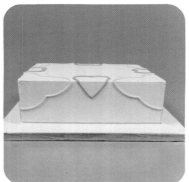

13. Pipe curved lines across the side of each corner (to meet the top lines) (No.3) (T).

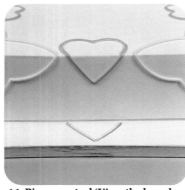

14. Pipe a central 'V' on the board at each side of the cake (No.3).

15. Pipe curved lines on board, as shown (No.3).

16. Pipe a line inside each No.3 curved line (No.1).

17. Filigree corner patterns (No.1) (T as necessary).

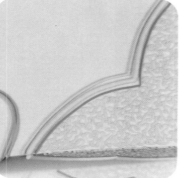

18. Pipe a line beside each No.3 line (No.2) (T as necessary).

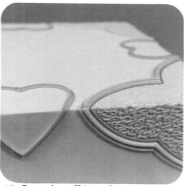

19. Overpipe all No.3 lines (No.2) (T as necessary).

20. Pipe a line beside each No.2 line (No.1) (T as necessary).

21. Overpipe each No.2 line (No.1) (T as necessary).

22. Pipe bulbs along base of cake inside each corner pattern (No.3).

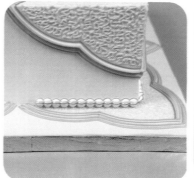

23. Overpipe bulbs (No.1).

24. Fix a roll of satin ribbon on each 'V'.

25. Pipe 2 curved lines on each ribbon (No.1).

26. Pipe a line beside each No.1 line on the ribbons (No.1).

27. Overpipe one line with small plain shells (No.1) and then pipe 3 graduated dots on ribbon front (No.1).

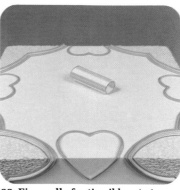

28. Fix a roll of satin ribbon to top centre of cake.

29. Fix artificial leaves and flowers of choice around central ribbon.

30. Pipe 2 bulbs at centre of each cake edge heart (No.3).

31. Fix runout hearts to bulbs.

32. Fix handmade doves to each heart.

Jane

JANE

1. Drawing showing template of stork.

2. Cover template with waxed paper and pipe-in the lower beak (No.1) (L.D. 10 m).

3. Pipe upper beak (No.1) (L.D. 10 m).

4. Place cocktail stick in position as shown.

5. Pipe over the cocktail stick to form leg and pipe-in the tail, as shown (No.1) (L.D. 10 m).

6. Pipe-in right leg on separate piece of waxed paper (No.1) (L.D. 12 hrs).

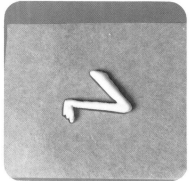

7. Remove right leg from waxed paper, upturn and overpipe (No.1) (L.D. 2 hrs).

8. Pipe-in head, neck and body and fix right leg in position (No.2) (L.D. 24 hrs).

9. Remove stork from waxed paper, upturn and pipe-in beak, head, body and left leg, as shown (L.D. 24 hrs).

10. Paint in eyes with edible colouring.

11. Pipe a bow on waxed paper, as shown (No.2) (L.D. 12 hrs).

12. Fix bow to stork's neck.

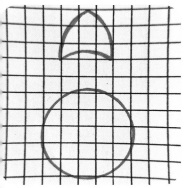

13. Drawing showing template of lily.

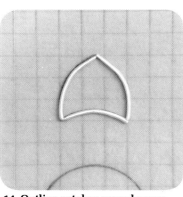

14. Outline petal on waxed paper (No.1).

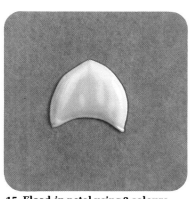

15. Flood-in petal using 2 colours of Royal Icing.

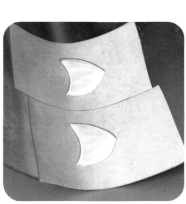

16. Leave petal to dry in curved position, as shown (L.D. 24 hrs). (5 required).

17. Outline and flood-in on waxed paper the lily's centre (L.D. 24 hrs).

18. Fix petals to centre.

19. Pipe spikes around edge of disc (No.1).

20. Fix baby to centre of lily.

21. Pipe curved lines on cake top in pattern shown (No.3).

22. Pipe a line around the base of the cake (No.3).

23. Overpipe the base line with scrolls (No.3).

24. Pipe a line each side of the cake top No.3 line (No.2).

25. Overpipe the cake top No.3 line (No.2) and then overpipe the base scrolls (No.2).

26. Pipe a line each side of the cake top lines (No.1), then overpipe all No.2 lines and scrolls (No.1).

27. Make a small hole in cake top, then fix the stork and lily in positions shown.

28. Pipe reeds around stork and lily, as shown (No.1).

29. Pipe name of choice and scrolls on cake top (No.1).

30. Pipe bulbs around cake-top edge (No.2).

31. Overpipe the bulbs with a line (No.1).

32. Fix ribbon around cake and board edge.

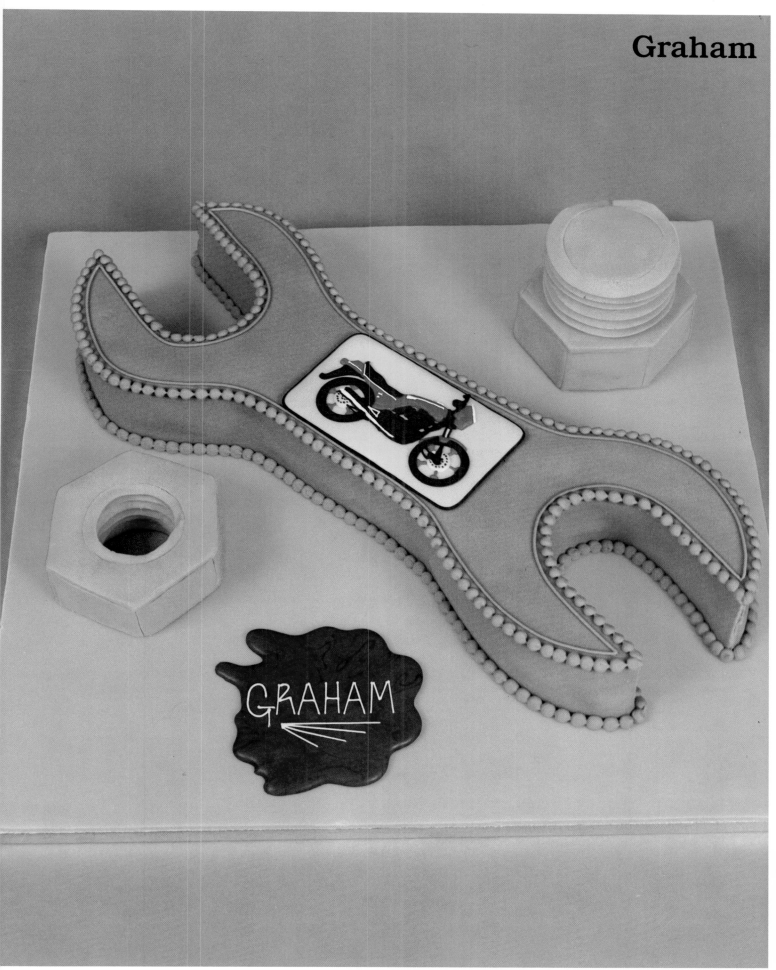

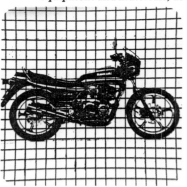

1. Diagram showing template of a motor-bike.

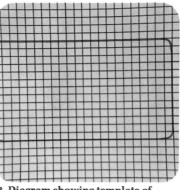

2. Diagram showing template of motor-bike plaque.

3. Outline plaque in black Royal Icing on waxed paper (No.2) (L.D. 1 hr).

4. Flood-in plaque in yellow Royal Icing (L.D. 24 hrs).

5. Place waxed paper over template and pipe-in red parts as shown (L.D. 20 m).

6. Pipe-in yellow parts, as shown (L.D. 20 m).

7. Pipe-in black parts, as shown (L.D. 20 m).

8. Pipe-in further black parts, as shown (L.D. 20 m).

9. Pipe-in further black parts, as shown (L.D. 20 m).

10. Pipe-in remaining red, white and black parts, as shown, to complete motor-bike (L.D. 24 hrs).

11. Two round sponge cakes required – 5″ diameter × 1″ thick.

12. One oblong sponge cake required – 5″ long × 2½″ wide × 1″ thick.

13. Slice each cake in half and jam the top on one half of each cake.

14. Cream over the jam.

15. Rejoin each cake.

16. Cut out the centre of each round sponge in the shape shown. (Retain centre).

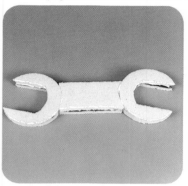

17. Trim the ends of the oblong sponge to fit the round sponges. Fix the 3 cakes together, as shown.

18. Cream over the whole SPANNER.

19. Roll out a thin strip of sugar paste and cover the sides of the SPANNER.

20. Roll out a thin sheet of sugar paste and cover the top of the SPANNER.

21. Cut each spanner end centre (which has been retained from 16) into a hexagon.

22. Remove the centre of one hexagon to form a nut.

23. Fix centre of NUT (retained from 22) to the other hexagon to form bolt. Cream all over.

24. Roll out, cut and fix sugar paste to areas shown.

25. Cut a long triangular strip of sugar paste to form the NUT and BOLT thread.

26. Wrap triangular strip around BOLT and wind it inside the NUT.

27. Cover a 14″ cake board with sugar paste and place SPANNER on it.

28. Pipe shells around edges (No.3). Then pipe a line inside the top shells (No.2).

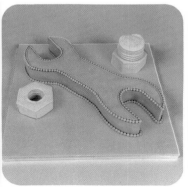

29. Place NUT and BOLT on board in the positions shown.

30. Fix motor-bike onto plaque and then fix plaque onto SPANNER.

31. Pipe partly coloured soft Royal Icing on waxed paper to form oil slick (L.D. 24 hrs).

32. Remove oil slick from waxed paper and fix to board. Write name of choice (No.1).

203

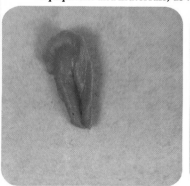

1. Pipe a single petal to the left on waxed paper (No.57).

2. Pipe a petal to the right (No.57).

3. Pipe a petal to the lower right (No.57).

4. Pipe a petal to the lower left (No.57).

5. Pipe an overlapping petal at bottom to complete the petals (No.57).

6. Pipe in heart of violet (No.1).

7. Pipe in flower stamen (No.1). Repeat 1–7 (L.D. 24 hrs) (24 violets required).

8. Pipe one side of leaf (No.57).

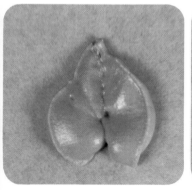

9. Pipe other side of leaf (No.57).

10. Etch in leaf veins with a paint brush and crimp leaf edges (12 leaves required).

11. Template.

12. Template.

13. Template.

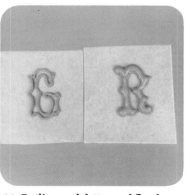

14. Outline each letter and flood-in with soft Royal Icing (No.1) (L.D. 24 hrs).

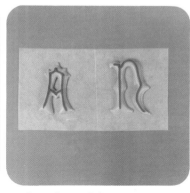

15. Overpipe each letter (No.1).

16. Place a round cake disc (of slightly smaller dimension) on cake top.

205

17. Using the disc as a guide, pipe a circle on cake top (No.3). Remove disc.

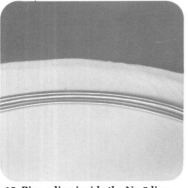

18. Pipe a line inside the No.3 line and then overpipe the No.3 line (No.2).

19. Pipe a line inside the No.2 line (No.1).

20. Pipe plain bulbs around top edge of cake (No.4).

21. Pipe equal sized bulbs around base of cake (No.4) (L.D. 1 hr).

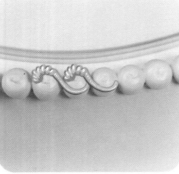

22. Overpipe each top bulb with an 'S' scroll so that the tail extends onto the 2nd bulb (No.2).

23. Overpipe each base bulb with an 'S' scroll so that the tail extends onto the 2nd bulb (No.2).

24. Overpipe all top scrolls (No.1).

25. Overpipe all base scrolls (No.1).

26. Pipe a line on cake board (No.3).

27. Pipe a line outside the No.3 line and then overpipe the No.3 line (No.2).

28. Pipe a line outside the No.2 line (No.1).

29. Pipe small scallops inside the cake top No.1 line and then outside the board No.1 line (No.1).

30. Fix letters to cake top and pipe curved flower stems (No.2).

31. Fix the violets and leaves to the stems.

32. Pipe 2 curved lines (No.2) and fix a pair of violets on cake side.

206

BEST

GRANDAD

WISHES

1. Make a triangular template out of card, as shown.

2. Pipe a line each side of the template (No.3).

3. Continue piping the lines vertically down the side of the cake (No.3) (T).

4. Continue piping the lines across the board (No.3).

5. Pipe a line outside each No.3 line (No.2) (T as necessary).

6. Overpipe each No.3 line (No.2) (T as necessary).

7. Pipe a line beside each No.2 line (No.1) (T as necessary).

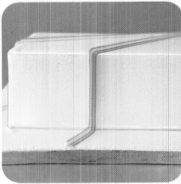

8. Overpipe each No.2 line (No.1) (T as necessary).

9. Filigree inside the triangular pattern (No.1) (T as necessary).

10. Pipe an 'S' scroll at the side of the cake-top corner shown (No.43).

11. Pipe an 'S' scroll at the side of the cake-top corner shown (No.43).

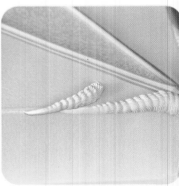

12. Pipe a 'C' scroll in the position shown (No.43).

13. Pipe a further 'C' scroll, as shown (No.43).

14. Pipe 4 more 'C' scrolls, as shown (No.43).

15. Pipe 4 more 'C' scrolls, as shown (No.43).

16. Pipe shells along top edge shown (No.43).

17. Pipe shells along the top edge shown (No.43).

18. Pipe a line along two sides of the base of the cake (beneath the scrolls) (No.43).

19. Pipe matching scrolls along the base of the cake shown (No.43).

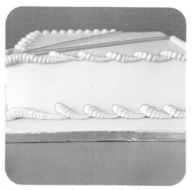

20. Pipe matching scrolls along the base of the cake shown (No.43).

21. Pipe matching shells along the base of the cake shown (No.43).

22. Overpipe each scroll (No.3).

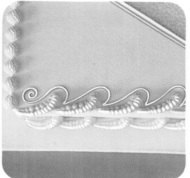

23. Pipe a line inside each cake-top 'C' scroll (No.2).

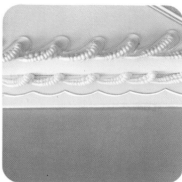

24. Pipe curved lines around board, as shown (No.2).

25. Overpipe each No.3 scroll with a wavy line (No.57).

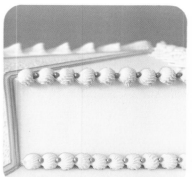

26. Pipe a dot between each shell (No.1).

27. Pipe a word of choice on the part of the cake top shown (No.2).

28. Pipe a word of choice on the part of the cake top shown (No.2).

29. Pipe a word of choice on the part of the cake top shown (No.3).

30. Overpipe each word (No.1).

31. Fix artificial flowers of choice and leaves to corner.

32. Fix ribbon of choice around the middle and board-edge of cake.

1. A 7″ round cake required.

2. Fix a 9″ thin cake board to cake top.

3. Fix a 9″ round cake on the board to form the TABLE (L.D. 12 hrs).

4. Roll out and cut a thin sheet of sugar paste to form a 19″ diameter TABLE CLOTH.

5. Fit the TABLE CLOTH over the TABLE (L.D. 12 hrs).

6. Mould a sugar paste 'dumb-bell' 1¾″ high.

7. Make two cuts into top of dumb-bell.

8. Ease the end pieces apart to form the CANDELABRUM (L.D. 12 hrs).

9. Pipe decorations on the CANDELABRUM (No.1) and fix 3 candle-holders in position (L.D. 12 hrs).

10. Pipe 2 lines on waxed paper against each other to form rectangle 1½″×1″ (No.2) (L.D. 1 hr) (2 required).

11. Filigree rectangles and then pipe 6-dot sequences around edge as shown (L.D. 12 hrs) (No.1).

12. Pipe 6-dot pattern around the bottom third of the TABLECLOTH to form a floral band (No.1).

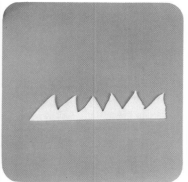

13. Roll out and cut a strip of sugar paste – 2″×½″ – then cut saw-teeth shape (2 required).

14. Roll up each strip to form NAPKINS.

15. Outline and flood-in on waxed paper 2 rectangles – each 1½″×1″ (L.D. 24 hrs).

16. Pipe decorations, as shown (No.1) (L.D. 2 hrs).

17. Fix rectangles together to form CARD and pipe curved rope against its spine (No.1) (L.D. 2 hrs).

18. Sequence showing formation of the flower bowl. (First form sugar paste ball; then pear shape and then bowl).

19. Pipe decorations on BOWL and then pipe flowers on top (No.1).

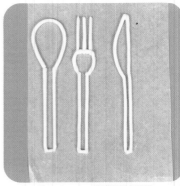

20. Outline 2 sets of CUTLERY – on waxed paper (No.1).

21. Flood-in with soft Royal Icing (L.D. 24 hrs).

22. Pipe decorations on CUTLERY handles (No.1) (L.D. 2 hrs).

23. Dip a cut cocktail stick into Royal Icing (L.D. 2 hrs) in upright position. Repeat until shape is formed (L.D. 12 hrs) 4 required.

24. Cut off cocktail sticks. Pipe 4 bulbs onto waxed paper and fix the WINE GLASSES onto the bulbs (L.D. 12 hrs).

25. Form WINE BOTTLE in manner described in 23.

26. Picture depicting Table top setting.

27. Pipe, on waxed paper, a spiral from centre to a width of ¾" to form BASKET base (No.2) (L.D. 2 hrs).

28. Pipe spiral line from base to form a BREAD BASKET (No.2) (L.D. 2 hrs). Decorate top rim (No.1).

29. Form sugar paste WINE BOTTLE REST.

30. Fix BOTTLE onto REST and decorate with basket effect (No.1).

31. Shape BREAD ROLLS from sugar paste to fit into BASKET.

32. Picture depicting the completed TABLE top.

1. Cover cake in normal way and then cut card to cover a triangular half of the cake.

2. Coat the uncovered half of the cake top in coloured Royal Icing and immediately remove card (L.D. 12 hrs).

3. Place card on coloured Royal Icing.

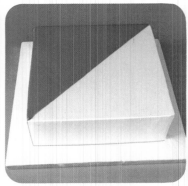

4. Coat uncovered half of cake top with different coloured Royal Icing. Remove card (L.D. 12 hrs).

5. Coat two sides of the cake and half the board in matching colour (L.D. 12 hrs).

6. Coat remaining two sides of the cake and other half of the board in matching colour (L.D. 12 hrs).

7. Pipe shells across the cake, as shown (No.43).

8. Pipe lines on cake top, as shown (No.2).

9. Pipe a line beside each No.2 line (No.1).

10. Pipe scallops beside each No.1 line (No.1).

11. Pipe an 'S' scroll on the top corner edge shown (No.44).

12. Pipe a matching 'S' scroll on the top corner edge shown (No.44).

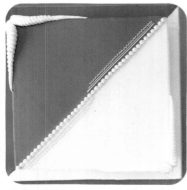

13. Repeat 11–12 at opposite corner.

14. Pipe 'S' lines on remaining top edges of cake (No.44).

15. Continue top shells down corners of the cake and across the board (No.43).

16. Pipe rosettes around the base of the cake (No.44).

214

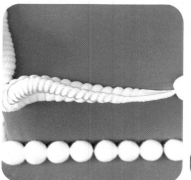

17. Overpipe each 'S' scroll (No.3).

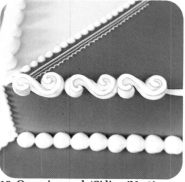

18. Overpipe each 'S' line (No.3).

19. Pipe a curved line beside each scroll, as shown (No.3).

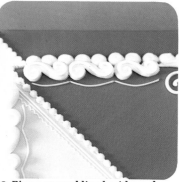

20. Pipe a curved line beside each 'S' line, as shown (No.2).

21. Overpipe each 'S' scroll (No.2).

22. Overpipe each 'S' line (No.2).

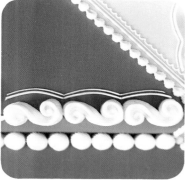

23. Pipe a line beside each No.2 line, as shown (No.1).

24. Overpipe each 'S' scroll (No.1).

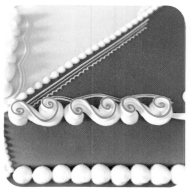

25. Overpipe each 'S' line (No.1).

26. Picture showing half the completed cake top.

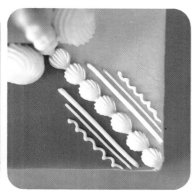

27. Repeat 8–10 on each of the dual coloured board corners, as shown.

28. Pipe a dot on each rosette (No.1).

29. Pipe a line around the board, as shown (No.2).

30. Pipe a line beside the board No.2 line (No.1).

31. Pipe message of choice on cake top (No.1), and then overpipe the No.1 line (No.1).

32. Fix artificial decorations of choice and ribbon to board edge.

NOTE: Before attempting to decorate this cake, please study the whole sequence of photographs and notes and ensure you have the proper equipment and materials, as well as sufficient time. Additional information can be found on pages 5–17.

1. One plain plastic scraper required.

2. Cut a 'V' into the scraper at half the height of the cake.

3. Coat cake and board in normal way using the scraper to form a central band around the cake side.

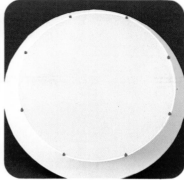

4. Mark top of cake into 8 equal divisions with piped dots, as shown.

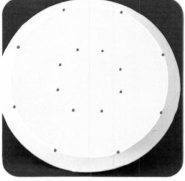

5. Mark inner top of cake into 8 equal divisions (in line with outer marks) with a dot, as shown.

6. Pipe a curved line between each pair of inner dots, as shown (No.3).

7. Pipe a line each side of each No.3 line (No.2).

8. Overpipe each No.3 line (No.2).

9. Pipe a line inside each inner No.2 line and outside each outer No.2 line (No.1).

10. Overpipe each No.2 line (No.1).

11. Pipe a spiral shell on cake-top edge (No.42).

12. Pipe a larger spiral shell on cake-top edge (No.44).

13. Pipe a spiral shell on cake-top edge (No.42). (Note: The 3 shells to lie between a pair of dots).

14. Repeat 11–13 between each pair of outer edge dots.

15. Repeat 11–13 around base of cake.

16. Pipe curved lines around cake top and board, as shown (No.2).

217

17. Pipe a line beside each of the No.2 lines piped in 16 (No.1) and then overpipe each of the No.2 lines (No.1).

18. Pipe an octagonal line on the cake top, as shown (No.2).

19. Pipe a line beside the No.2 octagonal line (No.1) and then overpipe the No.2 line (No.1).

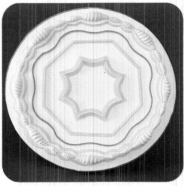

20. Pipe a wavy line on the cake top, as shown (No.2).

21. Pipe leaves on the wavy line using two colours of Royal Icing from a leaf bag.

22. Pipe a broken wavy line around the side of the cake, as shown (No.2) (T as necessary).

23. Repeat 21 around cake side.

24. Pipe curved lines on each large spiral shell, as shown (No.3).

25. Overpipe each No.3 line (No.2).

26. Overpipe each No.2 line (No.1).

27. Pipe loops on the cake top, as shown (No.2) then overpipe (No.1).

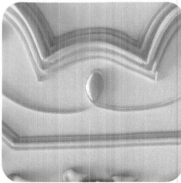

28. Flood-in each loop.

29. Pipe a dot against each loop (No.1).

30. Pipe scallops against each large curved base line (No.1).

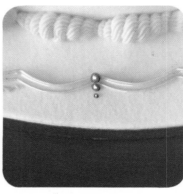

31. Pipe 3 graduated dots at each small curved base line division (No.1).

32. Fix candle-holders and candles on cake top and ribbon to board edge.

1. Pipe two straight lines across the top of the cake in the positions shown (No.2).

2. Pipe a connecting line across the centre of the cake top, as shown (No.2).

3. Pipe further lines in the positions shown (No.2).

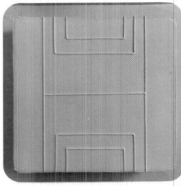

4. Pipe further lines in the positions shown (No.2).

5. Pipe further lines to complete a football field (No.2).

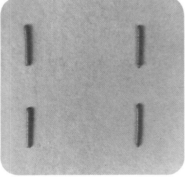

6. Pipe 4 × ½″ high flag posts on waxed paper, as shown (No.2) (L.D. 20 m).

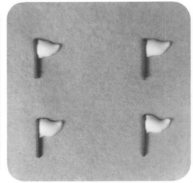

7. Pipe-in a flag on each post (No.2) (L.D. 12 hrs).

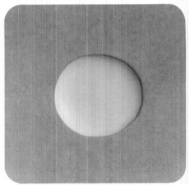

8. Outline and flood-in on waxed paper a 1″ diameter disc (L.D. 24 hrs) (4 required).

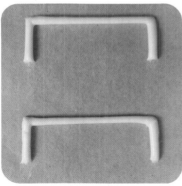

9. Pipe goal posts on waxed paper, as shown (No.4) (L.D. 12 hrs).

10. Paint lines on discs with edible colouring to represent footballs.

11. Pipe a word of choice on each football (No.1).

12. Form 2″ (approx) diameter sugar paste ball (L.D. 12 hrs).

13. Form two balls of sugar paste.

14. Now mould balls into shape shown.

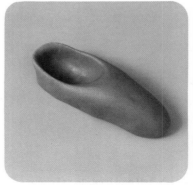

15. Shape into soccer boots, as shown.

16. Cut boot tops and pierce boot eyes, as shown.

17. Pipe lines on boots, as shown (No.1).

18. Pipe further lines on boots, as shown (No.1).

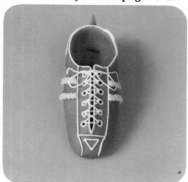

19. Pipe laces, as shown (No.1) (L.D. 12 hrs).

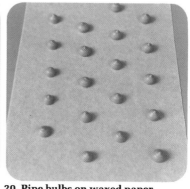

20. Pipe bulbs on waxed paper to form boot studs (No.2) (L.D. 12 hrs).

21. Fix studs to boot soles, as shown.

22. Pipe lines on the football in the positions shown (No.1) (L.D. 12 hrs).

23. Pipe shells around base of the cake (No.44).

24. Pipe shells along the parts of the cake-top edge shown (No.43).

25. Overpipe base shells with a line (No.3).

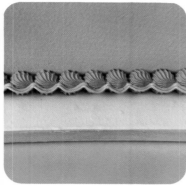

26. Overpipe the No.3 line (No.2).

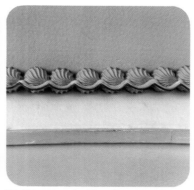

27. Overpipe the No.2 line (No.1).

28. Pipe message of choice on cake top, as shown (No.1).

29. Pipe a line at each board corner (No.2) and then pipe a line beside each No.2 line (No.1).

30. Fix ball and boots to cake top.

31. Fix goal and flag posts and pipe penalty spots on cake top (No.2).

32. Fix a football disc to each side of the cake and ribbon around board edge.

221

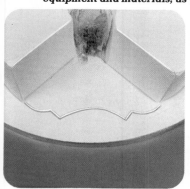

1. Pipe lines on board, as shown, joining the horseshoe ends (No.2).

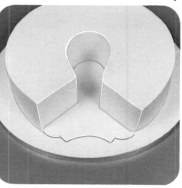

2. Flood-in the central area of the horseshoe to the outline (L.D. 12 hrs).

3. Pipe shells around the inside base of the cake (No.42).

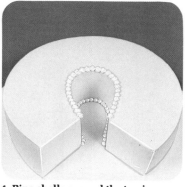

4. Pipe shells around the top inner edge (No.42).

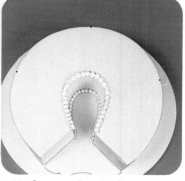

5. Mark outer edge of cake into 4 equal portions with piped dots.

6. Divide each portion into two and mark with piped dots.

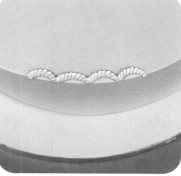

7. Pipe 4 curved ropes between each pair of dots (No.42).

8. Pipe 4 curved ropes along each horseshoe straight edge (No.42).

9. Pipe curved ropes around outside top edge of cake (so they inter-lock inner ropes) (No.42).

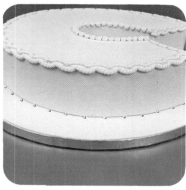

10. Mark base of cake with piped dots immediately beneath end of each inner top rope.

11. Pipe a curved rope against bottom side of cake between each pair of dots (No.42) (T).

12. Pipe curved (inter-locking) ropes on the board at base of cake (No.42).

13. Overpipe the top outer ropes with a curved line (No.3).

14. Overpipe the base outer ropes with a curved line (No.3).

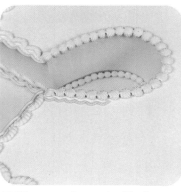

15. Pipe curved ropes beside the top shells (No.2).

16. Pipe a curved line beside each inner top rope (No.2).

223

17. Overpipe the top inner ropes (No.2).

18. Overpipe the top outer No.3 line (No.2).

19. Pipe a curved line under each top outer rope (No.2) (T).

20. Pipe a rope against each cake base rope (No.2) (T).

21. Overpipe the No.3 board line (No.2).

22. Outline the base design (No.2).

23. Pipe a line beside the cake top No.2 line (No.1).

24. Overpipe the top No.2 line (No.1).

25. Overpipe the top inner rope (No.1).

26. Overpipe the outer No.2 line (No.1).

27. Pipe a line under cake-side No.2 line and then against the No.2 line (No.1) (T).

28. Pipe curved ropes against the base ropes (No.1) (T).

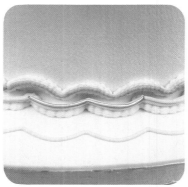

29. Overpipe the board rope line (No.1).

30. Pipe a line beside the No.2 board line and then overpipe the No.2 line (No.1).

31. Pipe 2 graduated dots between each top shell and then overpipe top outer No.1 line (No.1).

32. Pipe lines, as shown, to entrance and around cake base (No.1). Fix ribbon to board edge.

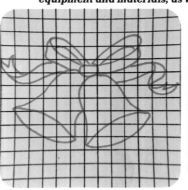

1. Drawing showing template of double-bell.

2. Outline double-bell on waxed paper (No.1) (4 required for each tier).

3. Flood-in areas shown (L.D. 30 m).

4. Flood-in further areas shown (L.D. 30 m).

5. Flood-in further areas shown (L.D. 30 m).

6. Complete flooding-in (L.D. 24 hrs).

7. Pipe 4 curved lines along each side of the cake top, as shown (No.1).

8. Pipe reverse curved lines on board (No.1).

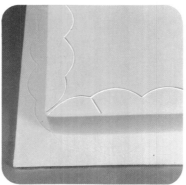

9. Pipe an angled line between the No.1 line and the cake edge (No.1).

10. Continue piping lines at same angle within the patterned area around cake top.

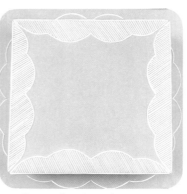

11. Picture showing cake top pattern complete with angled lines.

12. Pipe a line in the opposite direction, as shown (No.1).

13. Continue piping lines at same angle within the patterned area around cake top.

14. Picture showing cake top pattern complete with angled lines.

15. Repeat 9–13 on board pattern, as shown.

16. Pipe plain shells on cake top curved lines (No.2).

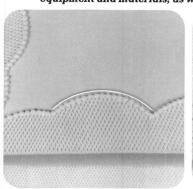

17. Pipe a line beside the shells (No.2).

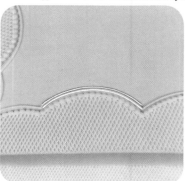

18. Pipe a line beside the No.2 line and then overpipe the No.2 line (No.1).

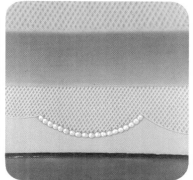

19. Pipe plain shells on board curved lines (No.2).

20. Pipe shells around base of cake (No.42).

21. Pipe an 'S' scroll on cake top edge (No.42).

22. Pipe a 'C' scroll over line-work on cake top (No.42).

23. Pipe another 'S' scroll on top edge of cake (No.42).

24. Repeat 21–23 from opposite corner of same cake top edge. Then repeat along each edge.

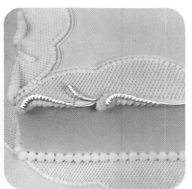

25. Overpipe the scrolls (No.2).

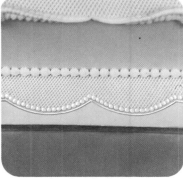

26. Pipe a line beside the board No.2 shells (No.2).

27. Pipe a line beside the board No.2 line and then overpipe the No.2 line (No.1).

28. Overpipe the scrolls (No.1).

29. Fix bell runouts to each side of cake.

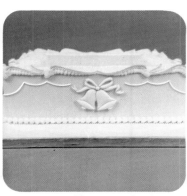

30. Pipe curved lines on side of cake, as shown (No.2) (T).

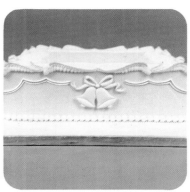

31. Pipe a line under the cake-side No.2 line then against the No.2 line (No.1) (T).

32. Fix sugar doves, artificial flowers of choice and ribbon, as shown.

Amelia

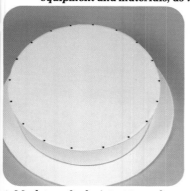

1. Mark top of cake into 18 equal spaces with small dots.

2. Pipe a line around the cake base (No.43).

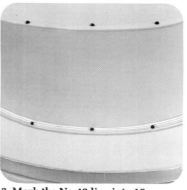

3. Mark the No.43 line into 18 equal spaces immediately beneath the top dots.

4. Pipe a scroll measuring ⅔rds the distance between 2 dots on top edge of cake (No.43).

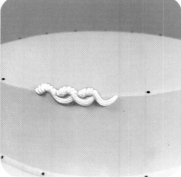

5. Continue scrolls around top edge of cake so there are 3 scroll heads between dots (No.43).

6. Repeat 4 on base line (No.43).

7. Repeat 5 (No.43).

8. Overpipe a top scroll (No.3).

9. Continue overpiping all top scrolls (No.3).

10. Overpipe a base scroll with another scroll (No.3).

11. Continue overpiping all base scrolls (No.3).

12. Overpipe a top scroll with another scroll (No.2).

13. Continue overpiping all top scrolls (No.2).

14. Overpipe a base scroll with another scroll (No.2).

15. Continue overpiping all base scrolls (No.2).

16. Overpipe a top scroll with another scroll (No.1).

229

17. Continue overpiping all top scrolls (No.1).

18. Overpipe a base scroll with another scroll (No.1).

19. Continue overpiping all base scrolls (No.1).

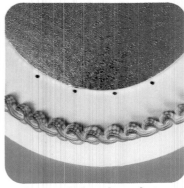

20. Place a cake board on cake top and mark out 18 spaces with small dots.

21. Remove cake board and pipe a curved line between each dot (No.2).

22. Pipe curved lines on side of cake beneath and symmetrical with top curved lines (No.2) (T).

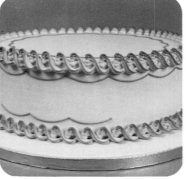

23. Pipe curved lines above base scrolls to match the curved lines in 22 (No.2) (T).

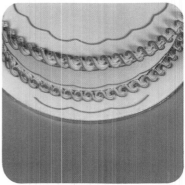

24. Pipe curved lines on cake board to match other curved lines (No.2).

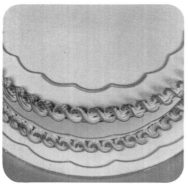

25. Pipe a line outside the No.2 line on cake top (No.1).

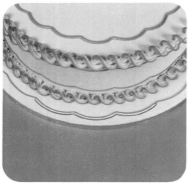

26. Pipe a line outside the No.2 line on cake board (No.1).

27. Pipe flower stem on cake side (No.2) (T).

28. Pipe second stem (No.2) (T). Repeat 27 and 28 around cake side.

29. Practise piping lily of the valley shape before piping directly to cake (No.1).

30. Pipe lilies of the valley around side of cake (No.1) (T).

31. Pipe a lily of the valley at each curve point on cake top (No.1).

32. Make 3 sugar bells (see instructions) and fix on top centre of cake. Pipe 3 short lines (No.1).

230

1. Drawing showing template of corner decoration.

2. Pipe curved line on waxed paper, as shown (No.4) (L.D. 2 hrs) (6 required for each tier).

3. Pipe 2nd line so that the bottom of the 1st line is overpiped (No.4) (L.D. 2 hrs).

4. Pipe the 3rd line so that the bottom of the 1st and 2nd lines are overpiped (No.4) (L.D. 12 hrs).

5. Remove from waxed paper, turn over and repeat 2.

6. Repeat 3.

7. Repeat 4.

8. Make 6 sugar bells and 12 sugar doves for each tier.

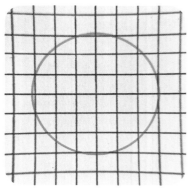

9. Drawing showing template of disc to be cut from paper.

10. Fold disc over top edge of cake and pipe a line around disc top (No.2).

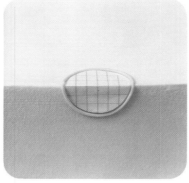

11. Pipe a line around disc on cake side (No.2) (T). Repeat 10–11 on each cake top edge.

12. Place disc at base of cake and pipe a line around disc on side of cake (No.2) (T).

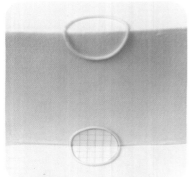

13. Pipe a line around disc on board (No.2). Repeat 12–13 around cake base.

14. Pipe a line beside each No.2 line (No.1).

15. Overpipe each No.2 line (No.1).

16. Pipe an 'S' scroll each side of each cake top pattern, as shown (No.3).

17. Pipe curved lines on cake top corners, as shown (No.2).

18. Overpipe each 'S' scroll (No.2).

19. Overpipe each 'S' scroll (No.1).

20. Fix corner decorations.

21. Pipe bulbs each side of each base pattern (No.3).

22. Overpipe the base bulbs with a line (No.2).

23. Overpipe the No.2 line (No.1).

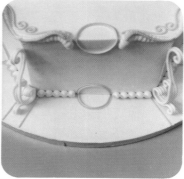

24. Pipe a line each side of each corner decoration, as shown (No.2).

25. Pipe 'L' lines on each cake board corner, as shown (No.2).

26. Pipe a line beside each 'L' line (No.1).

27. Overpipe each board No.2 line (No.1).

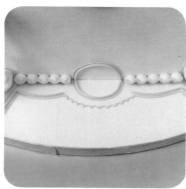

28. Pipe a curve of scallops between each 'L' (No.1).

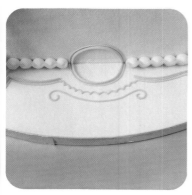

29. Pipe a curved line beside the scallops (No.1).

30. Fix a bell to each corner decoration.

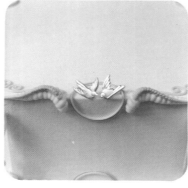

31. Fix doves to each cake top pattern.

32. Fix artificial flowers, fern and ribbon to board, as shown.

Good Luck

1. Drawing showing template of cat.

2. Pipe-in tail and front right leg on waxed paper (L.D. 10 m).

3. Pipe-in body and rear left leg (L.D. 10 m).

4. Pipe-in front left leg (L.D. 10 m).

5. Pipe-in inner ears (L.D. 10 m).

6. Pipe-in outer ears (L.D. 10 m).

7. Pipe-in face (L.D. 10 m).

8. Pipe-in eyes and tongue (L.D. 10 m).

9. Pipe a bow on waxed paper, as shown (No.2) (L.D. 2 hrs).

10. Fix bow to cat and pipe-in whiskers. Paint eyes in edible colouring (L.D. 24 hrs).

11. Outline and flood-in on waxed paper the letters of message of choice (L.D. 24 hrs).

12. Overpipe each letter of message (No.1).

13. Pipe dots each side of each No.1 line (No.1).

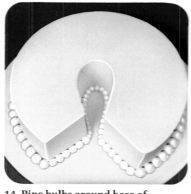

14. Pipe bulbs around base of coated horseshoe cake (No.3).

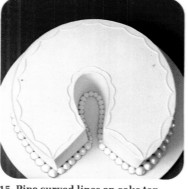

15. Pipe curved lines on cake top, as shown and then pipe a line around cake-top edge (No.2).

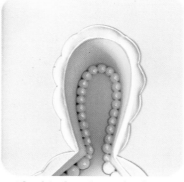

16. Flood-in the cake-top border. (L.D. 12 hrs).

235

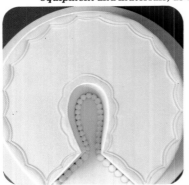

17. Pipe a line inside the No.2 curved line (No.2).

18. Pipe a line beside the No.2 line (No.1) and then overpipe the No.2 line (No.1).

19. Pipe a curved practice line (No.1).

20. Pipe practice dots and spikes on the curved line, as shown (No.1).

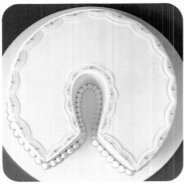

21. Now pipe 19–20 around top edge of cake in positions shown (No.1).

22. Pipe plain shells around top edge of cake (No.2).

23. Overpipe base shells with a line (No.2).

24. Overpipe base No.2 line (No.1).

25. Overpipe base No.1 line (No.1).

26. Pipe inward curving lines on board, as shown (No.2). (The points of the top and board lines to match).

27. Pipe a line beside the board No.2 line (No.1).

28. Repeat 19–20 on board, as shown.

29. Fix letters at angle on cake top using stiff Royal Icing.

30. Fix cat to cake top.

31. Fix artificial heather and horseshoe to cake top.

32. Fix pairs of artificial horseshoes around cake-side and ribbon around board.

1. Cut 4 discs of sponge cake – each 2¾″ diameter × 1″ deep.

2. Cut 1 disc of sponge cake – 2¼″ diameter; 1 disc – 1¾″ diameter; 2 discs – 1¼″ diameter (all 1″ deep).

3. Jam all disc tops except one of the smallest.

4. Pipe cream over the jam (No.4).

5. Join discs together to form bottle shape. Place in refrigerator for 2 hrs.

6. Remove 'bottle' from refrigerator and immediately trim rough edges to perfect shape.

7. Coat the 'bottle' with a thin layer of cream. Place in refrigerator for 1 hr.

8. Roll out and cut a sugar paste sheet – 10″×12″ – to envelop the 'bottle'.

9. Remove 'bottle' from refrigerator and immediately envelop in sugar paste sheet.

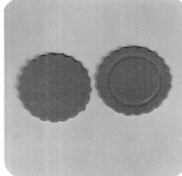

10. Roll out a thin sheet of sugar paste and cut a crinkled 2″ diameter disc. Imprint disc with a 1½″ diameter circle.

11. Fix the disc over the 'bottle' to form the bottle top.

12. Roll out, cut and fix a thin sheet of sugar paste to form the bottle label.

13. Roll out, cut and fix a smaller label of contrasting colour.

14. Roll out, cut and fix a crimped seal – supported around bottle neck with thin ribbon.

15. Pipe decorations on outer label and write on seal (No.1).

16. Pipe message of choice on label (No.2).

17. Cut 2 discs of sponge cake – each 3½″ diameter × 1″ deep.

18. Cut 2 discs of sponge cake – each 4″ diameter × 1″ deep.

19. Jam the tops of both 4″ discs and one 3½″ disc.

20. Cream over the jam.

21. Join discs together – small ones at the bottom and top – to form 'mug'. Place in refrigerator for 2 hrs.

22. Remove 'mug' from the refrigerator and immediately trim rough edges to shape.

23. Coat the sides of the 'mug' with a thin layer of cream. Refrigerate for 1 hr.

24. Roll out and cut a thin sheet of sugar paste – 13″×4″.

25. Leaving ½″ at top, wrap sheet around beer mug immediately after removing from refrigerator.

26. Roll out a thin strip of sugar paste – 13″×⅝″.

27. Wrap strip around the top ½″ of 'mug' so that ⅛″ protrudes.

28. Roll out and form a 4″ long sugar paste mug handle (L.D. 12 hrs).

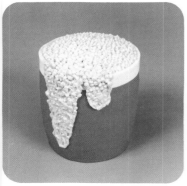

29. Cover 'mug' top and overspill with piped cream dots to form the froth.

30. Fix handle to beer mug (this can be pegged with cocktail sticks for additional support).

31. Roll out, cut and fix an oval crimped label.

32. Pipe message of choice on label (No.2) and then place BEER BOTTLE and MUG on serving tray.

Delia

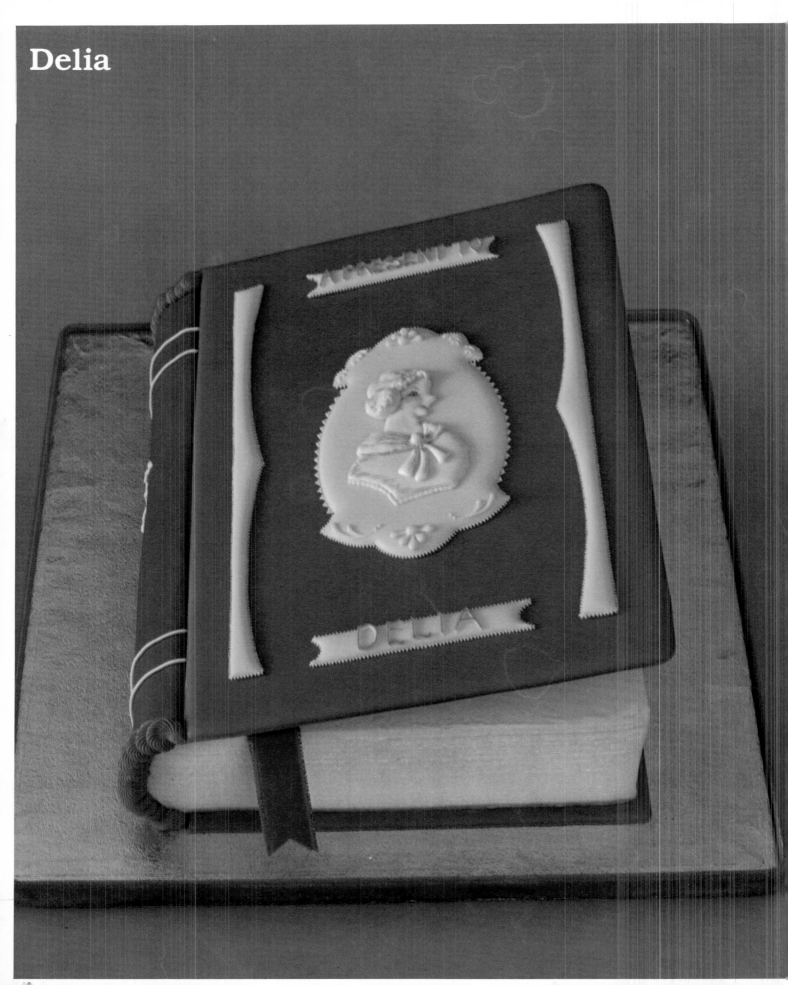

1. Square cake 7″×7″ required.

2. Cut a 1″ slice off one side.

3. Fix the slice to end of the cake and remove surplus. Trim side to form book spine shape.

4. Marzipan and coat cake in normal way.

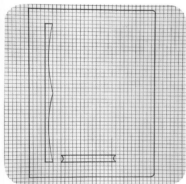

5. Drawing showing template of book cover 6½″×8¾″.

6. Outline book cover on waxed paper (No.2) then flood-in (L.D. 24 hrs).

7. Outline and flood-in on waxed paper the 7¼″ long shape shown (L.D. 24 hrs) (2 required).

8. Outline and flood-in on waxed paper the 3″ long shape shown (L.D. 24 hrs) (2 required).

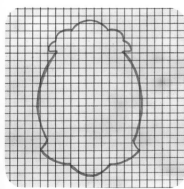

9. Drawing showing plaque template.

10. Outline and flood-in the plaque on waxed paper (L.D. 24 hrs).

11. Drawing showing template of Delia.

12. Pipe-in face and neck on waxed paper (L.D. 10 m).

13. Pipe-in bodice (L.D. 10 m).

14. Pipe-in hair (L.D. 10 m).

15. Pipe-in scarf ends on separate piece of waxed paper (L.D. 2 hrs).

16. Pipe-in fichu and then fix scarf ends to Delia with a piped bulb (L.D. 24 hrs).

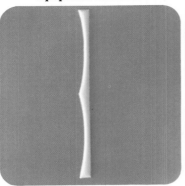

17. Pipe single dots against the edges of both the runouts of the shape shown (No.1) (L.D.12 hrs).

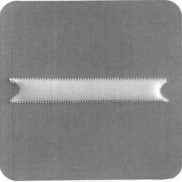

18. Pipe single dots against the edges of both the runouts of the shape shown (No.1) (L.D.12 hrs).

19. Pipe single dots against end edges and 6-dot sequences against each side of the plaque (No.1) (L.D. 12 hrs).

20. Fix Delia to the plaque and decorate, as shown, with edible colouring.

21. Decorate plaque with further piping, as shown (No.1).

22. Pipe message of choice on the two runouts shown (No.2) and then overpipe the message (No.1) (L.D. 2 hrs).

23. Fix all runouts to book cover, as shown.

24. Roll out and fix sugar paste strip to the spine of the book.

25. Coat sides of the book using a fine-toothed (sterilised) comb to create page effect (L.D. 12 hrs).

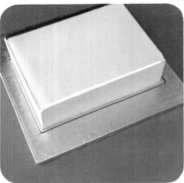

26. Pipe a line on the board to form the back cover of the book (No.2).

27. Flood-in between the cake base and the No.2 line.

28. Pipe imitation writing on cake top (No.1).

29. Fix cover at an angle to cake top and support until dry.

30. Pipe a rope at each end of the spine (No.44).

31. Pipe lines and imitation writing on the spine (No.2).

32. Cut and fix a ribbon book marker and fix matching ribbon to the cake-board edge.

242

DEAR TINA,
A HAPPY BIRTHDAY
FROM US ALL.

PROTOTYPE

1. Two pieces of sponge cake required – each 10″×10″×1″.

2. Jam the top of one piece.

3. Cream over the jam.

4. Join the cakes together.

5. Jam area 10″×7″ on cake top.

6. Cream over the jam.

7. One piece of sponge cake required – 10″×7″×1″.

8. Place 7 on creamed area.

9. Slightly trim top layer, as shown, and slope middle layer to form keyboard.

10. Cut back to form slight slope.

11. Cut 'V', as shown, along width of top.

12. Place cake on a 12″ square cake board and coat cake with cream.

13. Fix a strip of sugar paste around the base of the cake.

14. Cover the sloping front of the cake with a thin sheet of sugar paste.

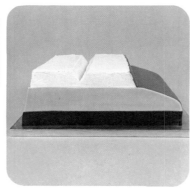

15. Cover the back and sides of the cake with sugar paste (leaving the top layer uncovered).

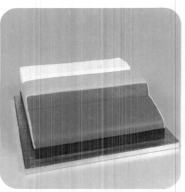

16. Cover top of front cake with a thin sheet of sugar paste so that it fits into the 'V'.

17. Cover the top back of cake with a thin sheet of sugar paste so that it fits into the 'V' and joins 16.

18. Fix a thin sheet of black sugar paste from the centre 'V' over the back to form the typewriter roller.

19. Form a top cover, as shown, from black sugar paste and fix.

20. Fix a thin sheet of sugar paste to the front sloping area to form keyboard base.

21. Cut shaped keys and spacer bars from sugar paste and fix in position.

22. Cut and fix the 2nd row of shaped keys from sugar paste, as shown.

23. Cut and fix the 3rd row of shaped keys from sugar paste, as shown.

24. Cut and fix the 4th row of shaped keys from sugar paste, as shown.

25. Cut and fix the remaining keyboard bars from sugar paste, as shown.

26. Pipe letters, numbers and symbols, as shown (No.1).

27. Cut and fix sugar paste control buttons and pipe numerals, as shown (No.1).

28. Fix a thin sheet of sugar paste into the 'V' and over the 'roller' to form paper.

29. Pipe message on 'paper' (No.1).

30. Cut and fix sugar paste paper guide.

31. Form sugar paste controls, as shown.

32. Fix controls.

245

Oliver

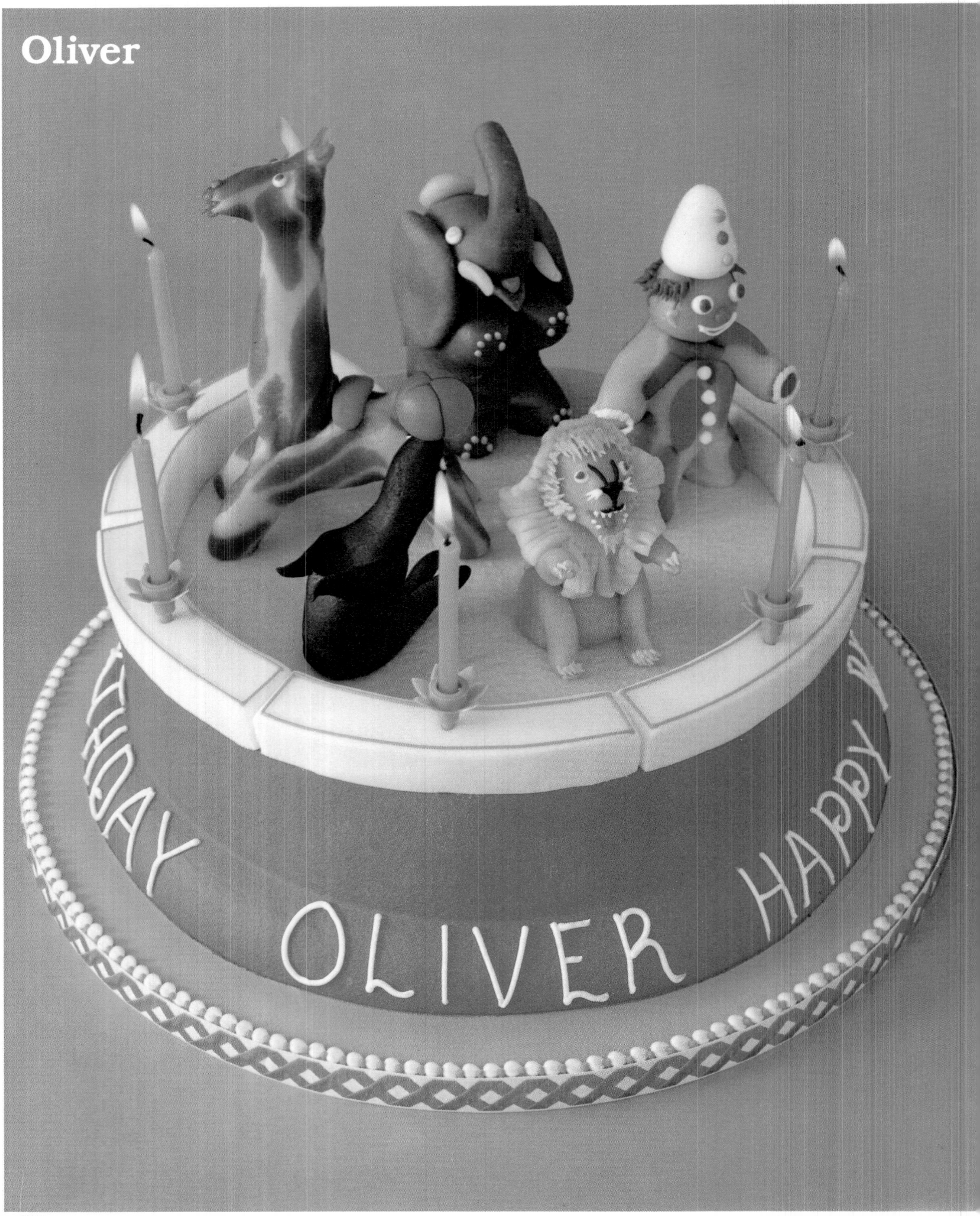

1. A marzipanned and coated 8" round cake required on a 12" board.

2. Cut a semi-circle from a plastic scraper.

3. Coat the side of the cake and use the scraper to give the effect shown (L.D. 12 hrs).

4. Stipple cake top and board with Royal Icing (L.D. 12 hrs).

5. Form a ball of marzipan.

6. Roll ball into the shape shown.

7. Cut marzipan into shape shown to form a seal.

8. Bend the seal to an upright position (L.D. 12 hrs). Complete the seal and ball, as shown.

9. Form 4 graded balls of marzipan, as shown.

10. Form each ball into the shape shown.

11. Fix each shape to form an elephant. Cut and decorate, as shown (L.D. 12 hrs).

12. Continue decorating the elephant, as shown.

13. Form one large, one medium (head) and 5 small balls of marzipan as shown.

14. Fix pieces from each small ball to the large ball, as shown.

15. Roll out large ball to form arms, body and legs.

16. Fix and shape the head, arms and body, as shown (L.D. 12 hrs). Decorate, as shown.

247

17. Form 3 balls of marzipan.

18. Form the balls into the shapes shown.

19. Cut, form and mount the shapes to form a lion (L.D. 12 hrs).

20. Decorate the lion, as shown.

21. Form 2 balls of marzipan, as shown.

22. Cover the large ball with pieces from the small ball and form into the shapes shown.

23. Fix shapes together to form a giraffe (L.D. 12 hrs).

24. Decorate the giraffe, as shown.

25. Roll out 7 blocks of sugar paste, as shown.

26. Fix blocks to create a circus ring on cake-top edge.

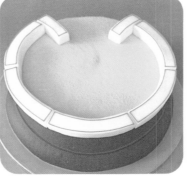

27. Pipe a line around the top edge of each block (No.1).

28. Pipe name of choice at the base of the cake front (No.2).

29. Pipe 'Happy Birthday' each side of the name (No.2).

30. Fix figures to cake top.

31. Fix candle holders with candles to circus ring.

32. Pipe shells and dots on cake board and fix ribbon to board edge.

248

1. Drawing showing template of representation tree trunk.

2. Drawing showing template of representation tree.

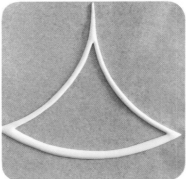

3. Cover tree trunk template with waxed paper and outline and flood-in, as shown (L.D. 1 hr).

4. Outline and flood-in the further parts shown (L.D. 1 hr).

5. Outline and flood-in the further parts shown (L.D. 1 hr).

6. Flood-in the centre, as shown (L.D. 24 hrs).

7. Pipe 6-dot sequences around the tree trunk edge (No.1) (L.D. 12 hrs).

8. Outline a flower on waxed paper using template as guide (No.1). (L.D. 2 hrs).

9. Flood-in flower (L.D. 24 hrs).

10. Cover tree template with waxed paper and outline and flood-in, as shown (L.D. 1 hr).

11. Outline and flood-in the further parts shown (L.D. 24 hrs).

12. Pipe 6-dot sequences and single dots around tree, as shown (L.D. 12 hrs).

13. Pipe sets of heart shapes on waxed paper (No.2) (L.D. 12 hrs) (20 sets required).

14. Place hearts in the position shown on waxed paper and fix with a central bulb (No.2).

15. Pipe spikes over the bulb (No.1) (L.D. 12 hrs).

16. Fix the pointed petal flower to the tree trunk and decorate, as shown.

17. Fix the tree and tree trunk to the cake top.

18. Fix a flower to the centre of each tree curve.

19. Pipe name of choice to cake top (No.2).

20. Overpipe the name (No.1).

21. Pipe shells around top edge of cake opposite tree (No.3).

22. Below the tree trunk, pipe a line (No.2), then a second line and a scalloped line, as shown (No.1).

23. Pipe shells around the cake base (No.3).

24. Overpipe the top shells with a line (No.2).

25. Overpipe the base shells with a line (No.2).

26. Overpipe each shell No.2 line (No.1).

27. Pipe a spike between each shell on the No.1 line (No.1).

28. Pipe a curved line around the cake board, as shown (No.2).

29. Pipe a line beside the board No.2 line (No.1).

30. Pipe a spike at each board line curve (No.1).

31. Except for the area below the tree trunk, fix a flower in each board curve.

32. Pipe scallops in remaining curves around the board (No 1) then fix ribbon to edge.

Richard

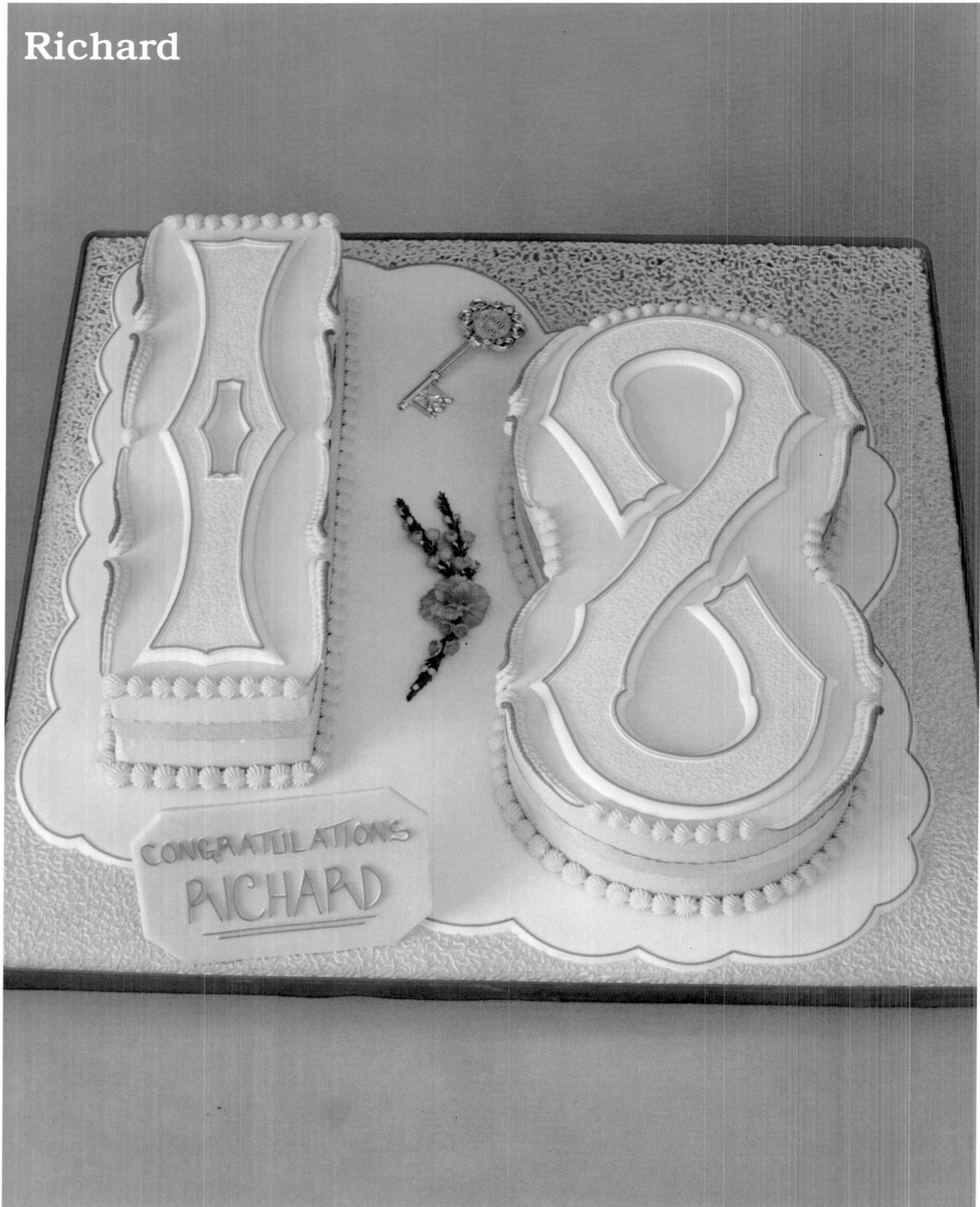

NOTE: Before attempting to decorate this cake, please study the whole sequence of photographs and notes and ensure you have the proper equipment and materials, as well as sufficient time. Additional information can be found on pages 5–17.

1. Two×4″ round cakes required.

2. One 4″ square cake also required.

3. Cut the 4″ square cake in half.

4. Fix the two halves end to end to form figure '1' and the two round cakes to form figure '8'.

5. Place the '18' on a cake board and marzipan and coat the cake in the normal way.

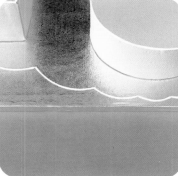

6. Outline the '18' with curved lines, as shown (No.2).

7. Flood-in the outlined area (L.D. 24 hrs).

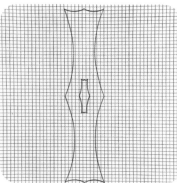

8. Drawing showing template of figure '1'.

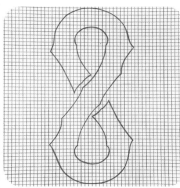

9. Drawing showing template of figure '8'.

10. Outline the figure '1' on waxed paper (No.2) and then flood-in (L.D. 24 hrs).

11. Outline the figure '8' on waxed paper (No.2) and then flood-in (L.D. 24 hrs).

12. Filigree outer areas of board, as partly shown (No.1).

13. Pipe shells around base of cake (No.43).

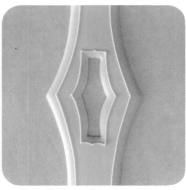

14. Pipe lines on the edge of figure '1' runout (No.1).

15. Pipe lines on the edge of figure '8' runout (No.1).

16. Filigree inside the No.1 lines (No.1).

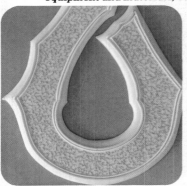

17. Pipe a line beside the No.1 lines (No.2).

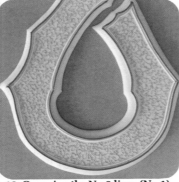

18. Overpipe the No.2 lines (No.1) (L.D. 2 hrs).

19. Fix the runouts to the cake top, as shown.

20. Pipe an 'S' scroll on cake-top edge, as shown (No.42).

21. Pipe an 'S' scroll on cake-top edge, as shown (No.42).

22. Pipe shells on cake-top edge (No.42). Repeat 20–22 at opposite end.

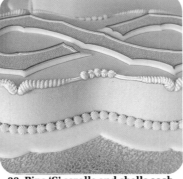

23. Pipe 'S' scrolls and shells each side of the figure '8', as shown (No.42).

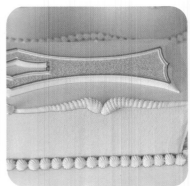

24. Pipe 'S' scrolls along each side of the figure '1' (No.42).

25. Pipe shells at each end of the figure '1' (No.42).

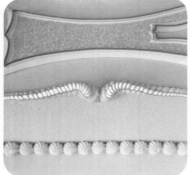

26. Overpipe each scroll (No.2).

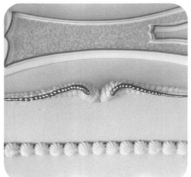

27. Overpipe each No.2 scroll (No.1).

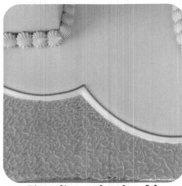

28. Pipe a line on the edge of the board runout (No.1).

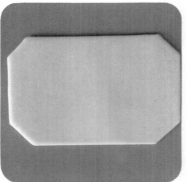

29. Roll out and cut a sugar paste plaque, as shown (L.D. 2 hrs).

30. Pipe message of choice on plaque (No.1).

31. Fix artificial decorations of choice between the figures.

32. Fix ribbon around the middle of each cake and plaque to the cake board.

1. Remove a 6″ diameter round cake from the centre of a 12″ round cake.

2. Marzipan and coat the 12″ cake in the normal way.

3. Flood-in the centre of the cake with Royal Icing (L.D. 12 hrs).

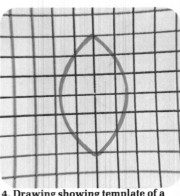

4. Drawing showing template of a petal.

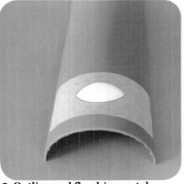

5. Outline and flood-in a petal on waxed paper (L.D. 24 hrs) in curved position (32 required).

6. Pipe lines on each petal, as shown (No.1).

7. Flood-in between the lines on each petal (L.D. 12 hrs).

8. Pipe additional curved lines on the petals in the positions shown (No.1).

9. Pipe plain shells around the inside base of the cake (No.3).

10. Fix the 32 petals evenly around the top edge of the cake.

11. Pipe shells around the inside top edge of the cake (No.32).

12. Pipe shells around the outside base of the cake (No.32).

13. Pipe a line each side of each petal, as shown (No.2).

14. Pipe a line each side of each petal on the side of the cake, as shown (No.2) (T).

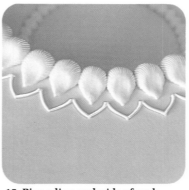

15. Pipe a line each side of each central shell, as shown (No.2).

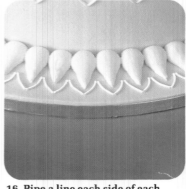

16. Pipe a line each side of each base shell, as shown (No.2).

256

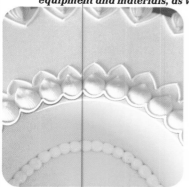

17. Overpipe each central top shell with a line (No.3).

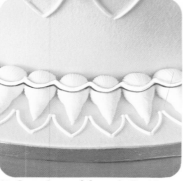

18. Overpipe each base shell with a line (No.3).

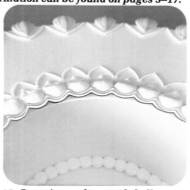

19. Overpipe each central shell No.3 line (No.2).

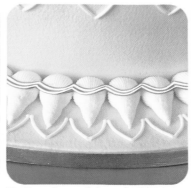

20. Overpipe each base shell No.3 line (No.2).

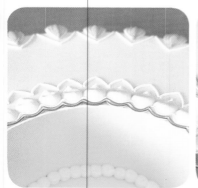

21. Overpipe each central shell No.2 line (No.1).

22. Overpipe each base shell No.2 line (No.1).

23. Pipe a line beside each petal No.2 line (No.1) (T as necessary).

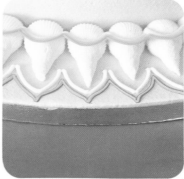

24. Pipe a line beside each board No.2 line (No.1).

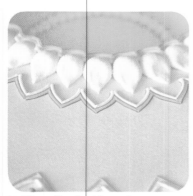

25. Pipe a line beside each centre edge No.2 line (No.1).

26. Picture showing piped bulb and line decorations.

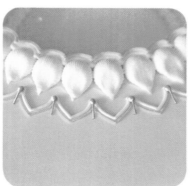

27. Pipe decorations at centre shell lines, as shown (No.1).

28. Pipe decorations at board shell lines, as shown (No.1).

29. Pipe message of choice on cake top (No.2) and then overpipe the message (No.1).

30. Overpipe the message again (No.1).

31. Place tissue paper in well of cake.

32. Fix ribbon to edge of board and place champagne bottle in well.

257

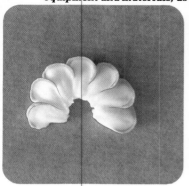

1. Pipe semi-circle of petals on waxed paper using two colours of Royal Icing (No.57). (12 required) (L.D. 1 hr).

2. Overpipe the petals (No.57) (L.D. 1 hr).

3. Overpipe the petals (No.57) (L.D. 1 hr).

4. Complete the flower shape, as shown (No.57) (L.D. 24hrs).

5. A serrated scraper is required.

6. On final coating use the serrated scraper on cake sides to obtain desired effect.

7. Mark cake-top edge into 4 equal portions with piped dots.

8. Pipe an 'S' scroll in one portion, as shown (No.43).

9. Continue piping 'S' scrolls along the edge, as shown (No.43).

10. Repeat 9 along the joining edge but pipe the scrolls in the opposite direction.

11. Pipe two bold 'C' scrolls in one portion of the top edge, as shown (No.43).

12. Continue piping the bold 'C' scrolls along remaining top edges (No.43).

13. Pipe a line around the base of the cake (No.43).

14. Repeat 8–10 at cake base.

15. Repeat 11 at cake base but in opposite direction.

16. Repeat 12 at cake base but in opposite direction.

259

17. Overpipe each top 'S' scroll (No.3).

18. Overpipe each base 'S' scroll (No.3).

19. Pipe a curved line inside top edge of cake, as shown (No.2).

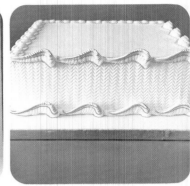

20. Overpipe each 'S' scroll (No.2).

21. Overpipe each top bold 'C' scroll with a line (No.2).

22. Overpipe each base bold 'C' scroll with a line (No.2).

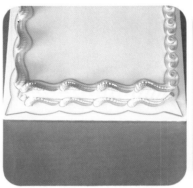

23. Pipe a curved line on the board the length of each 'S' scroll, and enjoined at corners with a 'V', as shown (No.2).

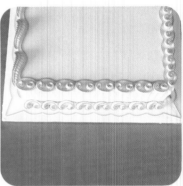

24. Pipe a curved line on the board the length of each bold 'C' scroll and enjoined at corners with a 'V', as shown (No.2).

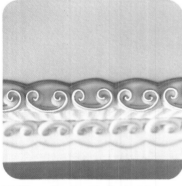

25. Pipe a line beside the inside top No.2 line (No.1) and then overpipe the No.2 line (No.1).

26. Overpipe each scroll (No.1).

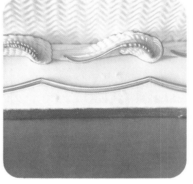

27. Pipe a line beside the board No.2 line (No.1) and then overpipe the No.2 line (No.1).

28. Pipe curved lines on cake top, as shown (No.2).

29. Fix flowers, as shown, and then pipe leaves to stems (Leaf bag).

30. Pipe a flower stem (No.2), leaves (Leaf bag) and fix a flower, as shown, at each corner of the cake.

31. Pipe message of choice to cake top (No.2) then overpipe the message (No.1).

32. Pipe a wavy line at each board 'V' line (No.1) and fix ribbon to board edge.

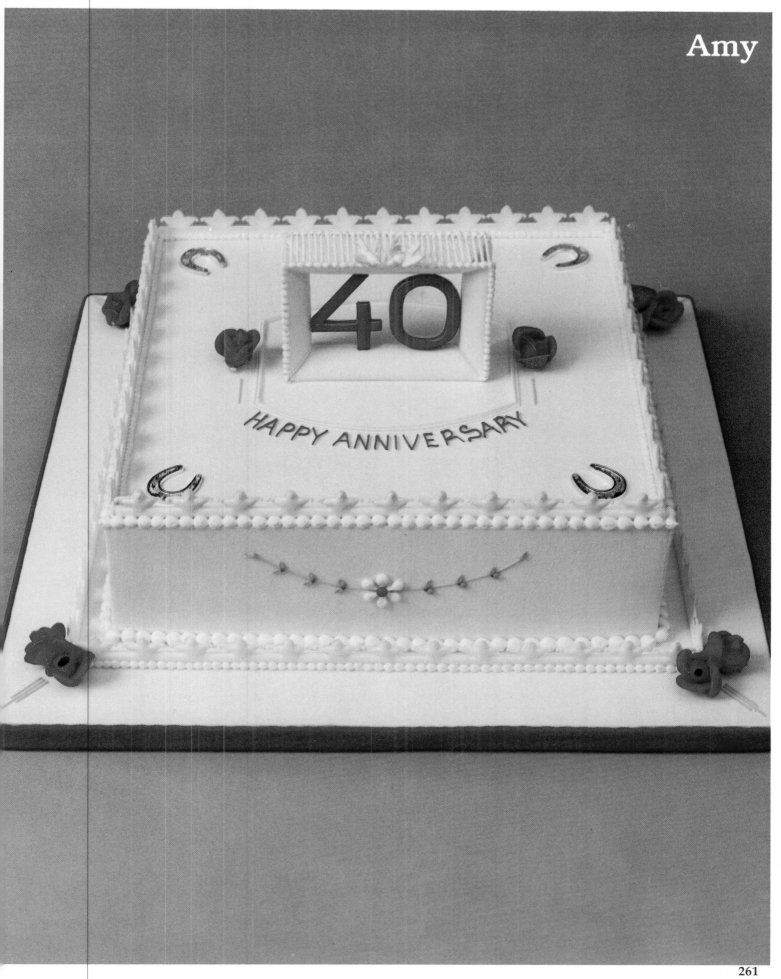

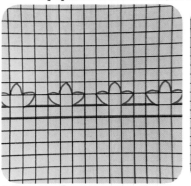

1. Drawing showing part section of border design template.

2. Drawing showing template of top ornament.

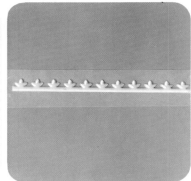

3. Outline and flood-in on waxed paper the border runouts to match cake top and board lengths (L.D. 24 hrs).

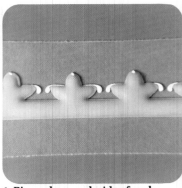

4. Pipe a drop each side of each runout motif (No.1) (L.D. 12 hrs).

5. Outline and flood-in on waxed paper part of the numerals, as shown (L.D. 2 hrs).

6. Flood-in to complete the numerals (L.D. 24 hrs).

7. Remove numerals from waxed paper, upturn and pipe a line around each numeral, as shown (No.1).

8. Flood-in reverse of numerals (L.D. 24 hrs).

9. Outline and flood-in on waxed paper 2 of each top ornament frame pieces (8 in all) (L.D. 24 hrs).

10. Fix 4 pieces together to make one frame. Repeat to make second frame.

11. Fix numerals into one of the frames.

12. Fix frames together, as shown.

13. Pipe a drop line from top to bottom of frame and continue around frame, as shown (No.2) (L.D. 2 hrs).

14. Pipe shells around frame edges (No.2).

15. Pipe shells around base of cake (No.3).

16. Fix board runouts, as shown.

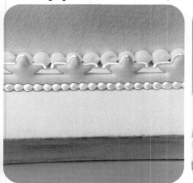

17. Pipe shells against board runouts (No.2).

18. Fix cake-top runouts, as shown.

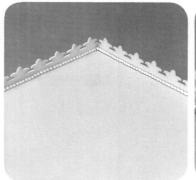

19. Pipe shells inside cake-top runouts (No.2).

20. Pipe shells around cake-top edge (No.3).

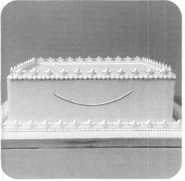

21. Pipe a curved line on each side of the cake (No.1) (T).

22. Pipe a central floral design on each curved line (No.2).

23. Pipe leaves on curved line, as shown (No.1).

24. Pipe coloured dots on floral design (No.1).

25. Fix ornament to cake top, as shown.

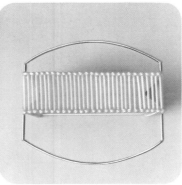

26. Pipe a line around the ornament, as shown (No.2).

27. Pipe a line beside the No.2 line (No.1).

28. Overpipe the No.2 line (No.1).

29. Pipe message of choice (No.1).

30. Pipe a line each side of the cake-top ornament (No.1) and fix flower of choice to it.

31. Fix artificial horseshoes and sugar doves to cake top, as shown.

32. Pipe lines on base corners, as shown (No.1) and fix matching flowers and ribbon to board edge.

263

Elizabeth

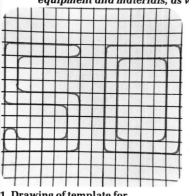

1. Drawing of template for numerals.

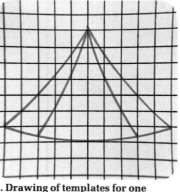

2. Drawing of templates for one large and one small triangular plaque.

3. Outline on waxed paper and flood-in the numerals (L.D. 24 hrs).

4. Outline on waxed paper and flood-in the large plaque (4 required for bottom tier) (L.D. 24 hrs).

5. Outline on waxed paper and flood-in the small plaque (4 required for top tier) (L.D. 24 hrs).

6. Make 160 sugar paste rosebuds for the two tiers (see instructions).

7. Cut a block of sugar paste – 4″×4″×1″ (L.D. 12 hrs).

8. Remove numerals from waxed paper, upturn and pipe a line along each edge (No.1).

9. Flood-in the reverse of the numerals with soft Royal Icing (L.D. 24 hrs).

10. Pipe scallops around each plaque edge (No.1).

11. Pipe a dot against each scallop, as shown (No.1).

12. Pipe words on each large plaque (No.1) (L.D. 12 hrs).

13. Pipe monogram on each small plaque (No.1) (L.D. 12 hrs).

14. Pipe scallops around edges of each numeral (No.1).

15. Pipe straight lines on numerals, as shown (No.1) (L.D. 12 hrs).

16. Pipe a line around base of cake (No.44).

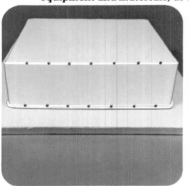

17. Mark each top and base side of the cake into 8 equal portions with piped dots.

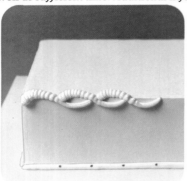

18. Pipe an 'S' scroll between each pair of top dots, as shown (No.44).

19. Pipe an 'S' scroll between each pair of base dots, as shown (No.44).

20. Overpipe the top scrolls (No.3).

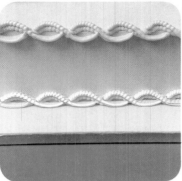

21. Overpipe the base scrolls (No.3).

22. Overpipe each No.3 scroll (No.2).

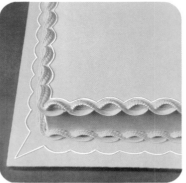

23. Pipe curved lines around cake top and then repeat on board. (The latter ending in a 'V' at each corner) (No.2).

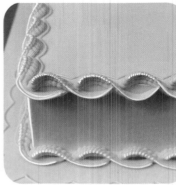

24. Overpipe each No.2 scroll (No.1).

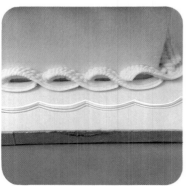

25. Pipe a line beside the No.2 board line and then overpipe the No.2 line (No.1).

26. Fix the appropriate plaque to each side of each tier.

27. Fix rose-buds to each side of cake, as shown.

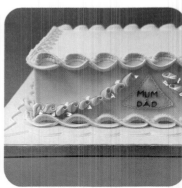

28. Pipe leaves between rose-buds (Leaf bag).

29. Fix sugar paste block and numerals to top tier.

30. Fix velvet ribbon to block edge and rose-buds to each corner. Pipe leaves (Leaf bag).

31. Pipe scallops and dots on top edge of block (No.1).

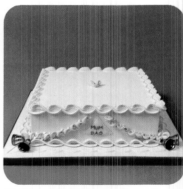

32. Fix artificial decorations of choice to cake board and matching ribbon to board edge.

1. Pipe pansy petal on waxed paper using two colours of Royal Icing (No.59).

2. Pipe second petal (No.59).

3. Pipe third petal (No.59).

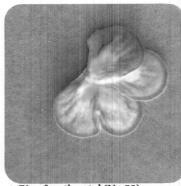

4. Pipe fourth petal (No.59).

5. Pipe fifth petal to complete pansy (No.59) (L.D. 24 hrs) (25 various coloured pansies required).

6. Paint centre of each pansy with edible colouring, as shown, and then pipe the stamen (No.1).

7. Picture showing 4 completed pansies.

8. Cut corners from a 9″ square cake. Marzipan, then coat in colours shown (L.D. 12 hrs between colours).

9. Picture showing side of cake.

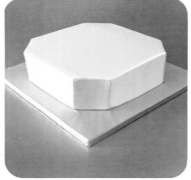

10. Picture showing corner of cake.

11. Pipe shells around each corner (No.3).

12. Pipe a curved line on the cake top between each corner, as shown (No.1).

13. Filigree each of the top areas shown (No.1).

14. Pipe a curved line on each side of the cake board (No.1).

15. Filigree each board area as shown (No.1).

16. Overpipe each No.1 line with shells (No.2).

268

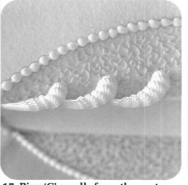

17. Pipe 'C' scrolls from the centre to the left of each top pattern, as shown (No.42).

18. Pipe 'C' scrolls from the centre to the right of each top pattern (No.42).

19. Pipe shells along each side of the cake base (No.42).

20. Pipe a line beside each top pattern (No.2).

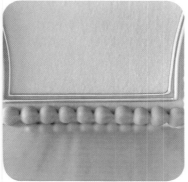

21. Pipe a line beside each No.2 line (No.1).

22. Pipe wife's initial at each corner of the cake (No.2) (T).

23. Pipe husband's initial at each corner of the cake (No.2) (T).

24. Pipe message of choice on the cake top (No.2) and then overpipe the message (No.1).

25. Pipe a curved line around message, as shown (No.2).

26. Pipe the further curved lines shown (No.2).

27. Fix pansies to curved lines, as shown.

28. Pipe leaves on to the lines (Leaf bag).

29. Pipe a curved line at each corner of the board (No.2).

30. Fix pansies to each corner line.

31. Pipe leaves to each corner line (Leaf bag).

32. Fix artificial decorations to each side of the cake and ribbon to board edge.

269

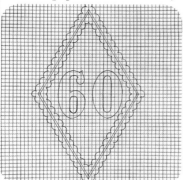

1. Drawing showing template of diamond shaped frames and numerals.

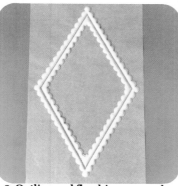

2. Outline and flood-in on waxed paper the inner and outer frames (L.D. 24 hrs).

3. Outline and flood-in on waxed paper each numeral (L.D. 24 hrs).

4. Outline and flood-in on waxed paper 2 diamond plaques (each 2¾″ long) (L.D. 24 hrs).

5. Outline and flood-in on waxed paper 2 curved plaques (each 2½″ across) (L.D. 24 hrs).

6. Place shaped cake on board, outline and flood-in the design, as shown (L.D. 12 hrs).

7. Pipe dots between inner and outer frames (No.2).

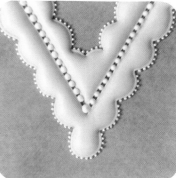

8. Pipe dots along inner and outer frame edges, as shown (No.1).

9. Decorate the '6' with piped dots and a floral design, as shown (No.1) (L.D. 12 hrs).

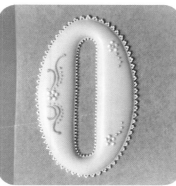

10. Repeat 9 on the '0'.

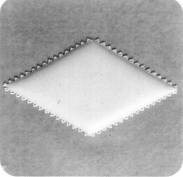

11. Pipe a series of dots forming triangular patterns around edge of each diamond plaque, as shown (No.1).

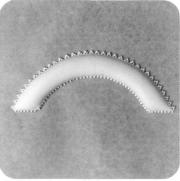

12. Pipe dots on inner curves of curved plaques and triangular pattern dots on outer curves, as shown (No.1).

13. Pipe initials of choice and floral decoration on each diamond plaque (No.1) (L.D. 12 hrs).

14. Pipe message of choice and floral decoration on each curved plaque (No.1) (L.D. 12 hrs).

15. Fix frame to cake top.

16. Fix numerals to cake top and pipe floral decoration on each frame corner (No.1).

271

17. Fix curved plaques to cake top.

18. Pipe 'S' scrolls at each end of the cake top (No.4).

19. Pipe 'C' scrolls at each end of the cake top (No.4).

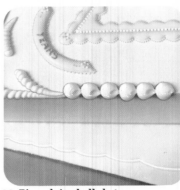

20. Pipe plain shells between scrolls on cake top edges (No.4).

21. Pipe plain shells around base of cake (No.4).

22. Pipe pattern inside scrolls at each cake-top end (No.2).

23. Overpipe all plain shells with a line (No.2).

24. Pipe a line beside the board runout (No.2).

25. Overpipe all shell No.2 lines (No.1).

26. Pipe a line beside the board No.2 line and then overpipe the No.2 line (No.1).

27. Pipe spikes on the shell No.1 line (No.1).

28. Pipe floral decorations on each side of the cake, as shown (No.1).

29. Pipe floral design at each curve of the board runout (No.1).

30. Fix the diamond plaque to the cake board and pipe a 'V', as shown (No.1).

31. Fix artificial leaves and flowers of choice to cake top.

32. Fix matching leaves and flowers around the cake base and ribbon around board edge.

272

HAPPY SAILING SIMON

1. An 8″ square cake required with combed sides (see Vincent).

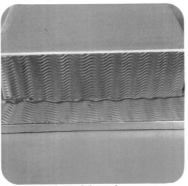

2. Coat and comb board.

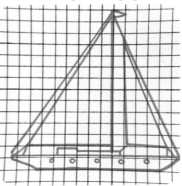

3. Drawing showing template of a yacht.

4. Drawing showing template of an anchor.

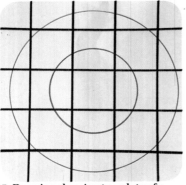

5. Drawing showing template of a lifebelt.

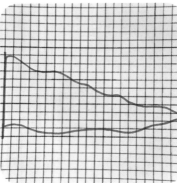

6. Drawing showing template of a pennant.

7. Outline and flood-in on waxed paper the yacht sails (2 yachts required).

8. Outline and flood-in the cabin area. (L.D. 2 hrs).

9. Outline and flood-in the hull and pipe-in the lines shown (No.2) (L.D. 24 hrs).

10. Paint the yachts in edible colouring.

11. Remove each yacht from waxed paper, upturn and repeat 7–10.

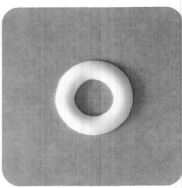

12. Outline and flood-in on waxed paper 8 lifebelt rings (L.D. 24 hrs).

13. Fix 4 pairs of rings together (back to back).

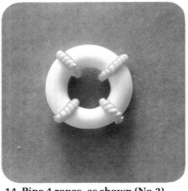

14. Pipe 4 ropes, as shown (No.2) (L.D. 2 hrs) then upturn and repeat (L.D. 2 hrs).

15. Outline and flood-in on waxed paper 8 anchors (L.D. 24 hrs).

16. Fix 4 pairs of anchors together (back to back).

17. Pipe ropes on each anchor, as shown (No.2) (L.D. 2 hrs).

18. Upturn each anchor and pipe the ropes, as shown (No.2) (L.D. 2 hrs).

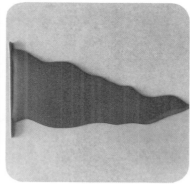

19. Outline and flood-in on waxed paper the pennant (L.D. 24 hrs).

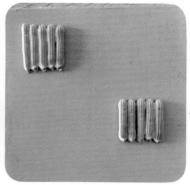

20. With 2 colours of Royal Icing in bag pipe 2 sets of 5 short lines on cake top (No.13).

21. Overpipe each set, as shown (No.13) (L.D. 2 hrs).

22. Pipe a scroll over one set, as shown (No.13).

23. Continue overpiping the set with scrolls, as shown (No.13).

24. Repeat 22–23 over the second set (to create breaker effect).

25. Pipe shells around the cake-top edge (No.13).

26. Pipe shells around the cake base (No.13).

27. Pipe lines of waves between the breakers, as shown (No.13).

28. Fix yachts to cake top.

29. Fix pennant to cake top and pipe message of choice (No.1).

30. Fix a pair of anchors to the front and back of cake with a piped rope (No.2).

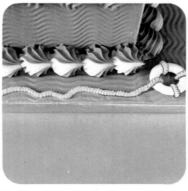

31. Fix a lifebelt to each corner with a piped rope (No.2).

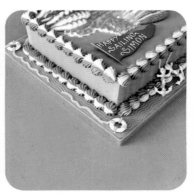

32. Fix ribbon to board edge.

Ruth

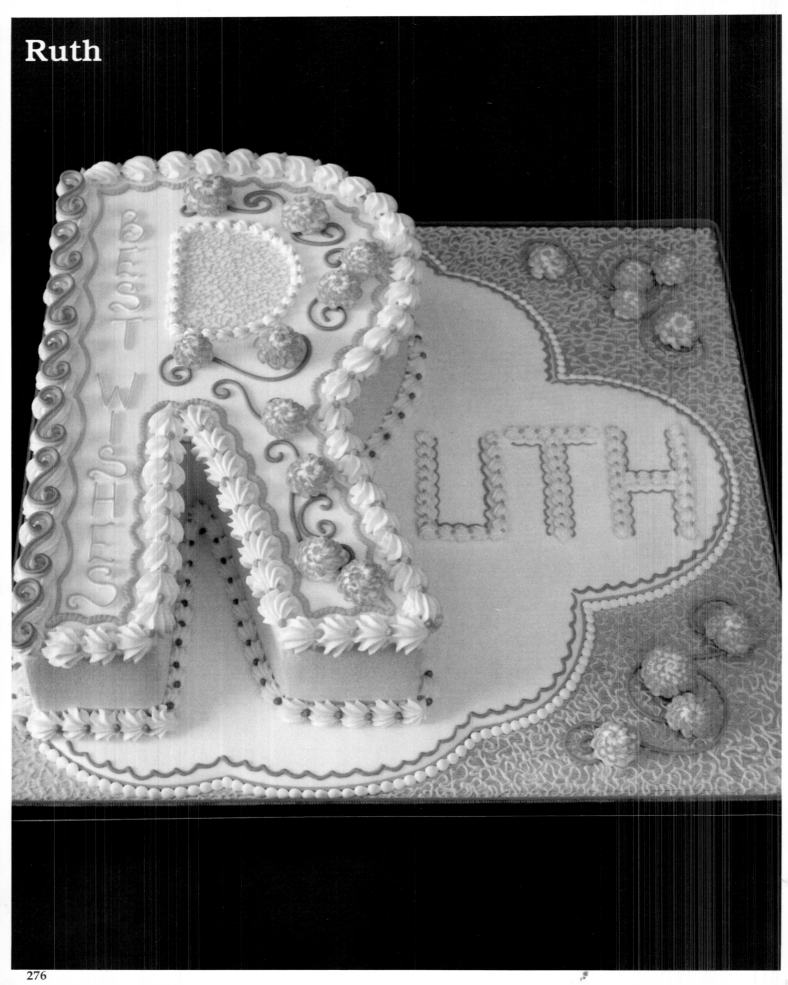

276

1. A marzipanned and coated cake in the shape of an 'R' required in position shown.

2. Form a ½" diameter dome from sugar paste and place on waxed paper (20 required).

3. Pipe a row of petals around the base of each dome (No.57) (L.D. 1 hr).

4. Pipe a second row of petals (No.57) (L.D. 1 hr).

5. Pipe a third row of petals (No.57) (L.D. 1 hr).

6. Pipe a fourth row of petals (No.57) (L.D. 1 hr).

7. Pipe a fifth row of petals (No.57) (L.D. 1 hr).

8. Pipe in stamens (No.1) (L.D. 24 hrs).

9. Pipe curved lines on the board, as shown (No.3).

10. Flood-in the area shown (L.D. 12 hrs).

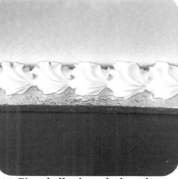

11. Pipe shells along the board back edge of the 'R' (No.7).

12. Pipe 'S' lines along the top back edge of the 'R' (No.7).

13. Pipe shells around the remaining base and top edges of the 'R' (No.7).

14. Pipe a 'D' in shells in the position shown on cake top (No.5).

15. Pipe a curved line beside each 'S' line (No.2).

16. Pipe a curved rope beside each cake-top shell (No.2).

17. Filigree the centre of the 'D' (No.1).

18. Overpipe each 'S' line (No.3).

19. Overpipe each 'S' line (No.2).

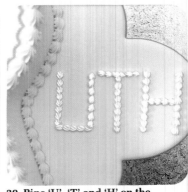

20. Pipe 'U', 'T' and 'H' on the cake-board runout in shells (No.5).

21. Pipe a dot between each cake-top shell (No.2).

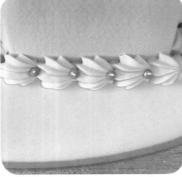

22. Pipe a dot between each cake-base shell (No.2).

23. Pipe a dot between each shell of the 'UTH' (No.1).

24. Pipe scallops around the 'UTH', as shown (No.1).

25. Pipe scallops around the board runout edge (No.1).

26. Pipe shells beside the board runout edge (No.2).

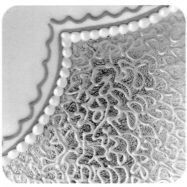

27. Filigree remainder of board (No.1).

28. Pipe message of choice on the 'R' (No.2).

29. Overpipe message (No.1).

30. Pipe curved lines on cake top, as shown (No.2).

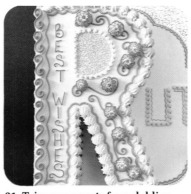

31. Trim sugar paste from dahlias and fix to cake top as shown.

32. Repeat 30–31 on cake board and fix ribbon to board edge.

1. Drawing showing template of plaques.

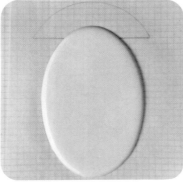

2. Outline and flood-in an oval plaque on waxed paper (L.D. 24 hrs).

3. Outline and flood-in 4 curved plaques on waxed paper (L.D. 24 hrs).

4. Pipe-in on waxed paper the parts of the figures shown (L.D. 20 m).

5. Pipe-in further parts of the figures, as shown (L.D. 20 m).

6. Pipe-in further parts of the figures, as shown (L.D. 20 m).

7. Pipe-in further parts of the figures, as shown (L.D. 20 m).

8. Pipe-in further parts of the figures, as shown (L.D. 20 m).

9. Pipe-in further parts of the figures, as shown (L.D. 20 m).

10. Pipe-in final parts of the figures (L.D. 20 m).

11. Paint figures with edible colouring (L.D. 24 hrs).

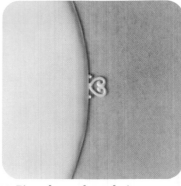

12. Pipe a heart-shape design on edge of oval plaque and add a dot each side (No.1).

13. Repeat 12 around plaque and then fix figures to plaque (L.D. 12 hrs).

14. Pipe ½″ high heart shape on waxed paper (No.1). Overpipe (No.1) and then pipe a dot (No.1) (L.D. 12 hrs) (8 required).

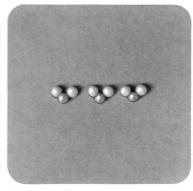

15. Picture showing sequence of dot edging.

16. Pipe dot edging around the 4 curved plaques and then pipe message of choice (No.1) (L.D. 12 hrs).

17. Fix all plaques to cake top in positions shown.

18. Pipe shells around top edge of cake (No.44).

19. Pipe shells around base of cake (No.43).

20. Pipe short vertical lines on cake sides in positions shown (No.2).

21. Pipe curved lines on cake board, as shown (No.2).

22. Fix artificial flowers in the positions shown at the base of the cake.

23. Pipe a suspended line from each short line to board line, as shown (No.2).

24. Pipe a suspended line each side of the suspended line (No.2).

25. Pipe a suspended line each side of the suspended lines (No.2).

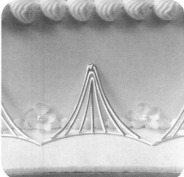

26. Repeat 25.

27. Repeat 26.

28. Pipe a bulb at each top join of the suspended lines and pipe shells against the board lines (No.2).

29. Pipe a parallel curved line on cake board (No.2).

30. Pipe a line beside the board No.2 line (No.1) and then overpipe each bulb with a line (No.1).

31. Pipe suspended tassels and a dot on each bulb (No.2) and then pipe a line beside the board No.1 line (No.1).

32. Fix artificial flowers, horseshoes, hearts and ribbon, as shown.

281

1. Drawing showing template of quarter moon.

2. Drawing showing template of the witch Griselda.

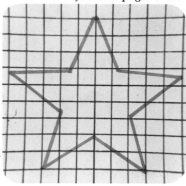

3. Drawing showing template of a star.

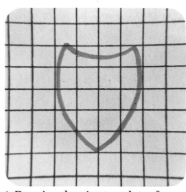

4. Drawing showing template of a halloween mask.

5. Outline and flood-in on waxed paper the part of the moon shown (L.D. 3 hrs).

6. Outline and flood-in the further parts of the moon shown (L.D. 3 hrs).

7. Outline and flood-in the further parts of the moon shown (L.D. 24 hrs).

8. Pipe eyelashes to moon's eye (No.1).

9. Pipe-in on waxed paper the parts of Griselda shown (L.D. 1 hr).

10. Pipe-in the further parts shown (L.D. 1 hr).

11. Pipe-in the further parts shown (L.D. 1 hr).

12. Pipe-in the further parts shown (L.D. 24 hrs).

13. Outline and flood-in the star on waxed paper (L.D. 24 hrs) (5 required).

14. Pipe 'V' lines on each star, as shown (No.1).

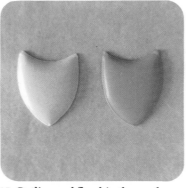

15. Outline and flood-in the mask shapes on waxed paper (L.D. 24 hrs) (4 required).

16. Paint each pair of masks with edible colouring.

17. An 8″ round coated cake on a coated board required.

18. Fix the moon to the cake top.

19. Fix stars to cake top.

20. Fix Griselda to the moon.

21. Pipe a 'C' scroll above the moon on the cake-top edge (No.3).

22. Enjoin a piped 'S' scroll with the 'C' scroll, as shown (No.3).

23. Repeat 21–22 around the part of the cake-top edge shown.

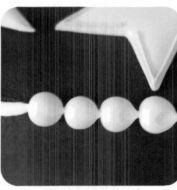

24. Complete the cake-top edge with piped shells (No.3).

25. Pipe shells around cake base (No.3).

26. Overpipe each scroll (No.2).

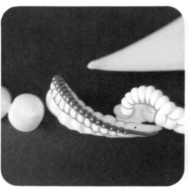

27. Overpipe each 'C' scroll (No.1).

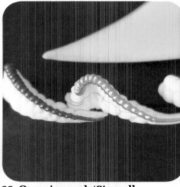

28. Overpipe each 'S' scroll (No.1).

29. Pipe a dot between each shell (No.1).

30. Fix stars to cake base.

31. Fix pairs of masks to cake side and pipe ties (No.1).

32. Pipe 'Halloween' on cake board (No.2) and fix ribbon to board edge.

Karen

Many Happy Returns

1. Drawing showing template of greeting card runout.

2. Outline and flood-in on waxed paper the back card (L.D. 24 hrs).

3. Outline and flood-in on waxed paper the front card (L.D. 2 hrs).

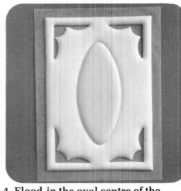

4. Flood-in the oval centre of the front card (L.D. 24 hrs).

5. Outline and flood-in on waxed paper the parts of the bow shown (L.D. 10 m) (5 required).

6. Outline and flood-in further parts of the bow, as shown (L.D. 10 m).

7. Outline and flood-in the further part of the bow shown (L.D. 10 m).

8. Complete bow with centre bulb (L.D. 24 hrs).

9. Using template, pipe a curved rope on waxed paper, as shown (No.2) (4 required).

10. Pipe and overpipe lines on waxed paper to form tassels (No.1) (L.D. 1 hr) (6 required).

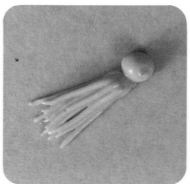

11. Pipe a bulb at each tassel top (No.2) (L.D. 24 hrs).

12. Pipe single dots along the scalloped sides (not corners) of the back card (No.1).

13. Pipe different coloured dots along the corner edges of the back card (No.1).

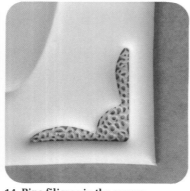

14. Pipe filigree in the corner spaces of the front card (No.1).

15. Pipe scallops against 3 sides of the front card (leaving spine free) (No.1).

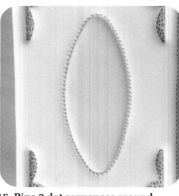

16. Pipe 3 dot sequences around the oval plaque (No.1).

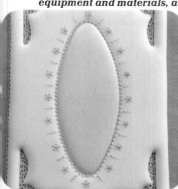

17. Pipe dot design around the oval plaque, as shown (No.1).

18. Pipe dots along the filigree edges, as shown (No.1).

19. Pipe message of choice on the oval plaque (No.1).

20. Overpipe and then underline the message (No.1) (L.D. 12 hrs).

21. Pipe message of choice and decorative motifs on the back card (No.1) (L.D. 12 hrs).

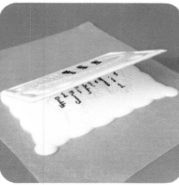

22. Fix and support cards in the position shown (L.D. 2 hrs).

23. Pipe plain shells along the spine of the card (No.1) (L.D. 12 hrs).

24. Fix card to cake top and then fix ropes, tassels and bow, as shown.

25. Pipe a line around the card, as shown (No.2).

26. Pipe a line beside the No.2 line, overpipe the No.2 line, pipe dots at corner edges (No.1).

27. Pipe 'C' scrolls along the edge shown of the cake top (No.42).

28. Pipe shells along the remaining top edges and the base of the cake (No.42).

29. Overpipe all scrolls (No.2) and then overpipe again (No.1).

30. Pipe dots between each shell, as shown (No.1).

31. Fix remaining bows and tassels to sides of the cake, as shown.

32. Fix artificial flowers, as shown, and ribbon to board edge. Remove the support.

1. A fruit cake baked in a 2pt. pudding basin required.

2. Marzipan the top.

3. Marzipan the side (L.D. 24 hrs).

4. Coat the cake with a thin layer of Royal Icing (L.D. 24 hrs).

5. Cover a 10″ round cake board with a thin sheet of sugar paste and place cake centrally on board.

6. Support a 7″ round cake board in upright position.

7. Pipe a line on a 16″×1″ sheet of waxed paper (No.44).

8. Overpipe the line with a series of 'S' lines in alternate colours (to form the handle) (No.44).

9. Immediately place the handle (still on the waxed paper) over the upright board (L.D. 24 hrs).

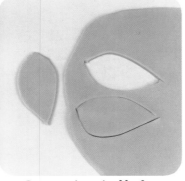

10. Cut 24 various sized leaf shapes from a thin sheet of sugar paste.

11. Nick each leaf edge and mark veins, as shown. Leave in curved positions to dry (L.D. 24 hrs).

12. Make 50 sugar paste roses of various sizes and rose-buds (see instructions).

13. Mark the top edge of the cake into 32 portions with piped dots.

14. Pipe vertical lines from top marks to base (No.1).

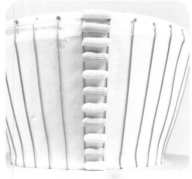

15. Pipe horizontal lines in alternate colours between 2 vertical lines (No.44).

16. Pipe a vertical line over the ends of the horizontal lines (No.3).

289

17. Pipe further horizontal lines in lighter colour, as shown (No.44).

18. Pipe between remaining spaces but using a darker colour (No.44).

19. Pipe a vertical line over the ends of the horizontal lines (No.3).

20. Repeat 17 in the next column, as shown.

21. Repeat 18, as shown.

22. Repeat 19.

23. Repeat 20.

24. Repeat 18. Then continue sequence around cake.

25. Picture showing finished basket-work on cake-side.

26. Pipe a line around the top edge of the cake and overpipe the line with a series of 'S' lines in alternate colours (No.44).

27. Repeat 26 at base of cake.

28. Fix roses, rosebuds and leaves to top of cake.

29. Remove handle from waxed paper and carefully fix to basket.

30. Fix a spray of leaves and roses to board.

31. Carefully fix a bow of velvet ribbon to handle.

32. Fix velvet ribbon to the edge of the cake board.

1. Mark the cake base into 16 portions with piped dots.

2. Pipe a 'V' on the board between each pair of dots (No.2).

3. Flood-in between the cake base and the No.2 line (L.D. 12 hrs).

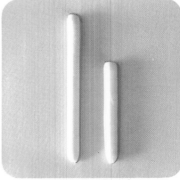

4. Pipe two lines on the cake top to form candles (No.4).

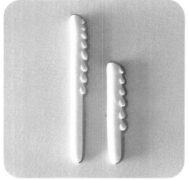

5. Pipe running shells on each candle (No.2).

6. Pictures 6–9 show sequence of making the candle flame. Pipe a line to form wick (No.1).

7. Pipe a long plain shell to form flame, as shown (No.3).

8. Pipe into the flame (No.2).

9. Pipe into the flame again (No.1).

10. Repeat 7–9 on each candle on cake and then pipe the lines shown (No.1).

11. Pipe a curved line, as shown (No.2).

12. Pictures 12–13 and 15 show the sequence of making holly and berries. Pipe a leaf shape (Leaf bag).

13. Using a paint brush, brush in characters of holly leaf.

14. Pipe leaves, as shown (Leaf bag).

15. Pipe practice berries (No.1).

16. Pipe berries on cake, as shown (No.1).

17. Pipe message of choice on cake top (No.1).

18. Overpipe message of choice (No.1).

19. Underline message, as shown (No.1).

20. Make and fix 2 sugar bells.

21. Pipe a musical note each side of the bells (No.1).

22. Pipe an 'S' scroll above the candles on the cake top (No.3).

23. Pipe a 'C' scroll, as shown (No.3).

24. Repeat 22–23 to cover the length of the top edge shown.

25. Pipe small shells along the remainder of the cake-top edge (No.3).

26. Picture showing completed cake to this stage.

27. Pipe plain shells around cake base (No.3).

28. Overpipe each scroll (No.2) and then overpipe each cake-top shell with a line (No.2).

29. Overpipe each base shell with a line (No.2).

30. Overpipe each scroll (No.1) and then overpipe each top shell line (No.1).

31. Overpipe base shell lines, pipe 'V' lines (No.1) then leaves (Leaf bag) as shown.

32. Fix and tie ribbon to side of cake.

1. Position an 8″ square cake, as shown, and marzipan and coat in normal way.

2. Roll out a piece of sugar paste to form book cover 4″×3″.

3. Make a block of sugar paste – 3½″×2½″×¾″ – to form book.

4. Shape book, as shown.

5. Fix book to cover.

6. Make and fix a sugar paste book-mark.

7. Pipe message of choice on book and decorate, as shown (No.1) (L.D. 24 hrs).

8. Place a piece of foil in an egg carton, as shown.

9. Roll out and cut 5×½″ diameter discs of sugar paste to form Christmas roses.

10. Press out each disc to form a petal shape, as shown.

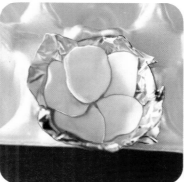

11. Moisten and fix the 5 petals on the foil, as shown (L.D. 24 hrs) (6 roses required).

12. Paint each rose, as shown, with edible colouring.

13. Pipe stamens to each rose (No.2).

14. Pipe tips to stamens (No.1).

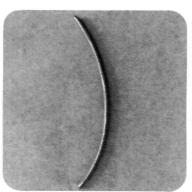

15. Pipe 7×4″ curved lines on waxed paper (various curves) (No.3).

16. Pipe short lines against each curved line to form fern (No.2) (L.D. 2 hrs).

295

17. Paint Royal Icing 'snow' on the fern (L.D. 24 hrs).

18. Picture showing fern curving in other direction.

19. Pipe a 'C' scroll on the part of the cake top shown (No.44).

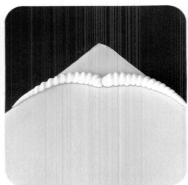

20. Pipe a matching 'C' scroll, as shown (No.44).

21. Pipe a rope on each top edge adjoining the scrolls (No.44).

22. Pipe a rope along each side of the cake base which lies beneath the top ropes (No.44).

23. Overpipe each scroll (No.42).

24. Filigree the cake board (No.1).

25. Cut a wedge of sugar paste to form a bookrest.

26. Fix wedge and book and pipe message of choice (No.2).

27. Overpipe message and pipe lines, as shown (No.1).

28. Position and fix ferns to the front of the cake, as shown.

29. Fix Christmas roses, as shown.

30. Fix a fern and a rose to the cake top.

31. Pipe a line along the two remaining cake top edges, as shown (No.1).

32. Fix ribbon to the board edge.

1. Serrated scraper required.

2. Marzipan and coat an 8″ round cake in the normal way but using the scraper on side.

3. Pipe a wavy line across the cake top (No.3).

4. Stipple top half of cake, as shown (L.D. 12 hrs).

5. Form a ball of sugar paste.

6. Now form the ball into a cone shape.

7. Cut into cone with scissors to obtain a tree effect.

8. Continue cutting down the length of the cone (L.D. 12 hrs) (5 trees required of various sizes).

9. Brush over each tree with Royal Icing.

10. Stipple Royal Icing over the top half of cake to obtain snow effect.

11. Fix fir trees, as shown.

12. Pictures 12–20 show sequence of making a snowman. Practice first by piping body (No.4) (L.D. 30 m).

13. Then by piping head (No.4).

14. Then by piping feet (No.4).

15. Then by piping arms (No.4) (L.D. 30 m).

16. Then by piping rings to form hat (No.2).

17. Then by piping dots and lines, as shown (No.1).

18. Then by piping a holly twig (No.1).

19. Then by piping holly and berries to the twig (No.1).

20. Finally pipe holly and berries on hat (No.1), then walking stick (No.2).

21. Repeat 12–20 twice on the cake top (to make different sized snowmen).

22. Pipe message of choice on cake top (No.1).

23. Overpipe the message (No.1).

24. Pipe curved lines around message (No.1).

25. Pipe shells around the top half of the cake, as shown (No.44).

26. Pipe shells around the base of the cake (No.44).

27. Pipe shells around the remaining top edge of the cake (No.3).

28. Overpipe each top No.44 shell with parallel lines and overpipe the base shells with a line (No.3).

29. Overpipe each top No.3 shell with a line and then overpipe each No.44 shell line (No.2).

30. Pipe icicles from cake-top edge (No.2).

31. Overpipe each of the lines shown (and continue around cake) (No.1).

32. Stipple a band around the cake board and fix ribbon to board edge.

299

Crispin

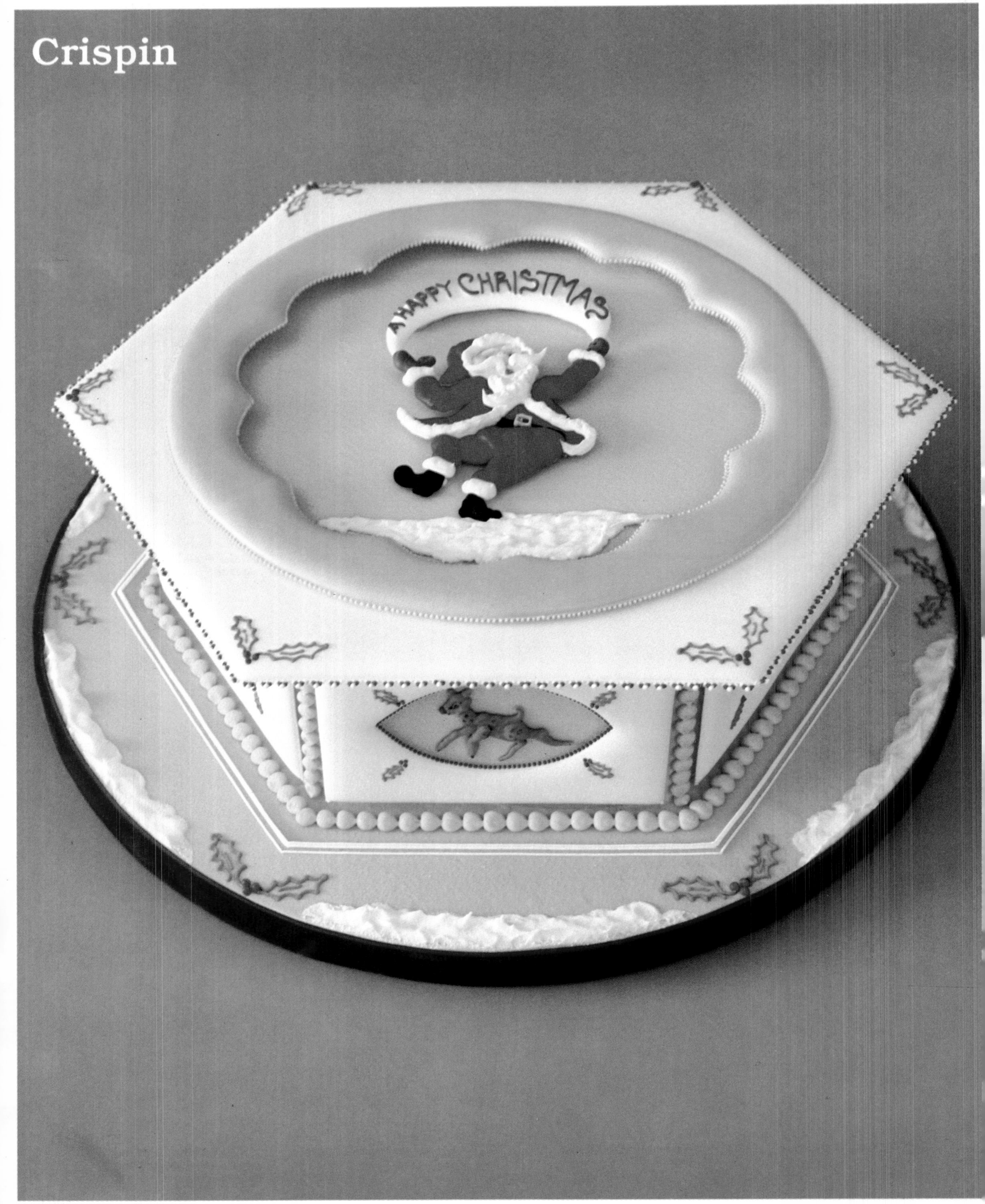

1. Drawing showing template of Father Christmas.

2. Pipe-in on waxed paper the parts of Father Christmas (L.D. 20 m).

3. Pipe-in further parts, as shown (L.D. 20 m).

4. Pipe-in further parts to complete Father Christmas (L.D. 24 hrs).

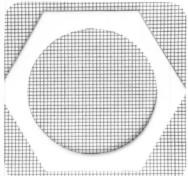

5. Outline and flood-in on waxed paper the large cake-top runout, as shown (L.D. 24 hrs).

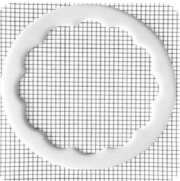

6. Outline and flood-in on waxed paper the small cake-top runout, as shown (L.D. 24 hrs).

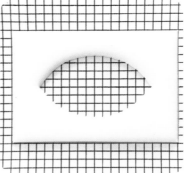

7. Outline and flood-in side panel runouts on waxed paper, as shown (L.D. 24 hrs) (6 required).

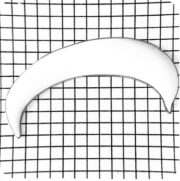

8. Outline and flood-in on waxed paper the banner, as shown (L.D. 24 hrs).

9. Drawing showing Christmas pudding.

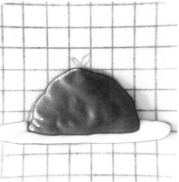

10. Pipe-in on waxed paper the parts of the Christmas pudding shown (L.D. 20 m) (2 required).

11. Pipe-in remainder of Christmas pudding, as shown (L.D. 24 hrs).

12. Drawing showing template of baby deer.

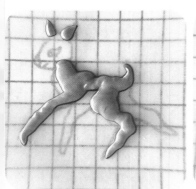

13. Pipe-in parts of the baby deer on waxed paper, as shown (L.D. 20 m) (2 required).

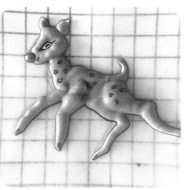

14. Pipe-in remainder of baby deer, as shown (L.D. 24 hrs).

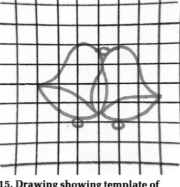

15. Drawing showing template of bells.

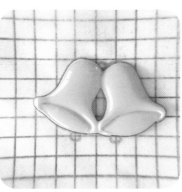

16. Outline and flood-in the bells on waxed paper, as shown (L.D. 24 hrs).

301

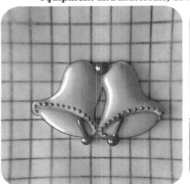

17. Pipe decorations on bells, as shown (No.1) (L.D. 12 hrs).

18. Pipe 6-dot sequence around outer edge of large runout and single dots along inner edge (No.1).

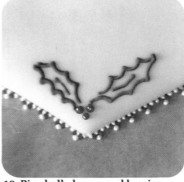

19. Pipe holly leaves and berries on each large runout corner (No.1) (L.D. 12 hrs).

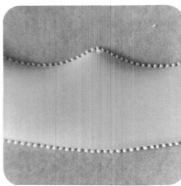

20. Pipe single dots along small cake-top runout edge (No.1) (L.D. 12 hrs).

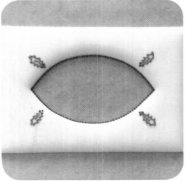

21. Pipe single dots along the inside edge of the cake-side runouts and decorate, as shown (No.1) (L.D. 12 hrs).

22. Pipe message of choice on banner (No.1) (L.D. 2 hrs).

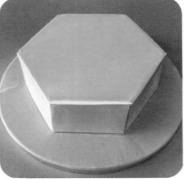

23. Prepare in the normal way an 8″ hexagonal cake on a 12″ round board.

24. Fix a cake-side runout to each side, as shown.

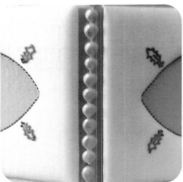

25. Pipe plain shells down each corner (No.3) (T).

26. Fix matching runout figures opposite each other, as shown.

27. Fix large cake-top runout, as shown.

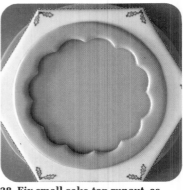

28. Fix small cake-top runout, as shown.

29. Fix Father Christmas and banner and then pipe 'snow' beneath his feet (No.1).

30. Pipe plain shells around base of cake (No.3).

31. Pipe a line on the board (No.2). Then a line beside and overpipe the No.2 (No.1).

32. Pipe cake-board decorations, as shown (No.1) and fix ribbon to board edge.

302

1. A dowel 9″ long×1″ in diameter required.

2. A piece of waxed paper 18″ long ×1″ wide required.

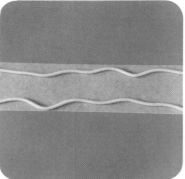

3. Pipe 2 irregular lines along the waxed paper, as shown (No.2).

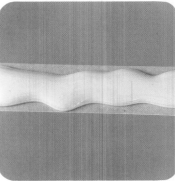

4. Flood-in between the 2 lines.

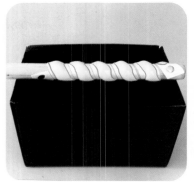

5. Immediately pin end of waxed paper and roll as shown; pin other end. Support (L.D. 24 hrs).

6. Drawing showing template of holly leaf.

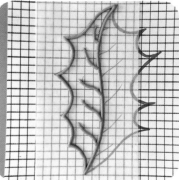

7. Pipe outline of half the holly leaf on waxed paper (No.2).

8. Immediately flood-in the half leaf, and fix over a curve, as shown (L.D. 24 hrs).

9. Repeat 7–8 for the remaining half leaf (6 leaves required).

10. Colour 2 pieces of marzipan, as shown.

11. Roll each piece into a square and place one upon the other.

12. Cut and roll the sheet into various sizes.

13. Cut and fix rolls into logs (6 logs required).

14. Decorate logs with Royal Icing and artificial robins (L.D. 12 hrs).

15. Mount a 4″ cake on an 8″ cake on a 12″ board. Marzipan and coat the cakes in the normal way.

16. Pipe a wavy line on board and a line around the edge of the board (No.2).

17. Flood-in between the 2 lines on the cake board (L.D. 2 hrs).

18. Flood-in remaining area of cake board (L.D. 12 hrs).

19. Fix each pair of holly leaf halves together (L.D. 2 hrs).

20. Paint leaf veins with edible colouring and then stipple Royal Icing on edges (L.D. 2 hrs).

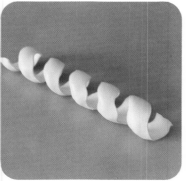

21. Gently slide the spiral from the dowel and then carefully remove waxed paper.

22. Place spiral on waxed paper and pipe a flame shape, as shown (No.4).

23. Pipe-in further colour to flame (No.3).

24. Pipe-in final colour to flame (No.2) (L.D. 24 hrs).

25. Pipe shells around base of the small cake (No.43).

26. Fix holly leaves in positions shown.

27. Pipe spikes around top edge and base of large cake, then pipe 'snow' between leaves (No.4).

28. Fix ribbon around centre of large cake and place logs on cake board, as shown.

29. Pipe a dome with stiff Royal Icing on cake top, as shown (No.32).

30. Immediately place spiral into dome.

31. Pipe berries around dome, as shown (No.3).

32. Fix ribbon to cake-board edge.

1. A sponge cake – 10″×10″ – required.

2. Cut sponge in half.

3. Cut one half into three, as shown.

4. Mount the 3 pieces on the first half, as shown, to form the sleighmobile.

5. Trim the front and back of the sleigh to shape shown.

6. Jam and cream the pieces together.

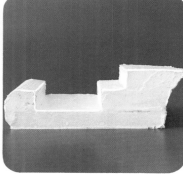

7. Cream all over the sleigh.

8. Line the sleigh seat with strips of sugar paste.

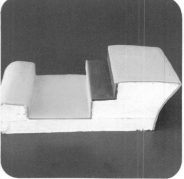

9. Cover top and ends of sleigh with sugar paste, as shown.

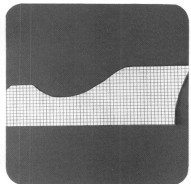

10. Cut a paper template for the side of the sleigh, as shown.

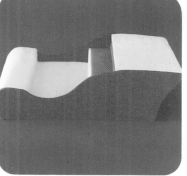

11. Using template, cut out and fix sugar paste sides.

12. Cover a 14″ round cake board with a thin sheet of sugar paste.

13. Mount sleighmobile on board.

14. Form two marzipan boots.

15. Fix boots to sleigh, form and fix marzipan trouser legs, as shown.

16. Form and fix a marzipan dome for the body.

17. Form and fix marzipan arms, as shown.

18. Form and fix marzipan head and nose as shown.

19. Form and fix marzipan hat, as shown.

20. Form and fix marzipan gloves, as shown.

21. Decorate head and hat with piped Royal Icing (No.2).

22. Decorate clothes with piped Royal Icing (No.2).

23. Make and fix a sugar paste joystick (which can be fixed with a cocktail stick).

24. Form two rocket boosters from sugar paste and fix candles and holders, as shown.

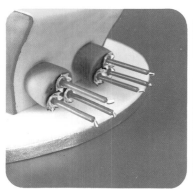

25. Fix rocket boosters to end of sleighmobile.

26. Make and decorate a variety of presents, as shown.

27. Pipe shells along each of the sleighmobile edges (No.42).

28. Pipe lines of shells, as shown (No.2).

29. Pipe antler decoration to front of the sleigh (No.2).

30. Fix presents to sleighmobile.

31. Pipe message of choice on cake board (No.2) then overpipe (No.1).

32. Pipe curved lines around message (No.1) and fix ribbon to board edge.

WARNING – CANDLES WILL BURN RAPIDLY CAUSING WAX TO DRIP

NOTE: Before attempting to decorate this cake, please study the whole sequence of photographs and notes and ensure you have the proper equipment and materials, as well as sufficient time. Additional information can be found on pages 5–17.

1. Drawing showing template of angel.

2. Drawing showing template of musical stave.

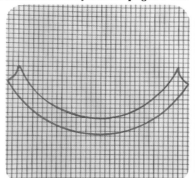

3. Drawing showing template of curved plaque.

4. Cover angel template with waxed paper and pipe-in the parts shown (L.D. 20 m) (two right and one left facing angel required).

5. Pipe-in the further parts shown (L.D. 20 m).

6. Pipe-in further parts shown (L.D. 20 m).

7. Pipe-in the further parts shown (L.D. 24 hrs) then paint the parts shown in edible colouring.

8. Picture showing a completed left facing angel.

9. Outline and flood-in the stave on waxed paper (L.D. 24 hrs) (4 required).

10. Outline and flood-in the plaque on waxed paper (L.D. 24 hrs).

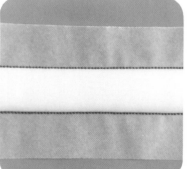

11. Pipe single dots along each edge of the stave (No.1).

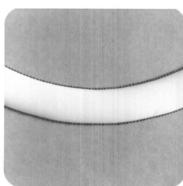

12. Pipe single dots along each edge of the curved plaque (No.1).

13. Pipe notes in white on waxed paper (No.1) then overpipe in black (No.1) (L.D. 12 hrs) (4 sets required).

14. Pipe the stave lines in white (No.1) then overpipe in black (No.1) (L.D. 12 hrs).

15. Pipe title as shown in white (No.1) then overpipe in black (No.1) (L.D. 12 hrs).

16. Fix notes to stave in the order shown and then pipe the vertical lines shown (No.1).

17. An 8" square cake, marzipanned and coated in the normal way, required.

18. Make 12 large and 6 small sugar bells.

19. Fix angels and plaque to cake top.

20. Pipe clouds around each angel, as shown (No.2).

21. Pipe a halo over each angel's head (No.2).

22. Fix a stave to each side of the cake.

23. Pipe shells along the central part of each top edge, as shown (No.43).

24. Pipe shells around the cake base (No.43).

25. Pipe a rope at each cake-top corner, as shown (No.3).

26. Overpipe each rope (No.2) and then pipe a line beside each rope (No.2).

27. Pipe a line beside each No.2 line (No.1).

28. Fix and decorate three pairs of small bells around plaque (No.1).

29. Pipe a line at each board corner (No.2).

30. Pipe a line beside each board No.2 line (No.1).

31. Fix and decorate a pair of bells at each corner (No.1).

32. Fix and decorate a bell below each stave and fix ribbon to board edge.

1. Serrated scraper required.

2. An 8″ round cake required. Coat in two colours and use scraper on the side.

3. Pipe a line around cake base (No.32).

4. Pipe a branch on the cake top, as shown (No.3) (L.D. 1 hr).

5. Pipe snow and mistletoe on branch, as shown (No.1).

6. Drawing showing template of robins.

7. Cover template with waxed paper and pipe-in the part shown (L.D. 20 m).

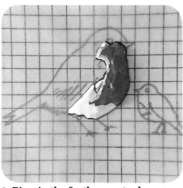

8. Pipe-in the further parts shown (L.D. 20 m).

9. Pipe-in the further parts shown (L.D. 20 m).

10. Pipe-in the further parts shown (L.D. 24 hrs).

11. Paint the robin, as shown, in edible colouring.

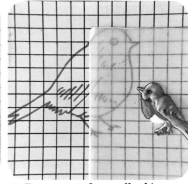

12. Repeat 7–11 for small robin.

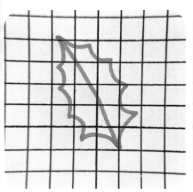

13. Drawing showing template of a holly leaf.

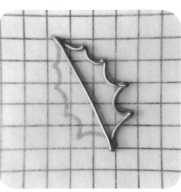

14. Cover template with waxed paper and outline the half of the leaf shown (No.1).

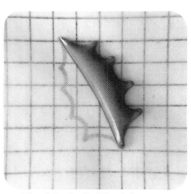

15. Flood-in the half leaf shown.

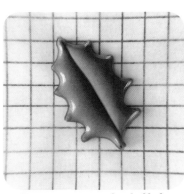

16. Repeat 14-15 on other half of the leaf.

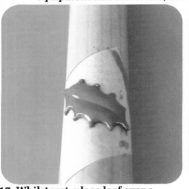

17. Whilst wet, place leaf over a dowel, as shown (L.D. 24 hrs) (24 leaves required).

18. Paint the leaf veins with edible colouring.

19. Fix robins to branch.

20. Pipe message of choice on cake top (No.2) and then overpipe (No.1).

21. Pipe snow on cake-base line (No.2).

22. Fix leaves around cake base, as shown.

23. Pipe a cluster of berries to each leaf (No.1).

24. Pipe bulbs around the top edge of the cake (No.4) (L.D. 1 hr).

25. Overpipe each pair of bulbs with an overlapping 'S' scroll, as shown (No.2).

26. Pipe overlapping 'S' scrolls around board, as shown (No.2).

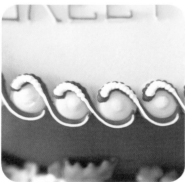

27. Overpipe the top scrolls (No.1).

28. Pipe the lines shown under the message (No.2) and then overpipe those lines (No.1).

29. Fix a spray of leaves to the cake top.

30. Pipe berries to the spray of leaves (No.1).

31. Fix leaves beside the message and pipe berries (No.1). Add 'snow' to all leaves.

32. Overpipe each board scroll (No.1) and fix ribbon to board edge.

1. Marzipan and coat an 8″ square cake in the normal way and then stipple the sides and board.

2. Drawing showing template of lady and gentleman.

3. Pipe-in on waxed paper the parts shown (L.D. 20 m).

4. Pipe-in the further parts shown (L.D. 20 m).

5. Pipe-in the further parts shown (L.D. 20 m).

6. Pipe-in the further parts shown (L.D. 24 hrs).

7. Decorate the figures as shown (L.D. 24 hrs).

8. Pipe fir tree on waxed paper starting from the top and working down to base (No.2) (L.D. 2 hrs).

9. Complete the fir tree by piping 'snow' and trunk (No.2) (L.D. 24 hrs).

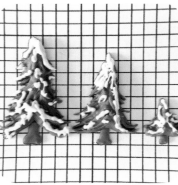

10. Repeat 8–9 to obtain 10 various sized trees.

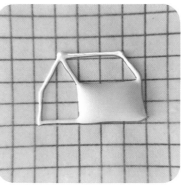

11. Outline the house on waxed paper (No.1) and then flood-in the part shown (L.D. 2 hrs).

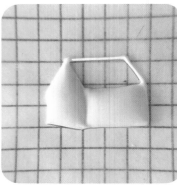

12. Flood-in the further part shown (L.D. 2 hrs).

13. Flood-in the roof (L.D. 24 hrs) and then decorate, as shown.

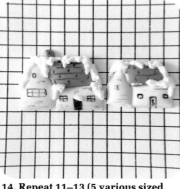

14. Repeat 11–13 (5 various sized houses required).

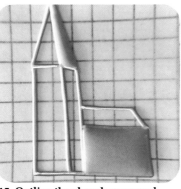

15. Outline the church on waxed paper (No.1) and then flood-in the parts shown (L.D. 2 hrs).

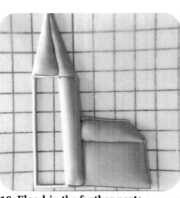

16. Flood-in the further parts shown (L.D. 2 hrs).

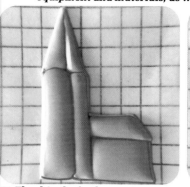

17. Flood-in the further parts shown (L.D. 24 hrs).

18. Decorate as shown.

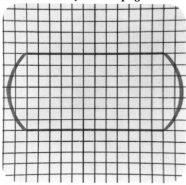

19. Drawing showing template of plaque.

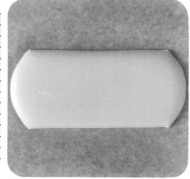

20. Outline the plaque on waxed paper (No.2) and then flood-in (L.D. 24 hrs).

21. Pipe curved lines on cake top, as shown (No.2) and then paint 'sky' with edible colouring.

22. Fix fir trees. Pipe snow as shown (No.2) (L.D. 1 hr).

23. Fix church, houses and trees to cake top. Pipe snow (No.2) (L.D. 1 hr).

24. Fix additional houses and trees. Pipe snow, as shown (No.2) (L.D. 1 hr).

25. Decorate path with filigree piping (No.1) and pipe bushes along path border (No.1).

26. Fix lady and gentleman to path.

27. Pipe shells along the cake-top edge as shown (No.7).

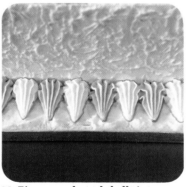

28. Pipe cone shaped shells in alternate colours from cake base (No.7).

29. Pipe spikes in alternate colours along top edge 'snow' areas (No.3).

30. Pipe a dot at the end of each cone shaped shell (No.1).

31. Pipe message of choice on plaque and then underline (No.1).

32. Fix plaque to cake top, artificial holly and ribbon, as required.

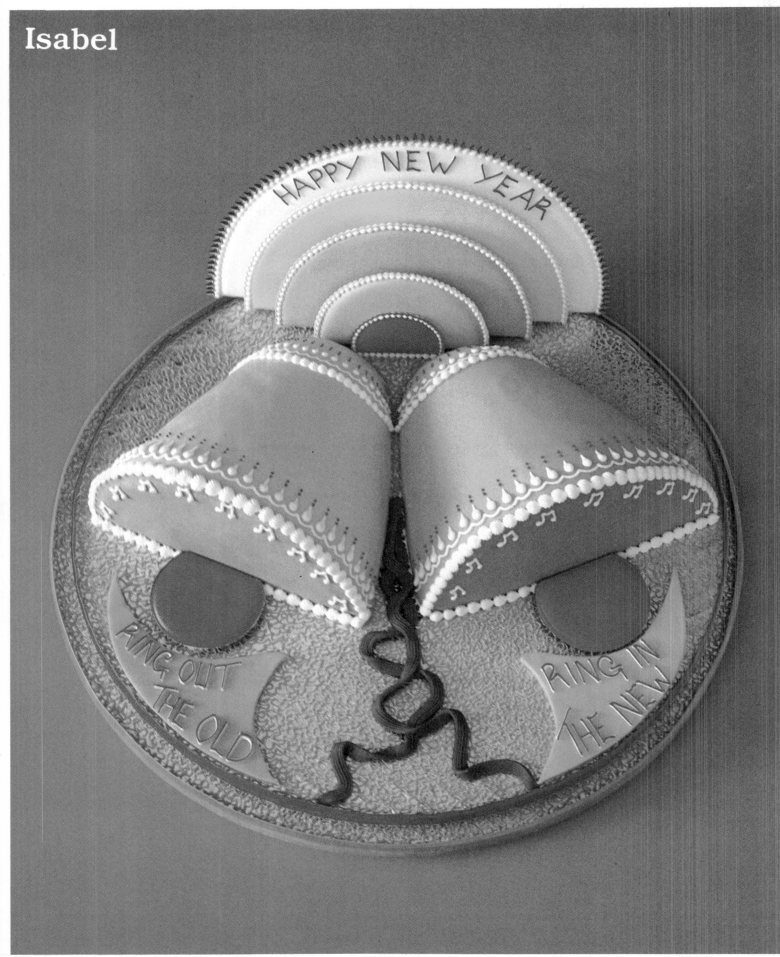

1. A cake baked in a 2pt. pudding basin required.

2. Cut cake in half and place in positions shown on a 15″ round board.

3. Mould and fix marzipan pieces to form bell shapes.

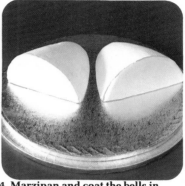

4. Marzipan and coat the bells in the normal way. Place bells and board on a 16″ round board.

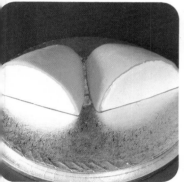

5. Roll out, cut and cover each bell in sugar paste in the colours shown.

6. Roll out, cut and cover each bell end in sugar paste in the colour shown.

7. Filigree the top of each board (No.1) (L.D. 12 hrs).

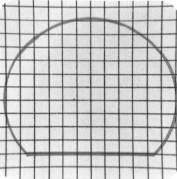

8. Drawing showing template of bell hammer.

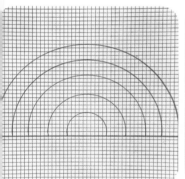

9. Drawing showing disc templates.

10. Outline on waxed paper the bell hammer (No.2). Flood-in (L.D. 24 hrs) (2 required).

11. Outline on waxed paper each disc (No.2) then flood-in (L.D. 24 hrs) (one of each required).

12. Pipe shells around the top edge of each disc (No.2) (L.D. 2 hrs).

13. Overpipe each shell with a line (No.1).

14. Pipe message of choice on the larger disc (No.1).

15. Pipe a spike between each shell on the larger disc (No.1) (L.D. all discs 12 hrs).

16. Pipe two bell ropes, as shown (No.22).

319

17. Pipe shells around the rim of each bell (No.43).

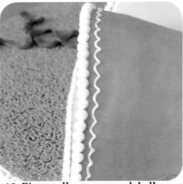

18. Pipe scallops over each bell, as shown (No.2).

19. Pipe a long shell from each scallop (No.2).

20. Pipe pairs of dots, as shown (No.1).

21. Pipe a row of shells over each bell, as shown (No.42).

22. Repeat 18–20.

23. Fix the smallest disc behind the bells with a row of shells (No.43). Support disc (L.D. 2 hrs).

24. Repeat 23 using the next sized disc.

25. Repeat 23 for each remaining disc, as shown.

26. Pipe 3 rosettes on the board at the centre of each bell (No.43) (L.D. 1 hr).

27. Fix each bell hammer on rosettes, as shown.

28. Pipe music notes around top edge of each bell (No.2).

29. Roll out, cut and fix the sugar paste shape shown above and in 31 (L.D. 2 hrs).

30. Pipe message of choice on left shape (No.2) and then overpipe (No.1).

31. Pipe message of choice on right shape (No.2) and then overpipe (No.1).

32. Fix ribbon to each cake-board edge.